CLEOPATRA'S CHILDREN

CLEOPATRA'S CHILDREN

By *Alice Curtis Desmond*

ILLUSTRATED WITH MAPS, CHARTS

AND PHOTOGRAPHS

DODD, MEAD & COMPANY

NEW YORK

ISBN: 0–396–06376–4
Library of Congress Catalog Card Number: 79-160859

Printed in the United States of America
by The Cornwall Press, Inc., Cornwall, N.Y.

*To Thomas C. Desmond
this book, my twentieth, like
all the others, is lovingly
dedicated*

ACKNOWLEDGMENTS

On finishing a book, an author remembers with gratitude all the people who have been of immeasurable help. Foremost, I want to thank my dear friend and editor at Dodd, Mead & Company, Miss Dorothy M. Bryan, for editing the manuscript, greatly improving it by suggesting many needed changes, but especially for her interest in *Cleopatra's Children* from start to finish. My thanks also go to my husband's office staff, Mrs. Alice Mason and Miss Marjorie Burnett, who saved me time by typing several drafts. But above all my gratitude goes to Thomas C. Desmond, who has cheerfully put up with a working wife, busy day after day at the typewriter, and for his help and encouragement during my long, difficult, and sometimes despairing years spent writing this book.

Mrs. Dorothy G. Moore, librarian at the Lake Placid Club, provided me with invaluable source material from their splendid library. Louis Barberon of the Librairie Lucien Dorbon sent me histories of North Africa in Roman times, long out-of-print, from his Paris bookstore. To the Bibliothèque d'Art et d'Archéologie de l'Université de Paris, I owe most of my data on Cherchel (Iol-Caesarea), shipped to me air-mail on microfilm. While from New York, Louis Cohen of the Argosy Bookstore furnished me with material I needed on many subjects.

The following persons aided me greatly in getting the pictures for this book: Donald R. Allen and Miss Janet L. Snow of the Art Reference Bureau, Ancram, New York; Otto L. Bettmann and Mrs. Beverly Mann of the Bettmann Archives; and Ewing Galloway, New York. I am grateful to Ginn and Company, Boston, Massachusetts, for permission to reproduce the pictures of (1) the Pharos Lighthouse, Alexandria, Egypt (from *Ancient Times*, copyright 1916 by James Henry Breasted, copyright renewed 1944 by Charles Breasted) and (2) the Assassination of Caesar and the Chariot Race in the Circus Maximus (from *Caesar in Gaul* by Benjamin L. D'Ooge and Frederick C. Eastman, copyright renewed 1945 by Benjamin S. D'Ooge). And Mrs. Athena M. Brock was most kind to let me use the photograph of the temple of Jupiter from *A History of the Ancient World* by George Willis Botsford, Macmillan, 1911.

In Europe, Maurice Chuzeville, official photographer of the Louvre, and M. Olagnier-Riottot, Conservateur du Musée des Art Africains, Paris, were equally helpful. I am grateful to Thames and Hudson, Ltd., London, for permission to reproduce several illustrations by Wheeler Wood from their book, *Roman Africa in Colour*, published in America by McGraw-Hill, and to Emmanuel Boudot-Lamotte of Paris for giving me the right to include four of his photographs from *Algérie*, published in France by B. Arthaud. While in North Africa, especially cooperative were: P. A. Février, l'Inspecteur des Antiquités, and M. Ahmed Benddeddonche, Conservateur des Monuments Historiques, Alger.

—ABCD

CONTENTS

ILLUSTRATIONS

xi

Nero
Caligula
Ruins of the Palaces of the Caesars, Palatine Hill, Rome
Relief on the Ara Pacis, Rome *Left to right: Antonia Minor,
    Octavia, Drusus, Livia, Antonia Major, and Lucius Aheno-
    barbus. Children in the foreground: Germanicus, Gnaeus
    and Domitia Ahenobarbus.*

MAPS AND DIAGRAMS

GENEALOGY CHARTS

CHRONOLOGICAL TABLE

B.C.

102   Julius Caesar born.

83   Birth of Mark Antony.

73   Herod the Great born.

68   Birth of Cleopatra VII of Egypt.

63   Octavian born.

57   Antony goes to Egypt with a Roman army to restore Ptolemy XI to the throne and meets his daughter, Cleopatra.

49   Caesar crosses the Rubicon to fight Pompey.

48   Caesar victor at Pharsalus in Greece. Antony commands the left wing of his army. Caesar pursues Pompey to Egypt. He falls in love with Cleopatra and restores her to the throne.

47   Caesarion born.

46   Cleopatra and her child join Caesar in Rome. Juba, the 6-year-old son of the king of Numidia, defeated by Caesar at Thapsus, forced to walk in his African triumph.

44   Caesar assassinated (March 15). Cleopatra and her son, befriend by Antony, return to Egypt.

B.C.

43–42   Octavian forms a triumvirate with Antony and Lepidus. Birth of Marcellus, the son of Octavia, sister of Octavian (43); and of Tiberius, to Livia and Claudius Nero (42).

41   Cleopatra joins Mark Antony in Asia Minor; wins his love and support; and brings him back with her to Alexandria.

40   Antony deserts Cleopatra and marries Octavia. Birth of Cleopatra's twins, Alexander Helios and Cleopatra Selene. Herod, tetrarch of Galilee, made king of Judaea by Antony.

39   Birth of Julia, daughter of Octavian and Scribonia; and of Antonia Major, daughter of Octavia by Antony.

38   Octavian divorces Scribonia and marries Livia. Drusus, her son by Claudius Nero, born.

37–36   Antony sends his Roman wife, Octavia, back to her brother. Cleopatra and the twins join him in Antioch. Marriage of Antony and Cleopatra. Antony goes to fight the Parthians and Cleopatra, returning to Egypt by way of Palestine, incurs the enmity of Herod. Birth of Ptolemy Philadelphus (to Cleopatra) and of Antonia Minor (to Octavia).

35–33   Octavia attempts a reconciliation with Antony but Cleopatra prevents it. Rhodon of Damascus, a spy of Herod's, comes to Egypt to be Caesarion's tutor. Antony stages a triumph in Alexandria. Marriage of Alexander Helios to the Princess Iotapa of Media. Coronation of Cleopatra and her children.

32   By divorcing Octavia, and announcing his marriage to Cleopatra, Antony breaks all ties with Rome. Octavian declares war on Antony and Cleopatra.

31   Battle of Actium (September 2).

31–30   Alexandria beseiged by the Romans. Antony and Cleopatra commit suicide. Caesarion and Alexander Helios put to death by Octavian.

29   Octavian master of the Roman world. Selene and Ptolemy, now Cleopatra's only living children, walk in Oc-

B.C.

tavian's Egyptian triumph. They live in Rome with Octavia. Selene meets Juba of Numidia.

27   Octavian becomes the Emperor Augustus.

25   Cleopatra Selene and Juba of Numidia are married. Augustus makes Juba king of his father's old kingdom and gives Selene, for a wedding present, the adjacent country of Mauretania. They go to live at Cirta, capital of Numidia, in North Africa. Julia is married to Marcellus. Herod's sons, Alexander and Aristobulus, sent to Rome to be educated.

23–21   Death of Marcellus. Selene and Juba move to Mauretania. They begin to build the city of Caesarea. Julia marries Agrippa (21); Marcella wed to Julius Antonius.

19   Marriage of Tiberius and Vipsania.

16   Alexander of Judaea marries Glaphyra, daughter of the king of Cappadocia. His brother, Aristobulus, weds Salome, a cousin. Marriage of Drusus and Antonia Minor.

15   Birth of Germanicus, son of Drusus and Antonia.

14   Ptolemy Philadelphus visits Mauretania.

13   Selene and Juba return to Rome. Find there Antipater, Herod's eldest son.

12   Ptolemy Philadelphus killed in a chariot race. The death of Agrippa. Tiberius forced by Augustus to divorce Vipsania and marry Julia. Tiberius and Drusus with the Roman army on the Danube.

11   Octavia dies.

10   Birth of Claudius, son of Drusus and Antonia.

9   Dedication of the *Ara Pacis*. Tiberius and Drusus with the Roman army in Germany. Death of Drusus.

8   Juba publishes the first part of his *History of Rome*.

7   Alexander and Aristobulus killed by their father, Herod.

6–5   Tiberius, to escape from his unhappy marriage with Julia, goes to Rhodes (6). Selene and Juba visit Rome again (5). Second part of Juba's *History of Rome* published.

B.C.

4   Birth of Jesus Christ (?). Herod murders his son, Antipater, and dies five days later.

2   Julia exiled. Julius Antonius, involved in a plot with her, commits suicide.

1   Birth of Ptolemy of Mauretania.

A.D.

1   Expedition of Gaius and Lucius, Augustus' grandsons, to the Near East. Juba writes his book on Arabia.

2   Juba continues his travels. He discovers the Canary Islands, the Madeiras, and visits Greece.

3   Juba takes as a second wife, Glaphyra, the widow of Alexander of Judaea. Disillusioned after a year, he returns to Selene.

5   Drusilla, a daughter, is born to Selene and Juba. Glaphyra marries Archelaus, king of Judaea, the brother of her first husband. Tiberius commands the Roman armies in Germany. Marriage of Germanicus and Agrippina, daughter of Agrippa and Julia.

6   Selene, Cleopatra's daughter, dies (March 3). Archelaus of Judaea banished to Gaul. Death (?) of his wife, Glaphyra.

8   Exile of Ovid.

9   Juba writes a book on Africa.

12   Birth of Caligula, son of Germanicus and Agrippina.

14   Death of Augustus. Tiberius becomes emperor. Julia dies in exile.

17–20 Ovid dies. Tiberius sends Germanicus to the Near East. His death in Syria. Vipsania dies.

23   Death of Juba of Mauretania. Ptolemy becomes king.

27   Pontius Pilate appointed governor of Judaea. Tiberius, tired of ruling, retires to Capri.

27–28 Ministry of Jesus Christ.

29   His crucifixtion. Livia dies.

33   Death of Agrippina for conspiring against Tiberius. Conversion of Paul of Tarsus.

A.D.

37   Murder of Tiberius by Caligula, who succeeds him as emperor. Birth of Nero, son of Agrippina II, sister of Caligula. Death of Antonia Minor.

40   Ptolemy of Mauretania killed by Caligula.

41   Caligula murdered by the praetorian guard. The soldiers proclaim Claudius, son of Drusus and Antonia, emperor.

42   Claudius makes Mauretania a Roman province. Drusilla, daughter of Selene and Juba, marries Antonius Felix, governor of Judaea.

44   Peter, disciple of Jesus, arrested by the Jewish king, Agrippa I (grandson of Herod), escapes from prison.

54   Claudius poisoned by his fourth wife, his young niece, Agrippina II. Nero, her son by Ahenobarbus, becomes emperor.

56   Paul of Tarsus, arrested in Jerusalem, appeals to king Agrippa II for the right to go to Rome and plead his case before Nero.

59   Nero has his mother, Agrippina, assassinated.

64–67   Great fire of Rome (64). Nero builds his Golden House. Persecution of the Christians. Peter and Paul martyred (67).

68   The Roman legions in Spain revolt and drive Nero from the throne. He kills himself and ends the Julio-Claudian dynasty.

CLEOPATRA'S CHILDREN

1

✿✿✿✿

MURDER EGYPTIAN STYLE

ON A LONELY STRETCH of beach where the eastern mouth of
the Nile River flows into the Mediterranean, Ptolemy XII of
Egypt and a group of hard-faced men, the young king's advisers, waited on the afternoon of September 29, B.C. 48, to
commit a murder. Ptolemy, a boy of thirteen, had been persuaded by his Egyptian tutor, Pothinus, and his Greek teacher,
Theodotus of Chios, to agree to the assassination of Pompey
the Great, defeated by Julius Caesar in Greece and coming
to seek refuge in Egypt.

"Caesar is the Roman general we must curry favor with
now," Theodotus told the boy-king. "He will deal harshly
with us if we befriend his rival."

So they waited for Gnaeus Pompeius that afternoon at the
frontier fortress of Pelusium, on the highway leading from
Palestine into Egypt. When his ship came in sight, Achillas,
commander of King Ptolemy's troops, and a Roman centurion
named Salvius, rowed out to bring the once-mighty Pompey
ashore. A rising young general, Gnaeus Pompeius Magnus had
won the title of "Great" by clearing the Mediterranean of
pirates. After which Pompey, Caesar, and Crassus formed the

first triumvirate (a three-man alliance), and ruled Italy together. Then came the inevitable rivalry with Gaius Julius Caesar, by that time governor of Gaul (Northern Italy, France, Holland, and Belgium), as to which of them should be first in Rome. Civil war broke out and Caesar pursued Pompey to Greece. On the 9th of August, 48, he caught up with him at Pharsalus, in Thessaly, where Pompey's forces were cut to pieces by Caesar's legions, hardened by eight years of fighting in Gaul.

Fleeing from the battlefield, Pompey escaped to Egypt, where he expected to be safe because of the help he had been, nine years before, to the present king's father, the dissolute Ptolemy XI, when his subjects deposed him. Pompey had sent a Roman army under Aulus Gabinius, proconsul in Syria, to force their hated king back on the Egyptians—for a price, of course. It was to raise the crushing sum of 10,000 talents, promised to Pompey by Ptolemy for restoring him to the throne, that the Egyptian people were still being taxed beyond endurance, for 1,600 talents of the debt owed Pompey had not yet been paid.

Unaware that the Egyptians hated the ground he walked on, Gnaeus Pompey unwisely fled from Pharsalus to Alexandria for protection. News of his arrival had preceded him to Pelusium, where Ptolemy XII was in camp with his soldiers. On the shore, the defeated general saw waiting to greet him the young king, his Greek teacher Theodotus, and some officers of the Roman garrison left by Gabinius in Egypt to keep the Ptolemies on the throne. Pompey felt himself among friends. He stepped out of the rowboat without hesitation on recognizing among the Romans, Lucius Septimius, one of his former centurions. "I remember you," Pompey said to him cordially. "We fought together in Syria."

It was the turncoat, Septimius, who struck the first blow.

As his old commander turned to face the boy-king, he walked up behind Pompey and stabbed him in the back.

They cut off Pompey's head to give to Caesar, whom the Egyptians were sure would reward them handsomely for ridding him of his rival. "Dead men do not bite," said Theodotus, giving the headless body lying on the sand a contemptuous kick.

* * *

For days after the crushing defeat of the Pompeians at Pharsalus, Marcus Antonius (in English, Mark Antony), who commanded the left wing of Caesar's army, searched the hills to which the survivors of the battle had fled. Where was Gnaeus Pompeius?

"It's too bad, but Pompey has slipped through our fingers," Antony returned to Julius Caesar's tent to report. "He wasn't among the prisoners brought in. We've searched the battlefield for his body. It's not there. Pompey has escaped, but where?"

"To Egypt, to get his reward for keeping those wretched Ptolemies on the throne," replied the victor of Pharsalus. "And I'm going after him."

Caesar lost no time in doing so, and, with his favorite 10th legion, he sailed for Egypt. As soon as his fleet dropped anchor in the harbor of Alexandria, a delegation of Egyptians rowed out to his *trireme* (a warship with three tiers of oars) to bring him a welcoming gift. When Theodotus unwrapped the bloody rags from around it, the Roman consul recoiled in horror, for the Egyptians had saved him the trouble of further pursuit by killing his son-in-law and bringing him his decaying head as a present.

Looking at Gnaeus' familiar face distorted in death, his lifelong ties with the dead man flashed through Caesar's mind.

Pompey had married Julia, Caesar's only child. Then, jealous of his father-in-law's success in Gaul, Pompey had done all he could in the senate at Rome to undermine his rival. The two men hated each other, and when Julia's death in childbirth broke the family tie uniting them, it became a struggle between Caesar and Pompey for supreme power.

On the 10th of January, B.C. 49, Caesar had marched his soldiers to the Rubicon (the present Pisatello, near Rimini), a little river that marked the boundary between Cisalpine Gaul and Italy. It was illegal for any governor to lead his troops out of his own province. "We can stop here," Caesar told his officers, "but, once over that bridge, we'll have to fight it out." He knew his men. They followed him, across the Rubicon, and marched on Rome. Caesar always moved with lightning speed. In three months, he had conquered all of Italy, and nearly caught Pompey and his forces before they escaped to Greece.

Caesar had come to Egypt intending to hunt down his son-in-law, and, for the sake of their dead Julia, allow him to commit suicide rather than face the disgrace of being taken back to Italy in chains. He was shocked to find that the Egyptians had decided Pompey's fate for him. When Theodotus gave him the signet ring he had often seen the triumvir wear, Julius Caesar, a hardened warrior, wept.

Furious at the smug way in which the Egyptians were taking it for granted that Pompey's death would meet with his approval, Caesar pushed the bloody head away. "Remove this ghastly thing!" he ordered an aide. "As for you—" The consul turned to the astonished Theodotus. "You'll hang for this!"

The Greek, who had plotted the assassination expecting a large reward, could scarcely believe what he heard. Instead of being grateful, Caesar was angrily shouting at him. Realizing that he had blundered, the fat little Greek could not get away fast enough. He ducked behind a tall centurion, and, when the Romans looked for him, he was gone. Theodotus managed to escape to Asia Minor, but, recognized in Antioch two years later, he was crucified for having dared to butcher a Roman general.

Meanwhile, Gnaeus Pompeius Magnus was buried with all the honors due a great soldier—and Caesar sent his signet ring to Italy, to let the senate know that, with Pompey dead, he was first in Rome.

* * * *

How dare the Egyptians kill Pompey for him! It showed an independence in them that Julius Caesar would not tolerate. Changing his mind about returning to Italy immediately, he decided to remain in Alexandria and let the Egyptians know who was master here.

The people of Alexandria were treated to a sobering sight as they lined the streets to watch the Roman consul land and step into his chariot. Twelve lictors marched before him carrying the *fasces*, a bundle of sticks with an axe in the middle, indicating his right to inflict punishment with rods or death with the axe. (From this Latin word we get "fascisti," and the emblem of the Italian Fascists in World War II was a bundle of such rods.) Behind Caesar came his legionaries, their faces grim under their leather helmets, as they escorted their general out to the Ptolemies' home on Lochias Point.

On commandeering the royal palace for his residence, Caesar found there two of the late king's children—Arsinoe, a girl of eighteen, and the younger of his two sons, both of whom had been named Ptolemy, a boy aged ten. Cleopatra and her elder Ptolemy brother were at Pelusium, on Egypt's eastern frontier, with their armies facing each other. After the death of her father, three years ago, Cleopatra, the eldest of his children and rightful heiress to his throne, had been driven out of Egypt by her brother Ptolemy's supporters. She had fled to Syria, where she managed to raise a small force of mercenaries. At the time of Caesar's arrival in Egypt, Cleopatra, now twenty, had marched back with her Syrians to try to regain the throne she had lost. But Ptolemy's larger army, commanded by General Achillas, blocked her return to Alexandria.

Their father had left a will in which he stated that Cleopatra was to succeed him and reign jointly with her older Ptolemy brother, whom, in accordance with Egyptian custom, she was to marry. As Ptolemy XI had appointed the Roman senate executors of his will, Caesar felt that he should carry out the late king's wishes. He sent messengers to Pelusium, and ordered Cleopatra and her brother to come to him at once.

Anxious to state his case before Cleopatra could plead hers, Ptolemy, accompanied by his Egyptian tutor Pothinus, arrived at the royal palace in Alexandria on October fifth. The interview he had with Caesar was pleasant enough. But when the boy-king, believing that he had convinced the Roman that he should rule Egypt alone, attempted to return to Pelusium, he was firmly told, "No, young man, you will stay right here."

Caesar now held Ptolemy and his tutor as hostages for his safety. But being imprisoned with the invader suited Pothinus perfectly. Having murdered one Roman, the crafty Egyptian began planning how to get rid of a second. With her protector dead, Pothinus would then dispose of the helpless Cleopatra, and, with the thirteen-year-old Ptolemy on the throne, he would be the real ruler of Egypt. As a first step, the Egyptian secretly sent word to Pelusium that Ptolemy had been captured, Achillas and his army must come and help the Alexandrians rescue their young king. Riots broke out and Caesar sent to Syria for more troops.

While he waited anxiously for them to arrive, the Roman

consul decided to be an arbiter in the family quarrel over the throne. He had in custody three of the Ptolemy children. But where was the fourth one? A week had passed since he had sent for Cleopatra. Was the girl foolish enough to think she could ignore his summons?

Caesar did not know it, but Cleopatra was as eager to see him as he was to see her. She knew that her brother had hurried to Alexandria—and she was not there to plead her cause. Nor could she see a way of reaching Alexandria. It was a hundred miles west of Pelusium, and between her and Caesar was encamped Achillas' army. "Somehow, I'll get by them," Cleopatra thought. From childhood, she had lived in fear of the assassin's knife, so her present predicament was nothing new to her.

In the first century before Christ, it was dangerous to be born a Ptolemy of Egypt, for you were likely to be murdered by your relatives or their hirelings. Since Ptolemy I had founded the dynasty, two hundred and fifty years before, brothers had slain their sisters, sons their fathers, and wives their husbands, if they stood in their way to the throne. In those times—so like ours of hate and violence—the Ptolemies were notorious for their crimes. To mention only their most recent one—Ptolemy XI, returning from Rome to find that Berenice IV, Cleopatra's elder half-sister, had seized the throne, murdered his daughter.

Berenice's death, seven years ago, had left Cleopatra, as heiress to the crown, vulnerable to death at any moment. So, grown accustomed to danger by now—and a determined young woman—she was not unduly afraid. Faced with the problem of how to get to Alexandria and into her former home, Cleopatra hired a fishing schooner, and, with a Sicilian named Apollodorus, went by sea from Pelusium to Alexandria, successfully bypassing Achillas' army. Landing on the island of Pharos, she transferred to a small boat and, after dark, was rowed by Apollodorus into the east harbor and up to the quay before the palace.

The Roman sentry was naturally suspicious when he saw the big Sicilian, as soon as he had tied up his boat, step ashore with a long bundle tied with rope over his shoulder. "What have you there?" he demanded.

Apollodorus' heart was pounding with fright against his ribs, but he managed to reply, "A Persian rug, a gift from my master for Julius Caesar. Sir, will you kindly have someone show me to his apartment?"

The guard hesitated. Apollodorus thought he was lost, that the soldier was going to demand he untie the bundle on his shoulder and show him the rug. To his relief, the Roman grunted, "All right, follow me," and he led the trembling Sicilian into the palace. He was passed on from guard to guard, and, finally, found himself ushered into a room where Caesar was seated at his desk, writing a letter.

The great man looked up and frowned, annoyed at the interruption. "What is it?" the Roman asked impatiently. But when the ropes around the bundle were cut and, instead of a rug, a young person emerged, he forgot his annoyance.

At first, Caesar thought his visitor was a boy, for Cleopatra was dressed in a short military tunic, with a sword at her side, like one of her soldiers. He soon realized his mistake. She snatched off her helmet, and when her blonde hair came cascading down about her shoulders, the astonished Julius Caesar, a grave man who seldom smiled, burst out laughing. He liked pretty girls—especially, girls with pluck and daring.

This is no made-up story. The Greek historian Plutarch, writing a hundred and fifty years after the event, tells us that this was the way the romantic meeting between the young queen and the middle-aged Roman general took place, and that they "talked all night." Cleopatra told Caesar how she had been driven off the throne of Egypt. He listened with admiration, already half in love with this charming woman, who, to fight for her inheritance, had the courage to return and face the dangers from which she had escaped.

2

HER FIRST ROMAN

THE GIRL-IN-THE-RUG was seated proudly beside Caesar, her hand in his, when, the next morning, he sent for her brother. Triumph shone in Cleopatra's eyes. Yesterday, she had been sad and forlorn, her small band of ragged Syrians facing Ptolemy's larger army. Without a friend in the world, she had crept back into her father's palace in danger of her life. Overnight, everything had changed. Now Cleopatra was not only Queen of Egypt once more, but she had won the backing of the most powerful man in the world.

On entering the room and finding his sister there, Ptolemy gasped. "I thought you were in Pelusium. How did you get here?" he demanded. Cleopatra did not deign to reply. Let him wonder! Fairly gloating, she sat quietly while Caesar berated the crestfallen boy for allowing Pothinus to drive his sister into exile.

"Your father's will states that you and your sister are to reign together," he told him, "and I must carry out his wishes. So neither my soldiers nor I will leave Egypt until Cleopatra again rules as your queen."

In sullen silence, the young Egyptian listened while the

stern Roman scolded him. Caesar made a pretense of being neutral in the royal squabble, but Ptolemy had only to note the tender glances the consul gave Cleopatra to realize which side he was actually on. According to the Roman historian, Dion Cassius, when Caesar's tirade ended, the thirteen-year-old king snatched the crown from his head, flung it at the older man in a fit of rage and rushed from the room.

* * * *

Four months later, Julius Caesar, to his amazement, was still in Alexandria. He had come in October, intending to stay but a few weeks—certainly, no longer than November. It was now February and he was receiving letters from the Roman senate, asking him why, with Pompey defeated, he did not return to Italy. But he had fallen in love with Cleopatra, and Caesar wished to stay until he saw her secure on the throne. Writing the senate that he must wait for the 37th Legion to arrive from Syria, the consul put off his departure from week to week.

He was nearly three times Cleopatra's age, but it did not matter, for Julius Caesar, at fifty-four, a tall slim man with a lean face and alert brown eyes, was still attractive to women, in spite of his bald head. He had been married three times. His affairs with the ladies were notorious. So it is unjust that Cleopatra has been blamed for causing the Roman invader of Egypt to fall so in love with her that he lingered on in Alexandria all that winter of 48-47, neglecting his career and his wife. Actually, it was an aging philanderer who set about winning the heart of a naive girl.

Her marriage to her thirteen-year-old brother was a mere formality to satisfy their Egyptian subjects, and, as far as we know, Cleopatra VII, born in the winter of B.C. 68 and now twenty, had never had a serious love affair until she met

GENEALOGY

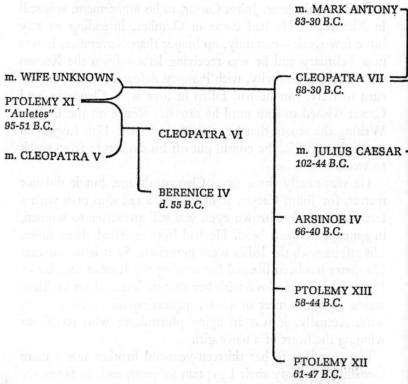

m. MARK ANTONY
83-30 B.C.

m. WIFE UNKNOWN

PTOLEMY XI
"Auletes"
95-51 B.C.

CLEOPATRA VI

m. CLEOPATRA V

CLEOPATRA VII
68-30 B.C.

m. JULIUS CAESAR
102-44 B.C.

BERENICE IV
d. 55 B.C.

ARSINOE IV
66-40 B.C.

PTOLEMY XIII
58-44 B.C.

PTOLEMY XII
61-47 B.C.

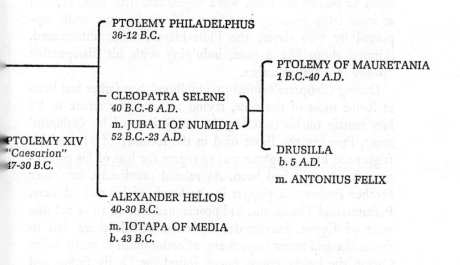

PTOLEMY XIV
"Caesarion"
47-30 B.C.

PTOLEMY PHILADELPHUS
36-12 B.C.

CLEOPATRA SELENE
40 B.C.-6 A.D.
m. JUBA II OF NUMIDIA
52 B.C.-23 A.D.

PTOLEMY OF MAURETANIA
1 B.C.-40 A.D.

DRUSILLA
b. 5 A.D.
m. ANTONIUS FELIX

ALEXANDER HELIOS
40-30 B.C.
m. IOTAPA OF MEDIA
b. 43 B.C.

Caesar. She had grown up, a neglected child, in the royal palace on Lochias Point. No one knows who her mother was, but it is thought that Berenice IV, murdered by her father, and Cleopatra VI, who died in infancy, were the children of Ptolemy's marriage to Cleopatra V, his sister; and that Cleopatra VII, Arsinoe IV, and the two Ptolemy boys were born of another woman—possibly, a harem favorite. Cleopatra's father, who went by the nickname of Auletes (the Piper) because he played the flute, was a degenerate little man. Grown so stout from gluttony that he could usually only walk supported by two slaves, the Flute-Player, when intoxicated, skipped about like a goat, indulging with his disreputable cronies in drunken antics.

During Cleopatra's unhappy childhood, her father had been in Rome most of the time, trying to bribe the senate to let him remain on his tottering throne. Reinstated by Gabinius' army, Ptolemy the Piper died in the summer of 51, and his frightened little daughter was to regret the loss of his protection, feeble as it had been. As related previously, her elder brother Ptolemy, a puppet in the hands of his evil advisers, Pothinus and Theodotus, had proclaimed himself to be the sole ruler of Egypt. Surrounded by enemies, Cleopatra fled to Syria. She had never known any affection until now. In Julius Caesar, the lonely young queen found the kindly father and protector she had longed for all her life.

As for the erudite Roman, a love affair with a girl not only endowed with charm but with brains as well was a new experience. Cleopatra had attended the *mouseion* (university) of Alexandria, founded by her ancestor Ptolemy I, where scholars from all over the civilized world came to study. There she had learned to speak six languages. But what pleased Caesar even more was that the young queen could trace her family back to his boyhood hero, Alexander the Great. The dynasty had been founded in the third century before Christ by one of Alexander's most trusted generals—Ptolemy, son of Lagus, a half-brother of the Macedonian king. After Alexander's death in B.C. 323, Ptolemy seized the Egyptian part of his former leader's empire and proclaimed himself to be the successor of the pharaohs.

Being of Greek descent, Cleopatra (whose name in Greek means, "Glory of Her Race") was probably not a brunette, as she is usually pictured, but blonde, like most Macedonian women. That she was small and slender we can be sure, or Apollodorus could not have carried her over his shoulder into the palace the night she met Caesar. Her profile, stamped on the coins she minted, shows her as no great beauty. So what did she have? "A sweetness in her voice," Plutarch wrote. And tact. When Caesar told Cleopatra about his epileptic fits, of which he was ashamed, because they often came upon him during a battle or when he was presiding over the senate, she consoled him.

"Epilepsy isn't an affliction but a gift of the gods," Cleopatra said. "Wasn't Hercules supposed to have been an epileptic?"

With his keen mind, Caesar was interested in everything, and in her golden chariot drawn by coal-black horses, Cleopatra drove him by the docks on the water front, to see Egyptian ships loading grain to be carried all over the civilized world. Then off they went, along the streets of Alexandria, that crossed one another at right angles. Built on a strip of land between Lake Mareotis and the Mediterranean by the Greek architect, Deinocrates, the capital of Egypt was the first town to be divided into regular blocks, as are our modern cities. Or the pair rowed across the harbor to the island of Pharos, to picnic at the base of the world's first lighthouse— and the model for all since erected—constructed by Sostratus of Cnidos, in the reign of Ptolemy II Philadelphus.

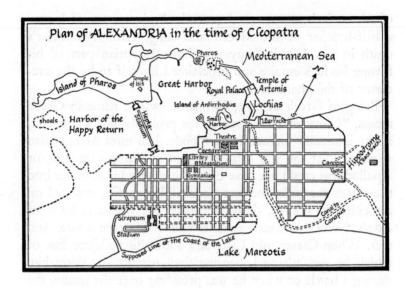

Plan of ALEXANDRIA in the time of Cleopatra

Mediterranean Sea
Pharos
Island of Pharos
Temple of Isis
Great Harbor
Royal Palace
Temple of Artemis
Island of Antirrhodus
Lochias
shoals
Harbor of the Happy Return
Heptastadium
Small Harbor
Barracks
Theatre
Caesareum
Library
Mausoleum
Gymnasium
Canopic Gate
Hippodrome Race Track
Serapeum
Stadium
Canal to Canopus
Supposed Line of the Coast of the Lake
Lake Mareotis

To Caesar, however, the most interesting sight in Egypt
was the Soma. In this cemetery, among the tombs of the
Ptolemies, was the embalmed body of Alexander the Great,
enclosed in a glass coffin. Brought by Ptolemy II from Babylon, where Alexander died, it lay in the city he founded after
his capture of Egypt. Ever since, as a child, Caesar had read
about the Macedonian, who, a king at eighteen, had conquered all the known world of his day by thirty, the Roman
had longed to be another Alexander. Having subdued Gaul
and Britain and looked out on the Atlantic, he wanted to in-
vade the East and gaze upon the Indian Ocean. But he was in
his fifties, well beyond the age of Alexander when the latter
had marched his army to India.

"You don't think," Caesar asked Cleopatra wistfully, "that
I'm too old to conquer the East?"

"Of course not, dear."

As she fondly patted his hand, Caesar thought how he
would not have talked this way six months ago. Once Pompey

was defeated, he had intended to settle down in Rome and devote himself to politics. But Cleopatra made him feel young again. He wondered, was she right in believing that he still had enough vigor left to conquer Asia as Alexander had done? His empire would then extend from Britain to India. From Rome, he would govern the world.

Alexandria was not Egypt, any more than Cleopatra was an Egyptian. Both were Greek. The capital of Egypt, a town at the western mouth of the Nile, resembled Athens more than it did Thebes or Memphis. Caesar wanted to go south, toward the source of the Nile, and explore the real Egypt, for it was one of the principal trade routes between Europe and India. But he did not dare turn his back on Pothinus, who was doing his best to discredit Cleopatra in the eyes of her subjects. By now, all Alexandria knew of the May-December romance in the royal palace. Their queen had not only lost her heart to a man old enough to be her father, they were told, but her sympathies were all with the Romans.

When Caesar's barber informed him that Ptolemy's tutor had sent to General Achillas at Pelusium a map of the defenses on Lochias Point, the Roman consul lost all patience. As Pothinus was leaving the dining room one night with the young king, an aide of Caesar's sprang out from behind a curtain and stabbed him.

Dazed with horror, Ptolemy stared down at his closest friend, sprawled on the floor, a dagger in his side. For a moment, he stood over the dead man, white and trembling, then, as fast as he could, the boy ran to Arsinoe's apartment.

"Pothinus has been murdered!" he gasped. "What shall we do?" And his sister replied, "Escape, or we'll be the next ones."

Ptolemy was too well guarded to get away, but Arsinoe managed to climb out of a window and join Achillas' army at Pelusium. Younger than Cleopatra, and wildly ambitious, Arsinoe longed to be queen in her sister's place. Angry with

Achillas, who refused to betray Ptolemy, she had him killed
and appointed her Greek tutor, Ganymede, as commander-in-
chief.

Under Queen Arsinoe, as she now called herself, the Egyptian army marched on Alexandria with a force five times that
of the Romans. The uneven struggle began with a naval battle,
during which Caesar set fire to the enemy fleet anchored in
the *Eunostos* (Harbor of the Happy Return), as the western
basin was called. It spread through the town and reached the
university library, where 40,000 papyrus rolls were destroyed.

With the city in flames, Arsinoe's troops, who had come
from Pelusium by sea, landed on the island of Pharos that, on
the order of Ptolemy I, had been connected with the main-
land by a causeway (the Heptastadium), nearly a mile long.
Halfway across it, the Egyptians were stopped by Caesar,
leading the defense in person. He had marched his legionaries
out onto the mole that divided the east basin before the palace
from the Harbor of the Happy Return. It was a hand-to-hand
struggle. Suddenly, all around Caesar's soldiers, there was wild
confusion, for some Alexandrians had come out along the
causeway in their rear. Trapped between the two enemy
forces, the panic-stricken Romans began to jump from the
mole.

Swept off the embankment with the others, Caesar landed
in the water among a mass of soldiers, weighed down by heavy
armor, swimming for their lives. His bald head made a fine
target for the Egyptian archers on the mole, but, somehow,
he kept going and reached the marble steps of the palace, to
pitch forward exhausted into Cleopatra's arms.

Four hundred Romans drowned that day. But, within a
week, the 37th Legion arrived from Syria. Aid also came from
an unexpected friend. Antipater of Idumea had supported
Pompey, but Pompey was dead, so he marched from Palestine
with 3,000 Jews to offer his help. In gratitude, Caesar made

Antipater *procurator* (governor) of Judea, and his son, Herod, governor of Galilee.

Since the Romans now outnumbered the Egyptians, Caesar decided to go after Arsinoe's army that had retreated up the Nile. But, first, he must get rid of Ptolemy. Caesar was confident of victory, and, if the little king remained with him, it would be hard to explain to the senate why he did not make him joint ruler with Cleopatra. So, having sent for the young pharaoh, the Roman asked him, "How would you like to join Arsinoe?"

Ptolemy knew he was being sent to his death. "Why can't I stay here?" the boy pleaded.

"What will the Egyptians think of you?" Caesar exclaimed. "If I'm willing to set you free, and you refuse to go, do you know what the world will call you? A coward! Ptolemy, you want to rule Egypt, don't you? Then, be a man. Go back to your army and fight me openly, as their leader and king."

For several minutes the Egyptian boy stood facing the tall Roman in trembling indecision. Then, realizing that what Caesar said was true—if he wished to be king, he must learn to act as a leader—Ptolemy agreed to help his sister Arsinoe command the Egyptians in the coming conflict with the Romans.

A week later, the two armies met up the Nile. Attacked by the enemy on three sides, the Egyptians' retreat to the river turned into a rout. In the panic to escape, Ptolemy's overloaded boat capsized. Next day, his body, encased in golden armor, was found floating, face down, in the muddy waters of the Nile.

Ganymedes was drowned too, Arsinoe was captured, and, on March 27, B.C. 47, Julius Caesar entered Alexandria for the second time in triumph. Cleopatra stood proudly by his side in the chariot, as he was driven through the city between cheering crowds. It was a different welcome from the one

that Caesar had received on arriving in Egypt, the previous
October. Delegations of the leading citizens came humbly to
beg his forgiveness.

He would be merciful, the Roman told them. He would not
burn Alexandria to the ground, but the 1,600 talents still owed
Pompey for reinstating Ptolemy XI must be paid him, and he
would stand no more nonsense about who was to rule Egypt.
Cleopatra was to reign with her surviving brother, the eleven-
year-old Ptolemy XIII, as consort. Her sister Arsinoe, who
had dared oppose him, Caesar sent to Rome in chains to take
part in his triumph.

With Egypt independent in name only, Julius Caesar felt
that he could take a vacation. Spring had come and Olympus,
her Greek physician, said that a cruise up the Nile would be
beneficial to the queen's health, for the Roman consul had
been in Egypt for six months, and Cleopatra was expecting
a baby.

Caesar had loved many women. But not even his first wife
Cornelia, the one love of his youth, whom he had married at
seventeen and lost at thirty-four, had satisfied his every need
as did Cleopatra. In spite of her wild, impulsive ways, when
occasion demanded it, she could be every inch a queen. Now,
in three months, Caesar would have the joy of cradling their
child in his arms. The baby was due in July. His only off-
spring, Julia, the daughter he had by Cornelia, was dead.
Neither Pompeia, his second wife, nor Calpurnia, his present
one, had given him a child. And the prospect of becoming a
father again, at fifty-five, thrilled him. Of course, the baby
would be a boy. It must be. Caesar had longed all his life for
a son.

3

HONEYMOONING ON THE NILE

CLEOPATRA LIKED TO LOOK from her palace windows at the ships sailing out of the harbor with cargoes of Egyptian linen, papyrus and grain. The products of Asia also passed through the port of Alexandria. In the fragrant warehouses along the water front were stored the perfumes, the scented oils, the ivory, spices and silks brought from Arabia, India and China.

Trade with the Orient had made Egypt rich. The goods imported from the south by way of the Red Sea were landed at the port of Berenice, carried by caravans of camels across the Arabian desert, and brought down the Nile on rafts. Merchants, mostly Greek, awaited their arrival in the bazaars of Alexandria, to buy and sell. Their Arab sailors were skilled at crossing the Indian Ocean by means of the prevailing winds that blew in opposite directions at certain seasons of the year. Using the summer monsoon, their little dhows sailed east to fetch goods from India and China. Then in the wintertime, when the winds reversed themselves, they were literally blown back to Egypt.

None of the Ptolemies had ever cared to venture far from Greek Alexandria, but Cleopatra, living on the old trade route to Asia, longed to see what lay up the Nile. So she urged the trip on Caesar. Anything to keep him with her a few months longer! Over her hung the dread that, with Egypt crushed, he would return to Rome. She knew her Roman lover had remained in Alexandria longer than he had meant to, or felt he should, and the senate was certainly of that opinion. It was only Caesar's eagerness to see his child that kept him from returning to Italy and his legal wife.

"Why don't we explore the way to India your army will take some day?" Cleopatra kept saying.

So in May, B.C. 47, the pair left Alexandria in a *thalamegus* (a houseboat used by wealthy Egyptians on the Nile), with triangular silk sails, a pilot at the helm, and the rowers singing as they raised and lowered the oars. Escorting Cleopatra's ship was a fleet of smaller boats, full of soldiers. Caesar had brought them along so his legionaries would know what conditions the Romans must face when they came up the Nile again on their way to conquer India.

On leaving the fertile delta behind, the queen and her Roman found themselves in another Egypt. For the next four weeks they would follow the Nile as it flowed between the Libyan and Arabian deserts. When the pyramids at Giza loomed up on the west bank of the river, Caesar felt as though he had stepped back several centuries, for life in Upper Egypt had hardly changed since the days of the pharaohs.

The flotilla of boats stopped at mud-brick villages, where descendants of the pyramid-builders lined the banks of the Nile to gaze at their queen. The sophisticated Greeks of Alexandria considered the Ptolemies mere mortals, but to these simple *fellahs* (peasants) of Upper Egypt, Cleopatra was not only their queen, but a living deity—Isis, the Egyptian Venus. This worship of their rulers (a custom inherited from the pharaohs) was a new idea to Caesar. Brought up in the democratic Roman republic, he had never seen such homage paid to a monarch. At Thebes, when Cleopatra stepped from her ship onto the quay, her subjects, falling on their knees, touched their foreheads to the ground as the goddess-queen walked to her chariot.

The next morning, everyone in Thebes was hurrying out to a huge stone building at Karnak to see Queen Isis offer a sacrifice to Ammon, king of the gods. Along the road lined with human-headed sphinxes, came the procession, moving slowly toward the temple. Dust rose from the feet of marching soldiers and from the wheels of a long line of chariots. Caesar rode in the last one. Behind him, lying in a litter borne on the shoulders of eight Nubian slaves, was Cleopatra. Usually, she wore Grecian dress, a long pleated chiton or tunic, held in by a girdle at the waist. Instead, today, a sheer linen robe reached to her gold sandals. The plaited, black, artificial hair of a wig fell to her shoulders; while on her head was the tall, double crown adorned with the emblems of Upper and Lower Egypt, the vulture and the cobra. Cleopatra might have been the queen of one of the pharaohs. The awed crowds knelt at the sight of her, their faces in the dust.

The queen's litter bearers carried her into the temple and through a series of courtyards, each divided from the next by stone pylons, to the entrance of the sanctuary. Here, a group of white-robed priests waited, with the food offerings she was to present to the ram-headed god of fertility.

Wearing the ibis mask of Thoth, god of wisdom, the high priest stepped forward to open the bronze doors of the shrine. Only he and Cleopatra, earthly representatives of Ammon, were allowed to enter this sacred place. So the Egyptian drew back in surprise and anger at the sight of the tall, bald-headed man, with a red cape over his uniform, who had boldly followed the queen to the door of the sanctuary.

Cleopatra had dreaded this moment. All the way up the Nile, she was relieved to find that her subjects still believed the Ptolemies, like the pharaohs, to be divine beings, descended to earth to rule over them. Assured of her own divinity, the goddess-queen wondered how she could persuade the Egyptians to accept Caesar as her husband. Roman law did not recognize the marriage of a Roman and a foreigner, but, from the day Cleopatra knew she was pregnant, an Egyptian marriage with him, if not a Roman one, had been uppermost in her mind. Somehow, she must legalize their child about to be born.

"Open those doors," the goddess Isis commanded.

"Not to the Roman," replied the high priest firmly. "Not to the man who has seduced our queen and enslaved the Egyptian people."

"He is not a Roman or even a mortal, but a deity like myself, the great Ammon come down to earth in human form."

It was a brave speech but Cleopatra, facing the stern-eyed priest, was trembling. He looked like a cynical man who preached the old state religion, but no longer believed himself in the myth of the Egyptian rulers' miraculous descent from the gods. Would he refuse to open the shrine? For a ghastly moment she thought so. Then, to her immense relief, something spectacular happened to bolster her claim—the hot sun on Caesar's bald head brought on one of his epileptic fits. He let out a cry, fell to the ground, and rolled about in convulsions.

"See, it is the spirit of Ammon entering into the Roman," Cleopatra informed the high priest. "Now will you let my celestial husband enter his sanctuary?"

Fortunately, the attack was a mild one. As the Egyptian unlocked the bronze doors, the Roman got to his feet and followed the goddess-queen into the dimly-lit shrine. The high priest fumigated with incense the gold statue, with the horned-head of a ram, rising above them in the darkness. Queen Isis sprinkled it with water from the sacred lake. Then she motioned to Ammon-Caesar to place the food offerings before his own image. He did so, in a trance, the dazed state that follows an epileptic fit.

When the royal pair returned to the ship, Caesar did not remember what he had done. But when Cleopatra told him that, in the temple at Karnak, the spirit of Ammon, supreme deity of Egypt, had entered into him, the Roman was pleased. "I like being divine," he said.

Royal adultery with the gods was not a new idea to the Egyptians. Many of the pharaohs had claimed celestial birth. When the high priest of Karnak told the people that he had actually seen the great Ammon come down to earth and enter the person of Julius Caesar, the cynical Alexandrians laughed, but the majority of the Egyptian people accepted the new deity as their queen's husband. What if he did have a wife in Rome? Gods and goddesses were above the laws of conduct that govern the common man in the popular belief. They could have several husbands and wives. They could get married or not, as they pleased; and, of course, any child of Ammon and the Queen of Egypt would be legitimate.

* * * *

Four weeks after leaving Alexandria, the royal flotilla reached Coptos (now Kypt), the start of the trade route from the Nile over to the Red Sea. Caesar talked there with merchants and camel drivers who had been across the Arabian desert to Berenice, the most southerly Egyptian port on the Red Sea, and obtained from them all the information he could about crossing to Arabia and India. Then Caesar and Cleopatra returned to Alexandria, and, having been away for two months, they settled down on Lochias Point to await the birth of their child.

On his desk Caesar found the usual letters from the Roman

senate, demanding to know why he remained so long in Egypt. He ignored them. Italy, in charge of Mark Antony, who had been sent back to Rome after the battle of Pharsalus to govern in his name, was in chaos. What of it? Nothing now could have induced Julius Caesar to leave the woman he loved, who might be facing a difficult time. He had a right to be apprehensive. When Caesar was born, his mother had been unable to have a natural delivery. The doctors were obliged to take Aurelia's child from her by an abdominal incision. That is how the operation known in obstretics as a Caesarean section received its name, from Aurelia's famous baby who came into the world by the aid of a surgeon's knife.

One morning in July, B.C. 47, Caesar was taking a bath when Cleopatra's Greek doctor, Olympus, rushed into the room. "What is it?" the consul asked.

"The queen is in labor. Her child is badly placed. I shall have to use forceps."

Caesar turned pale, remembering his mother. Not waiting to dry himself, he grabbed up a dressing gown, slipped it on over his wet body, and hurried into Cleopatra's room. Several other doctors surrounded the queen's bed. She lay on it, moaning softly. It was more than Caesar could bear to see Cleopatra suffer. He kissed her, then fled and waited, his heart pounding, in the adjoining dressing room.

After several hours, the child was born, feet first, instead of in the normal way, head first, which the Romans thought was a bad omen. The consul was summoned. He hurried into the room, took only a quick glance at the newborn infant lying on a table (Caesar said later, he thought it had died), and, hurrying over to Cleopatra's bed, took her tenderly in his arms.

The baby did indeed appear to be dead. The other doctors thought so, but Olympus decided to make certain. He picked the child up, dipped it into a basin of hot water, and slapped it gently all over. To everyone's surprise, the infant uttered a faint cry. At the sound, Caesar turned around. He took a good look at the naked child. Suddenly beside himself with joy, he rushed over, grabbed up the baby, and held it out to Cleopatra. "My son!" he cried. Happy tears rolled down his cheeks.

There could be only one name for him, Cleopatra's baby must be named after his proud father. In Egypt, he would be known officially as Ptolemy XIV, but his parents called him Caesarion (Little Caesar).

As all Egypt rejoiced over the birth of the boy who some-day would be their pharaoh, Caesarion's father, two weeks after his birth, was forced to leave Alexandria. For nine months he had ignored the angry commands of the senate that he return to Rome. Now he must bestir himself. Caesar was needed almost anywhere in the empire but in Egypt. In Asia Minor, south of the Black Sea, Pharnaces, king of Pontus, was causing trouble. And there was a battle to be fought in North Africa against Gnaeus and Sextus, Pompey's sons, who, with the aid of King Juba of Numidia, had raised an army to re-venge Pharsalus. But Cleopatra's lover promised to send for her and their child when he was finished settling these prob-lems in Africa. He wanted them to join him in Rome.

So one day, with reluctance, the Roman consul once more buckled on his military uniform and sailed out of the harbor of Alexandria, leaving Cleopatra, with baby Caesarion in her arms, waving to him from the roof garden on the palace. "We won't be separated long," Caesar had promised her, as they kissed good-by.

It would be a year. While she waited to be summoned to Rome, Cleopatra had a bas-relief carved on a wall of the temple at Hermopolis, showing her wedding with Ammon. The god, who appears in human form, greatly resembles

Caesar. Surrounding the celestial pair—Caesar and Cleopatra—
are other divine beings, rejoicing at the birth of their son.
Actually, Caesarion's human parents were as illustrious as
any gods or goddesses. Next to Italy, Egypt was the most important nation in the Roman world and a far wealthier country. Little Caesar's father would become the dictator of Rome;
his mother was now secure as Queen of Egypt. No child was
ever born with a brighter future.

4

❦❦❦❦

TODAY EGYPT AND ROME,
TOMORROW THE WORLD

LEAVING EGYPT, Caesar crossed the Mediterranean to Zela in Asia Minor and, in four hours, destroyed the army of Pharnaces, King of Pontus. Then he sailed for North Africa. There, Pompey's sons, Gnaeus and Sextus, and two of their father's friends, Cato and Scipio, with the help of King Juba of Numidia, were continuing the civil war that Caesar thought had ended at Pharsalus. He marched against them, and at Thapsus (Sousse in Tunisia), on the 6th of April B.C. 46, defeated a second Pompeian army.

By July, Caesar was back in Rome. Cleopatra had arrived with baby Caesarion. She was living in his villa on Janiculum Hill. And he began planning to celebrate his victories. There would be four triumphs, for Gaul, for Asia, for Egypt, and for Africa. To impress the Roman people, Caesar arranged that they should follow one another at intervals of several days.

The first triumph, over Gaul, took place on a hot August afternoon. By one o'clock, crowds lined the Via Sacra, the principal street in the Forum, through which the procession would pass. From the Campus Martius (Field of Mars) outside the city walls, amid a fanfare of trumpets, came the senators and the white oxen to be sacrificed, their gilded horns garlanded with flowers. Then lurid posters of battle scenes mounted on wheeled platforms rolled by, showing Caesar leading his legions to one German victory after another. These were followed by wagons heaped with gold and silver booty from the conquered cities of Gaul. Next came the Gallic captives, dragging their chains. Behind them, in a four-horse chariot stood Julius Caesar, wearing a purple toga. A slave held a laurel wreath over the victorious general's bald head as he passed by, his lean, sun-tanned face wreathed in smiles.

Slowly, the procession moved through the Forum, tightly packed with people, to the foot of the Capitoline. There, the Gallic chiefs were led off to the Mamertine prison to be strangled; and Caesar, having climbed the flight of steps leading up the hill to the temple of Jupiter, laid his laurel wreath in the lap of the statue of the god and sacrificed the white oxen.

At his second triumph, celebrating Caesar's defeat of the King of Pontus with such ease, a banner simply read: *Veni, vidi, vici* (I came, I saw, I conquered). With these brief, boastful words, known to every student of Latin, Caesar had informed the senate of his quick victory over Pharnaces' army.

Two days later, it was his conquest of the Egyptians. The Romans were shown a statue of the boy-king Ptolemy and a model of the Pharos lighthouse. Arsinoe, fettered with chains, was made to walk at the head of a long line of prisoners. Next came animals native to the Nile, the sides of their cages let down so the spectators could shiver with fear and delight at the sight of lions, panthers, and crocodiles. Finally, bringing up the rear, was something the Romans had never seen—a giraffe. Yet it was not at this strange beast, but at a young woman seated in the reviewing stand, that most of the people were looking. Everyone wanted to get a glimpse of the siren who had kept their ruler so long in Egypt.

The eyes of thousands were on her face. So had been Caesar's gaze, as his chariot rumbled by in a cloud of dust. For him, there was only one person at his triumph. There she was, on the dais, seated near Calpurnia. The Queen of Egypt had refused to be present on Caesar's day for Gaul and his day for Asia because he insisted that his wife, for appearances' sake, should also sit there. But Cleopatra had come today to see Arsinoe stagger by, loaded down with chains. She hated her younger sister, who had tried to steal her throne.

At his fourth triumph over Africa, a week later, Caesar exhibited another strange animal—a camel—first seen by the Romans at the battle of Thapsus. Otherwise, the parade was a warning to Caesar's enemies that they had better give up Pompey's cause for lost. The crowd was shown what had happened to Scipio, to Cato, and their African ally, King Juba of Numidia. Following a display of Juba's war elephants, forty of them in Indian file, each trunk clasping the tail before it, there were posters that pictured Scipio, after the surrender, leaping into the sea; Cato, drinking poison; Juba and the Pompeian general, Petreius, fighting a duel to the death rather than be beheaded. How Caesar would have enjoyed dragging them after his chariot in chains! Unfortunately for him, they had killed themselves; and Pompey's sons had escaped to Spain. All he had to show the Romans from his African campaign were their first camel, forty elephants, and a six-year-old boy.

Following the gruesome picture of King Juba's suicide came his son. Little Juba was made to walk alone, behind the other Numidian prisoners, so the Romans could get a good look at him. Was he to die after the triumph? His jailers had said that was the usual fate of important prisoners taken by the Romans in war. Juba stared straight ahead. *I mustn't let these people* see that I'm afraid, he thought. I must be brave, like my father was.

In the suicide-pact after Thapsus, Juba of Numidia had stabbed to death the Pompeian general Petreius, then ordered one of his slaves to run a sword through him. Crouched, terrified, in a corner of the tent, six-year-old Juba II had seen his father die in agony. The ghastly scene still swam before his eyes, as, dragging his chains, but head held high, the brown-skinned African boy walked proudly along the Via Sacra, between the two lines of hostile white faces.

When the procession reached the base of the Capitoline, little Juba and the other Numidian captives were led back to their dark cells under the Mamertine prison. At the precise moment when the majority of them were being strangled, Caesar, in the temple of Jupiter above, was presenting his trophies of victory on the altar and giving thanks to Jove.

* * * *

On the night of his African triumph, Julius Caesar was host to the Romans at a sumptuous banquet. King Juba's elephants stood holding flaming torches in their trunks to light the scene, as the citizens of Rome sat down to feast at tables set up in the public squares. This was only the beginning of weeks of festivities. Actors performed in the theater; there were chariot races; gladiators fought with one another and with wild beasts.

Clad in purple, a wreath of flowers hiding his baldness, Caesar presided over these celebrations, Cleopatra at his side, while Calpurnia remained alone at home. All Rome gossiped about them, for the consul had returned to Italy in love with everything Egyptian. In those days, Rome was a small, over-crowded town, where the average person lived uncomfortably in one of many five-story tenements, called *insulae* (island blocks), built around dark courtyards, with no piped water above the ground floor. Anxious to rebuild the place, with Alexandria in mind, Caesar drew up plans for a new city with broad avenues, Greek-pillared temples, and marble government buildings. And he had an Egyptian mathematician, Sosigenes, reform the Roman calendar, making the year consist of 365 days (seven months of 31 days, four of 30, and one of 28), adding an extra day every fourth year. In honor of Caesar's birthday, the month of Quintilis was renamed Julius (July).

This new Julian calendar (still in use today) was Cleopatra's idea, which did not endear it to the Romans. The arrival from Alexandria of the Queen of Egypt, accompanied by her one-year-old son and twelve-year-old brother-husband, Ptolemy XIII, had caused a scandal. People lined the streets to get a glimpse of the "Egyptian harpy" being carried in a litter, with her child on her lap, out to Caesar's villa across the Tiber (now the Vatican district). The Romans felt great sympathy for Caesar's legal wife, the stately, middle-aged Calpurnia, who was handling a difficult situation with dignity.

Sensing their antipathy toward her, the twenty-two-year-old Queen of Egypt seldom appeared in public, once her elderly lover's triumphs were over, but remained quietly in the house on Janiculum Hill he had lent her. The west side of the Tiber was not a good address in those days. Caesar lived on the fashionable east side of the river, in the Forum, with his wife. But, as often as he could, he came to visit Cleopatra and his son.

Little Caesar was slow in learning to walk. He kept falling down, and he was not talking. This worried his parents. They did their best to keep the child amused with a nursery full of toys. He was now playing with a set of letter blocks, given the boy to teach him the Latin alphabet, a hobbyhorse, and a map of the Roman empire. Since he was not quite two years old, the gift of a map was a bit premature. But Julius Caesar liked to sit Caesarion on his lap and point out to his son where he had been—to Gaul, to Britain, to Asia Minor and Africa— and show him where he was going.

In February of 45, it was to Spain. Obliged once more to put himself at the head of his troops, Caesar left for Munda. He had a third army, led by Pompey's sons, to fight, and was so busy he could snatch only a few hours' sleep at night. But it did not prevent him from thinking constantly of his son. In his letters to Cleopatra, he asked her to write to him about the boy. How much had Caesarion grown? And had he begun to talk?

When Caesar returned from Spain to celebrate his fifth triumph for the victory at Munda on March 17th, with the Pompeian forces crushed at last, Little Caesar had grown amazingly. He greatly resembled his father, the Roman historian Suetonius tells us, "both in his looks and walk." And he was talking incessantly. Caesar had come home to a chatterbox.

The boy was outrageously spoiled. He ruled the household. When Caesar came to his suburban villa to work on a revision of his *De Bello Gallico* (the famous *Commentaries*, about his campaigns in Gaul), Caesarion liked to interrupt his father in his study. On being let in, the child ran to his "dear Papa," who caught him up in his arms and kissed him. And there would be no more work done on the *Commentaries* that day.

Little Caesar also loved his mother dearly. Mornings, when Cleopatra went to watch her son being dressed by his *nutrix* (nurse), a Greek slave named Zoe, selected so the boy would learn Greek as naturally as Latin, he was wild with delight. Caesarion kept kissing his "dear Mama" and insisted upon her tying on his sandals. Cleopatra, too, was happy. Only one thing was lacking. Caesar loved her and not the high-born Calpurnia, a descendant of the second king of Rome, whom he had married for political reasons, yet the months passed and Caesar did not divorce his wife or speak to Cleopatra of a Roman marriage.

She hoped he would, for Caesar had made himself dictator for life, and he was powerful enough to do almost anything he wanted, even abolish the law forbidding a Roman to marry a foreigner. But when Cleopatra brought up the subject, he replied, "Oh, it wouldn't do to have a divorce now, when I'm about to ask a great favor of the Romans!" A king in all but name, Caesar longed to assume the actual title and make his power hereditary. But, having rid themselves of the Tarquins and established a republic, the Romans wanted nothing more to do with kings.

Not quite daring to seize the crown by force, Julius Caesar, short of declaring himself king, began to act like one. He was the first Roman to have his head on a coin, and he had a statue of himself placed in the temple of Jupiter, with those of the seven kings of Rome. In these honors, he included Cleopatra. In his new temple in the Forum, dedicated to Venus, from whom Caesar claimed descent through Julus, son of Aeneas, he erected a solid gold statue of the young Queen of Egypt, "Divine Sister of Venus," with two huge British pearls in its ears—a sign, some thought, that Caesar expected Cleopatra to be regarded as a goddess. This was offensive to a good many Romans. And the malicious gossip they repeated about the "Egyptian" (that Caesarion couldn't possibly be Caesar's child) upset the dictator's friends, especially Mark Antony.

Tall, heavily built, with thick curly hair, and muscles like a gladiator's, Antony resembled his mythical ancestor, Hercules. A good-natured man, who enjoyed life and lived for the day, he was a frequent guest at the villa on Janiculum Hill. Cleopatra was always glad to see him. As a girl, thirteen years ago in Alexandria, she had found Mark Antony attractive. In the autumn of B.C. 57, his cavalry had led the way from Syria into Egypt at the head of the soldiers sent by Pompey to restore her father, Ptolemy XI, to the throne. Cleopatra was a precocious eleven-year-old then; the handsome Roman cavalry colonel, twenty-six; and she developed a "teen-age" crush on him.

"Remember, I kissed you?" Mark Antony reminded her now. Cleopatra blushed and replied, "Of course, I remember." But she didn't tell him how it had thrilled her, her first kiss!

Since joining Caesar's staff in 54, Antony had served him loyally. When the governor of Gaul was hesitating at the Rubicon, wondering whether to cross the stream and declare himself Pompey's enemy, Antony had galloped from Rome to urge him to push on. So now, resenting the criticism of Caesar one heard on all sides, he begged Cleopatra to tell the dictator how unpopular his lordly airs were making him. It was rumored that he intended to overthrow the republic, to make himself king and Cleopatra queen, and the Romans wondered, had the man's epileptic fits affected his mind?

"The crown isn't something that Caesar can force the Romans to give him," Antony said. So several months later, Cleopatra was surprised to learn that, to test public opinion, he had taken part with the dictator in a well-rehearsed scene. In February, the Romans honored Lupercus, the god of fertility. The ceremony began when two young men ran through the streets, whipping every woman they met. This was supposed to make the women pregnant. The whip was called a *februa;* a word that has given us the name of our month of February, in which the Roman festival was held.

On February 15, B.C. 44, as hundreds of spectators crowded into the Forum to watch the fun, Mark Antony came bounding along the Via Sacra, striking to the right and left of him with his februa. He had been chosen this year as one of the men to whip the women. Antony remained a boy all his life. This was the kind of horseplay he enjoyed. Followed by a hilarious mob, he stopped before the dias upon which Caesar was seated to witness the merrymaking, and, half in jest and half in earnest, placed a laurel wreath on the dictator's head and proclaimed him king of Rome.

A few people cheered, but many more loudly voiced their disapproval, and Caesar, seeing that the idea was not being well received by the crowd, had sense enough to refuse the crown—for the present. At which Antony, as if it had all been a joke, and he had merely acted on impulse, pranced away, followed by his gay friends.

Caesar was left a disappointed man. He realized that the time was not yet right for him to transform the Roman republic into a monarchy. First, he must conquer India. When he had won for them an empire such as the Romans had never dreamed of, they would give him anything he wanted.

5

FALLING SICKNESS

EAGER TO EXTEND his conquests until the whole world was at his feet, Caesar began making plans for one last campaign to crown his career. He intended to leave Rome in March 44 B.C. and go to India by way of the Nile (the journey he had taken with Cleopatra), but his generals, afraid of pirates in the Red Sea, persuaded him to take Alexander's land route across Asia Minor.

Cleopatra learned with dismay that her lover would be away for two years and he refused to divorce Calpurnia until his return. Was Caesar getting tired of her? Had he won her love merely to get control of Egypt? But when she saw the fond look in the aging dictator's eyes as he gazed at his son, Cleopatra knew her fears were absurd. Didn't Caesar tell her constantly that he was only going to conquer India so that Caesarion, at his death, would inherit an empire such as even Alexander the Great had never imagined? He was wild about the boy.

With Caesar as her husband, and Caesarion his heir, Cleopatra saw herself queen of the world. The possibility that such a thing might happen alarmed the Romans. "I detest the Queen (of Egypt)," Cicero wrote. He wasn't the only one who hated her. About this time occurred the mysterious death of Ptolemy XIII, who had come to Italy with his sister. The fourteen-year-old pharaoh may have died of natural causes. But everyone knew there wasn't much family love among the Ptolemies, and the Jewish historian, Flavius Josephus, blames Cleopatra for the crime. "Ptolemy XIII was poisoned by his sister," Josephus wrote, "because he stood between her son and the throne (of Egypt)." Nor was Caesarion any better liked. Many Romans were old enough to remember the child's grandfather, and the drunken capers that Auletes of Egypt had cut in Rome during the years he spent there. If Caesar became king, was the grandson of silly old Ptolemy the Piper to inherit the empire?

One day, Little Caesar was taken by his father to a theater built by Pompey on the Campus Martius, where the senate was meeting while their building in the Forum was being repaired. There were long speeches that the child was too young to understand. Seated beside Zoe, he dropped off to sleep.

Then his nutrix (nurse) was shaking him awake, for Caesarion's father had stepped down from the *rostra* (platform) and was coming over to fetch him. There were steps ahead, but, taking his small hand, Caesar helped the boy up them onto the dais. Little Caesar was lifted in the air and seated on a desk overlooking the senate chamber. Frightened, he looked down upon rows of strange faces.

"Fellow Romans, I present to you my beloved son," Caesarion heard his father say. "I am leaving to travel to far places and face great dangers, but I hope to win India for the empire. You may be sure that, if my boy was sixteen and had reached manhood, he would be going with me. As he is still a child, not quite three, I leave him in your charge. Take good care of him, for he is more precious to me than life. Someday

he will be king of Egypt, but he will also be a loyal Roman,
I hope worthy at my death to succeed me."

When his father finished speaking, there was polite ap-
plause, but only from the most loyal of Caesar's supporters.
The majority of the senators sat looking glum. The dictator
lifted Caesarion from the desk and, once again holding his son
by the hand, helped him down the steps of the rostra. The
child ran obediently, like his father told him to, back to his
nurse.

Listening to all this was a pale, lean fellow named Gaius
Cassius Longinus, with an angry look in his eyes. He had
served under Pompey at Pharsalus and never ceased to be
Caesar's enemy. All through his speech, Cassius had longed to
stride up to the dais and plunge a knife into the dictator's
breast. He hated tyrants. And wasn't that what Caesar had
become?

When the senate adjourned, Cassius went across the chamber to join his brother-in-law, Marcus Junius Brutus, and the
two young men walked home together.

"Did you hear Caesar publicly acknowledge Cleopatra's
child to be his son and say that the boy was to succeed him?"
Cassius exclaimed. "Brutus, didn't I tell you that Caesar in-
tends to found a dynasty? He has made himself dictator for
life, but, mark my words, not satisfied with that, when he
returns from India, he'll crown himself. By Jupiter, haven't
we had enough of kings?"

"Indeed, we have," agreed Brutus. He was very proud of
being descended from Lucius Junius Brutus, who had led the
uprising against Tarquinius, the last king of Rome, and freed
the city from the rule of one man.

"Your ancestor founded our republic, do you want Caesar
to destroy all he stood for?" Cassius asked. "We've endured
a lot from him, but this is too much. I tell you, Marcus, before
that man brings our beloved republic to an end, he must die."

For some time Cassius had been saying that, for the good of the state, Julius Caesar should be assassinated. Today, hearing him publicly proclaim Cleopatra's son to be his child and heir, Cassius felt the time for the murder had arrived. Under Caesar, what had the republic become? A farce! Too much of a coward to do the deed alone, Cassius enlisted accomplices. By the first of March they numbered sixty. The conspirators all had grievances against the man they planned to kill. His generals, like Labienus and Decimus Brutus, resented Caesar's taking the credit for all his victories, when often, during a battle, he had been in his tent, having an epileptic fit. Others were indignant over the rumor that he intended to transfer the capital of the empire from Rome to Cleopatra's Alexandria. Brutus was the hardest to convince. Because of an old love affair with his mother, Caesar had made Brutus governor of Cisalpine Gaul. Could he plot the murder of his benefactor?

"You, most of all, Marcus, should be with us," Cassius said to him. "As his descendant, it's your duty to defend the republic which was the creation of the first Brutus."

So Marcus consented to join the conspiracy. A meeting was held at Cassius' home. With everyone in agreement that Caesar's ambition to establish an hereditary monarchy was a threat to the liberty of the Roman people and so he must die, there was little left to do but plan his assassination. March 15, the Ides of March (middle of the month) on the Roman calendar, was chosen as the day, because that was the last time the dictator would preside over the senate before he left for Asia Minor.

"Don't say a word about this to anyone," Cassius told his fellow conspirators. But with so many people in on the plot, the secret was not well kept. Caesar was warned by a soothsayer, (fortuneteller) that, on the Ides of March, he might be murdered, to use caution that day and stay home. But previous attempts to kill the dictator had made him indifferent to danger. By March 13, when he dined with Cleopatra, he had forgotten the soothsayer's warning.

Caesar was only fifty-eight but he looked seventy tonight, for, tired from overwork, he was suffering from frequent epileptic fits. Sixteen legions had been sent ahead to Greece. He was leaving Rome on the 19th of the month, to join them in Athens. And he had many things on his mind. So had Cleopatra. She and Caesarion were sailing for Alexandria after Caesar left, and she wished to discuss with him some things about the boy that worried her.

"He acts so strangely, at times," Cleopatra said. "He grins in a foolish way, and stares at you blankly. Then, after a minute or two, he's all right again. Do you think it's anything to worry about?"

Ever since, as a baby, Little Caesar had kept falling down, the fear that he would inherit his father's epilepsy (a disease the Romans called "Falling Sickness" because a person often falls and hurts himself during an attack) had haunted his parents. The thought being too dreadful to face, Cleopatra brought up another problem. "Then he's afraid of so many things, like the dark. Someone has to sit by his bed every night until he goes to sleep."

This was a minor matter Caesarion's parents could bring themselves to discuss. When the meal ended, Caesar said, "Befor I leave, I'll go and kiss him good-night again. Perhaps, we can have a little talk." So, later that evening, before going home to Calpurnia, the dictator went into the *cubicula* (bedroom) where his son lay in bed, but not asleep.

"What's this I hear about you being afraid of the dark?" Caesar said, sitting down by his bed and taking the child's hand. "Aren't you ashamed of yourself? A big boy almost three! Why, at your age, I wasn't afraid of anything. Do you think, if I had been a coward, I could have conquered Gaul?

And your mother wasn't afraid to come back to Egypt and fight for her throne. I'm going to India to win an empire for you. Someday, you may lead a Roman army to even greater conquests. Do you think that your soldiers will want to follow and obey you if they think you're afraid?"

Tears rushed to Caesarion's eyes. Throwing his arms around his father's neck, he sobbed, "Papa, I love you!"

Caesar's heart melted. It was impossible to scold the dear little fellow. "You're going to try to be brave and make us proud of you?" he asked and, kissing his son tenderly, laid him back on the pillow and went away.

He was never to see him again.

6

MURDER ROMAN STYLE

ON THE MORNING of March 15th, the conspirators, daggers hidden under their togas, were waiting in the corridor outside the senate chamber. As the hours passed and Caesar did not come, they grew worried. Had the plot leaked out? Cassius sent Decimus Brutus, one of Caesar's most trusted generals in Gaul, to the dictator's home in the Forum to find out what was the matter.

On entering his house near the temple of Vesta, Brutus found Caesar at breakfast. He had spent a restless night. So had Calpurnia. She had dreamed of seeing her husband lying dead. This morning, Calpurnia was so upset that she was begging him not to go to the senate but to stay home.

"It's the Ides of March," she reminded him, "when the soothsayer said that something terrible might happen to you."

"But, *Imperator* (general, from which our word emperor is derived), you must come." And Decimus Brutus used the one inducement he knew would tempt his former commander. "The senate, as a farewell gift, has voted unanimously to make you king."

Caesar's heart leaped with joy. He had hoped that they

would give him the crown before he left Rome. "It's a trap! Oh, please don't go!" Calpurnia tried to warn her husband. But nothing could keep him home now.

Calling for his litter, the dictator went off in high spirits with Decimus Brutus to Pompey's theater, on the Campus Martius. As he walked through its portico, Caesar saw Mark Antony standing beside a statue of Pompey. He stopped to chat with him. Then the dictator entered the hall where the senate met. The whole assembly rose respectfully to their feet, as he took his place on the rostra.

From this point on, the conspirators had planned every move. Cimber walked up to the dais, ostensibly to ask for a pardon for his exiled brother. Cassius and the others, as if in support of the appeal, came forward. Caesar stood up, frowning. Why was there no mention of his being made king? And why was everyone crowding so close around him? Angry suspicion in his eyes, he ordered the men to step back. Instead, Cimber snatched the dictator's toga from off his shoulder. That was the signal agreed upon. Knives flashed out, as the murderers closed in on the unarmed man.

Casca struck the first blow. Then the others fell upon him —Cassius struck, Cimber struck, Ligarius struck, Decimus Brutus (his trusted general) struck. Caesar, streaming with blood, managed to stagger out to the portico. At the base of Pompey's statue, he fell to the marble floor. *"Et tu, Brute?* (You, too, Brutus?)" were Julius Caesar's last words as he saw Marcus Brutus, his young protégé, coming at him with dagger raised. Brutus' blade dug in, and Caesar died, stabbed twenty-three times to make sure he was dead.

At the time of the murder, Mark Antony was standing only a short distance away. He rushed to the dictator's defense. But his path was blocked by the murderers. Believing themselves to be patriots, they ran out of the theater, their togas

spattered with Caesar's blood, waving their knives and shouting, "The tyrant is dead! We've saved the republic!"

In horror, Antony looked down at the bloodstained corpse,
lying at the base of Pompey's statue. Would the conspirators
return and murder him next? Knowing that they might, Antony, slipping out of the building, hurried by way of back
streets to his home on Esquiline Hill. His wife Fulvia almost
fainted when Antony, rushing in, told her what had happened.
"I must hide," he gasped. "Now no friend of Caesar's will be
safe."

On hearing of the dictator's murder, people locked themselves in their houses, expecting more bloodshed to follow.
Mark Antony, as Caesar's closest associate, was in great danger.
He turned his home into a fortress. Gladiators, with swords
drawn, stood guard at all the entrances. But even before making plans for his own safety, Antony thought of Caesar's
young widow and her child, alone and unprotected, across the
Tiber. A trusted slave was sent to warn Cleopatra that she
too might be murdered, as well as Little Caesar. She was not
to leave the house.

Rome was stunned. The dictator was dead, and since the
Romans did not recognize Caesar's Egyptian marriage, he
had left no legitimate descendant. There would be a mad
scramble for power. Antony knew he must act quickly. The
next day, escorted by his bodyguard of armed gladiators, he
rode to the dictator's home in the Forum to get possession of
his will. He must know whom Caesar had named to succeed
him. Perhaps, himself?

The dictator's body had been carried to a spot nearby in
the Forum. And Calpurnia had gone there to weep over his
corpse. Antony had never liked Caesar's cold, domineering
wife, but now he felt sorry for the poor woman. Her eyes
red from crying, Calpurnia kept saying, "Oh, if he had only
listened to me, and not gone to the senate—" Wishing to leave

Calpurnia alone with her grief, Antony lost no time in stating the reason for his visit. "I would like to see Caesar's will," he said.

It was with the Vestal Virgins (their temple was a kind of Records Office), Caesar's widow told him. "But I have a copy. I'll get it for you."

A half hour later, Antony was back on the Esquiline, seated in his library, reading what Faberius, Caesar's secretary, had written and the dictator had signed. Glancing over the will, Antony had the surprise of his life. He was completely ignored! Three grandnephews—Lucius Pinarius, Quintus Pedius, and Gaius Octavius—inherited the dictator's fortune, which amounted to approximately five million American dollars. If a son was born to Calpurnia after his death, Caesar asked several friends to act as the child's guardians. His real estate in Rome, including the villa in which Cleopatra was living, was left to the Roman people. Every citizen was to inherit 300 *sesterces* (about $15 in American money). In a codicil, Caesar named Octavius (in English, Octavian), the eldest of his nephews, as his adopted son and chief heir, leaving him three-quarters of his estate. There was no reference to Cleopatra, not the slightest mention of his real son.

* * * *

All Rome flocked to the Forum to see Julius Caesar lying in state. On March 20th, his corpse was to be burned on the Campus Martius, outside the city walls. The day before, Mark Antony went to look for the last time at the man he had loved and admired. Finding a large crowd weeping around the slain dictator, Antony, holding up Caesar's toga, red with blood, made them an eloquent speech. He told the people of the dictator's gift to them—each citizen of Rome to receive 300 sesterces. Touched by his generosity, the crowd grew hysterical with grief. Seizing benches, tables, anything that would burn, they built a pile of wood and burned the corpse then and there.

The next day, not wanting Cleopatra to hear the unpleasant news from anyone else, Antony rode across the Tiber to tell her about Caesar's will. In a garden by the house, he found the young widow seated on a bench, her child beside her. Cleopatra had wept until she could weep no more. She was calm, in a state of shock. With his big eyes in his old little face, how like Caesar the boy looked!

"Have you told him?" Antony asked.

"I tried to, he kept asking why his father didn't come to see him. Last night, I showed him the star Venus. I told him that his dear Papa had gone up there to join his ancestress, the goddess Venus. But, from the sky, he was watching over him. I think now Caesarion knows he'll never see him again."

They sat for a while in silence. Then, much as Antony hated to do it, he had to tell Cleopatra about the will. She listened in shock amazement. "Octavian, his adopted son and heir? What about his own child and me?"

"Neither of you are mentioned."

Cleopatra burst into tears. With a stroke of his pen, the man she had loved and trusted had reduced her from being queen of the world to being simply queen of Egypt. And she might not be that for long, with Caesar, her protector, dead. As for Caesarion, once crown prince of the earth, what would his future be now? But there was no use tearing up the document in Antony's possession or forging another, Calpurnia had been smart enough to give him only a copy. The original was "with the Vestal Virgins"—or so she said.

"That clause, where Caesar appoints guardians for any child born to Calpurnia after his death, shows it's an old will," Cleopatra was quick to point out. "Why, Calpurnia has been beyond the childbearing age for years! There must be a newer will, in favor of Caesarion."

"If there was," replied Antony, "Calpurnia has burned it."

Caesar's wife had obtained her revenge. What would Cleopatra do? Try to get Caesarion declared by the senate as the rightful heir before Octavian returned to claim his inheritance? Or run away?

"Why, that's absurd, what have I to fear of a youth of eighteen?" Cleopatra exclaimed, when Antony suggested that she return to Egypt and wait there to see what happened. "Octavian is hardly more than a boy, without a single supporter."

She tried to remember Gaius Octavius, this grandnephew of Caesar's, the son of C. Octavius by Atia, the daughter of his sister Julia. The dictator had scarcely known him as a child, but had taken a fancy to the young man during his Spanish campaign against the sons of Pompey. Still weak from pneumonia, the delicate, often-ill Octavian had joined his great-uncle in Spain and fought at his side. Cleopatra had also heard of him in Rome. It seemed that Octavian had rescued Juba, the little Numidian prince, from prison after Caesar's triumph. Admiring his courage as he walked in chains through the Forum, Octavian had taken the young African to live with him. Juba was a bright boy. Octavian intended to have him educated.

At present, Caesar's nephew was at school in Apollonia, Illyria (now Albania), studying military tactics with Marcus Vipsanius Agrippa, a boyhood friend. Cleopatra implored Antony, before Octavian could return to Rome, to present her son's claim before the senate. He gladly agreed to help. It was to Antony's selfish interest to see that Octavian, who might become a dangerous rival, did not succeed his uncle. On the other hand, if he was regent for Cleopatra's child, Antony would rule Rome until Caesarion became of age.

So a few days later, the slain dictator's closest associate rose in the senate and put forward Caesarion's claim to be Caesar's son and heir.

"Nonsense! If he believed Cleopatra's boy to be his, why didn't Caesar mention him in his will?" demanded those who preferred Octavian.

* * * *

Ten days after Caesar's death, Antony was about to go for a swim in the Tiber one morning when a short, blond, young man, with a sickly pallor, appeared at his house. It was Octavian. His mother, Atia, had notified him of his uncle's death, and, accompanied by his friend Agrippa, he had hurried back to Rome. In a quiet but firm voice, Octavian announced that, as his adopted son and chief heir, he wanted his three-quarters share of Caesar's estate. Antony, furious, had to hand over the gold.

The chief assassins, Cassius and Brutus, had fled to Greece, and Rome formed itself into two factions over who was to succeed the late dictator. Some supported Caesar's nephew; others, Caesarion. Then, to everyone's surprise, Octavian, whom no one at first had taken seriously, began to gain supporters, for the average Roman refused to question Caesar's will. Why should they, when in it every citizen would get 300 sesterces? Italy was in for another civil war. So tense did the situation become that, in April, a month after Caesar's death, Antony rode across the Tiber one evening to beg Cleopatra to return to Egypt and let him handle her affairs in Rome.

"Do you want something to happen to Caesarion?" Antony pleaded. "You underestimate Octavian. Under that reserved manner of his, he is ruthless, full of cold cunning. As long as Caesarion lives, Octavian will never feel secure. So don't you think he wouldn't like to get his hands on your boy. Why, even this house isn't yours! Caesar willed all his land on the Janiculum to the Roman people for a park—"

He never finished that sentence for the still of the night was shattered by the clatter of chariot wheels. Hurling up the driveway, they screeched to a stop before the house.

Rushing to the window, Antony saw, to his horror, that the courtyard was filled with chariots, disgorging helmeted and breastplated soldiers. He quickly closed the shutters. Who were these men? Octavian's bodyguard, Antony knew, sent by him to kidnap the Queen of Egypt and murder her son. Snatching up Caesarion, he asked Cleopatra, "Which way?" There wasn't a moment to lose. They heard steps outside and loud voices. Someone was hammering on the door.

Little Caesar began to cry. What was happening? Frightened, the boy clung to Antony as he ran across the room. Drawing back a curtain, Cleopatra opened a door and led the way down some stairs into total darkness. They had only gone a few steps, stumbling in the dark, when the thud of heavy hobnail boots could be heard in the room over their heads.

"They're inside," Antony warned. "Keep very quiet."

Cleopatra had taken Caesarion from Antony's arms. "*Hs-s-s*—" she whispered, for the child, terrified by the darkness, was crying hysterically, loud sobs that might be heard.

At the foot of the stairs, they felt their way, up to their knees in water, along a long vaulted passage. His *cloaca* (sewer), that brought water to the house of a rich Roman, also served him as a hiding place. But how safe were they? At any moment, the door at the top of the stairs might open, the light of flaming torches flash in their eyes, and they would hear the sound of wading feet coming nearer and nearer to the dark, slimy corner where they were crouching.

The fugitives hid in that cold, wet darkness for twenty minutes. It seemed like three hours. Each time a rat ran by, or a big black spider dropped on him, Caesarion clung in a panic to his mother. Then, gradually, the commotion above them ceased. The house grew quiet and, after hesitating a long time, the fugitives ventured back upstairs. Looking around her, Cleopatra exclaimed, "The beasts!" The rooms that Caesar had filled for her with exquisite furniture and statuary were a mass of debris. Octavian's soldiers had wrecked the house.

Going to the door, Antony stood stunned by what he saw in the courtyard. There was no sign of his chariot and horses, but his charioteer and his four bodyguards lay sprawled on the gravel, dead. Antony turned to Cleopatra. "Now will you go back to Egypt?" he demanded.

7

✂︎✂︎

BEWARE OF OCTAVIAN

ON APRIL 13, B.C. 44, a farmer driving a *plaustrum*, a canvas-covered country wagon with solid wooden wheels, stopped at four o'clock in the afternoon before Cleopatra's house. A woman wearing a hooded, knee-length *paenula* (a rough woolen cape worn by poor Romans), with a child in her arms, ran out. Placing the boy in the back of the farm wagon, among some empty wine barrels, she climbed up onto the seat beside the old man. He cracked his whip and the two mules trotted off.

Taking back streets to avoid being seen, they reached the Porta Trigemina, one of the gates of Rome, and set off along the Via Ostiensis, heading for the coast. It was to be an anxious journey, for Octavian had soldiers patrolling every road leading out of the city, with orders to arrest any woman traveling with a three-year-old child.

The mules were old, they seemed to creep past the farms that lined the left bank of the Tiber as it flowed to the sea. At one village they heard cries of "Stop! Stop!" but the old farmer used his whip instead and they didn't stop. It was five o'clock when they jolted to a halt to feed and water the mules.

While she waited in the yard of the inn, the woman ran around to the back of the wagon where, under the canvas hood, the child was huddled. "Be quiet! Don't make a sound!" she whispered.

They went on again, stopping only when it was necessary. In a cluster of houses, halfway to the coast, some soldiers halted them. One of the men seized the mules by their bridles and demanded, "Hey, you, old man! What have you got in the back of that cart?" Another, peering in under the canvas top, started to investigate. Just then, a third man exclaimed, "It's only old Jason! He brings fruit, vegetables, and wine from Mark Antony's farm at Ostia up to his house in Rome. I know Jason, he passes here every week, let him go."

Jason whipped up his mules and on they went.

A storm was blowing in from the sea and, as they neared the coast, the canvas hood on the wagon seemed about to fly off. But by seven o'clock they reached Ostia, the nearest sea-port to Rome. Stopping at a villa outside of the walled town, Jason pounded on the door. He waited and pounded again. Still no answer. Then, through the garden beside the house came a short, bald-headed man carrying a fishing pole.

"I'm back from catching a mess of fish," Grattius Faliscus, poet and sportsman, explained to Cleopatra the pole in his hand. "Come in. Antony sent me word that a friend of his would be in need of hospitality. I was expecting you. You must be hungry, I'll get you some food."

Held in his mother's arms, Caesarion watched Jason drive on to Antony's farm. Then the refugees waited while Faliscus opened the door. They slipped inside. Faliscus quickly closed it behind them. No one saw them enter that tiny, white stucco house.

"How do you like my hideaway?" the poet asked. "I've just bought it, as a place to come to and get some writing done. I'm working on a long poem, five hundred hexameters, on the joys of fishing. I like it in Ostia, nobody knows me. I live simply, without any servants. I hope you won't mind my cooking."

On a stove, some pots stood on trivets above the glowing charcoal. Picking up one of them, filled with steaming onion soup, Faliscus placed it on a table with some flat, circular loaves of black bread. Cleopatra sat down and, taking Caesarion on her lap, tried to feed him. But the child was too tired to eat. So the exhausted little boy was placed on the only bed in the little one-roomed house, and, before his mother had finished undressing him, he was asleep.

"I'll spend the night out in the stable with my horse," Faliscus said. "She's a dear friend, I don't mind in the least."

But several hours later, when her host had gone, Cleopatra, unable to sleep, still sat by the table where the poet had left her, listening to the storm. It was getting worse. The rain beat on the tiled roof, the wind rattled the wooden shutters, and tears streamed down her cheeks. Cleopatra had no idea as to what the future held or how she would get to Egypt. Bitterly, she compared her present plight with her arrival in Italy, two years ago.

"It would be too dangerous for you to go to my *villa rustica* (country estate) in Ostia," Antony had told her. "That is the first place Octavian will look for you." So, in Faliscus' seaside retreat that only a few of his intimate friends knew about, Cleopatra waited for Mark Antony to join her. Of the excitement her departure had caused in Rome, she knew nothing.

When one morning, two days later, the door opened and Antony walked in, Cleopatra ran to throw her arms about the handsome, curly-haired giant, she was so glad to see him. The news he brought was not reassuring. That day (April 15, 44 B.C.), Cicero wrote to his friend Atticus, "The Queen of Egypt left Rome two days ago." People even knew that she had gone to Ostia, to try to sail for Alexandria.

"By now, Octavian must have every ship watched," Antony said, "and how I can get you to Egypt, I don't know. Meanwhile, you're safe here with Grattius. He has been in Greece for three years, and has only just returned to Italy, so he cannot have seen you in Rome. I told him that you were an important person in great danger, fleeing the country, but he doesn't suspect who you are."

The wind and rain still shook the house. But, after a hasty meal, Antony went out into the gale and trudged off down the road to the walled city of Ostia. An hour later, he returned, feeling more cheerful. At a tavern he had met a sea captain named Sarbo, who was leaving for Cyrene, on the North African coast, with some pilgrims who had been in Rome. He was willing to take two more passengers on to Egypt aboard the *Triton*. But Captain Sarbo refused to sail while the sea was so rough. With Rome alerted that the Queen of Egypt had fled to Ostia, any delay was dangerous. But what could they do? From a window, Cleopatra and Antony peered anxiously at the sky.

It was afternoon before the storm blew out to sea, and a boy came to tell them that Captain Sarbo's *Triton* was ready to sail. "Oh, not now!" exclaimed Cleopatra. Italy's leading grain and olive oil port of Ostia was a busy commercial city of red-brick apartment buildings, vast warehouses, and the forum, temples, theater, taverns, and public baths common to every Roman town. The life of the port centered around a mile of docks along the Tiber, where cargoes from all over the Mediterranean were unloaded, to be sent by barge up the river to Rome. At this time of day, the water front would be crowded with Egyptian wheat merchants, Greek ship pilots, stevedores, muleteers, ferrymen and slaves. How could they get on board the *Triton* without being seen?

While the boy waited outside, Faliscus and Antony made plans with Cleopatra. "I can get you through the town," the poet told her. "Hide in the back of my *lectita* (chaise), and I'll drive you as far as the Porta Marina. Beyond that, I cannot go. It's private property, owned by the grain and oil companies. No vehicles but theirs are allowed; or any people, except on foot."

It was a long walk from the Porta Marina, out onto the pier along which the cargo ships were moored. How could they get past Octavian's men, who would surely be on the dock, watching any boat about to sail? Antony finally thought of a way, but the success of his plan depended upon not a slip being made.

"When we get out of Grattius' wagon at the Porta Marina, you'll start off alone, and I'll follow with Caesarion," he informed Cleopatra. "You'll be fairly safe. It's your son they're after, but don't worry about him. I'll get him on board, somehow. We must go separately, however. No one must suspect that we know each other. On the long walk from the Porta Marina to the *Triton*, you'll be alone. Have you the courage to do it?"

Cleopatra wondered whether she had, but Antony didn't wait for her reply. He went out to the garden, where the boy sent by Captain Sarbo was waiting. "Run to the tavern in Ostia," he instructed him, "and tell everyone there that the Queen of Egypt left for Alexandria yesterday."

* * * *

Late in the afternoon of April 15th, the *Triton* was getting ready to sail. Standing near the foot of the gangplank, his eyes searching the people going on board, was one of Octavian's soldiers. Among the passengers, mostly pilgrims from North Africa, returning home with their luggage and all the things they had bought in Rome, the soldier hardly glanced at a bare-legged youth who hurried by, wearing a hooded paenula. It was a woman with the three-year-old child for whom he was watching.

His attention was drawn to the stir around two people who followed some distance behind in the crowd. What was this— a short, bald-headed man had a tall young woman by the arm? The soldier saw that it was necessary that he support her, for the girl, so stout she could hardly waddle, was obviously pregnant. People were looking at her and laughing. "Ye gods, will she have her baby before she gets on board?" exclaimed a flower vendor.

"More likely twins, from the size of her," someone else said.

The girl seemed to the soldier to enjoy all the interest she was causing. She minced along, shaking her long black curls, and clowning with the other travelers. Not looking where she was going, the girl banged into an old woman. "Hey, look out there—" she cried, in a deep male voice.

The old woman let out a yelp. "That's a man. Look!" She pointed after the "girl," who, picking up her *palla* (a long woolen mantle Roman women wore over an ankle-length tunic or *stola*), had made a dash for the ship. Leaping on board, "she" disappeared below.

Octavian's soldier rushed over to the gangplank, where the captain had already given the order to raise the anchor. "I demand to search this boat!" he cried.

"Certainly," replied Sarbo, "but you'll have to go with us to North Africa if you do, for we're casting off."

A few seconds later, Antony, having left his female disguise, his black wig, and his precious burden in Cleopatra's cabin, jumped ashore just as the *Triton* moved away from the wharf. Waiting for him on the dock was Faliscus—the short, bald-headed man who had helped Antony smuggle Caesarion on board the ship.

"That was the Queen of Egypt, of course," the poet said to him. "I knew she was Cleopatra, the minute I saw her. Why did you risk your life for that woman? Who cares about what happens to Cleopatra since Caesar's death? It's Octavian you should be friendly with now. His soldier might have arrested you for smuggling Cleopatra's child on board under your stola. Why did you do it?"

"Because I like excitement."

"I can think of safer ways to amuse myself. You're in love with her, aren't you?"

"Yes," admitted Antony, "ever since she was a homely little girl of eleven."

Meanwhile, from the ship, Cleopatra watched the town of Ostia growing smaller. She thought fondly of Mark Antony, the only person in Rome who had helped her. There hadn't even been time to thank him. Unfastening the belt that kept Caesarion suspended under his stola, Antony had dropped the boy on the berth and dashed out of the cabin.

With a heavy heart, Cleopatra wondered what lay ahead. She had lost Caesar's love and protection. Now there was no place for her and her son except in Egypt. And she would have to fight Arsinoe, as she had fought her brother Ptolemy, to regain even that crown. For her sister, by Cleopatra's request released from prison after Caesar's triumph, had returned to Alexandria and seized the throne. I was a fool to let Arsinoe live, Cleopatra reproached herself.

Her bitter thoughts were interrupted on hearing behind her the cry of the epileptic. Recognizing the scream from having nursed Caesar through his attacks, Cleopatra rushed over to the berth on which his son lay tossing. He was breathing hard, his eyes rolled wildly, and a bloodstained foam was already on the boy's lips. During a fit, little could be done, Cleopatra knew, except to try to keep an epileptic from hurting himself while unconscious. She pushed the handle of a dagger she always carried between Little Caesar's back teeth, to prevent him from biting his tongue, then held his hands for fear that, in flinging himself about, the boy would get hurt. Gradually, his convulsions subsided, he grew limp and dropped off to sleep.

There was no use pretending any longer that Caesarion had not inherited his father's disease. His mother burst into tears. Prolonged emotional stress, Caesar had told her, brought on his epileptic fits. All that Little Caesar had been through recently had been too much for him. Poor Cleopatra! Her troubles were only just beginning. She must not only face the future alone, but with an epileptic child.

8

HER SECOND ROMAN

PERCHED BY A WINDOW of the palace at Alexandria, Little Caesar, wearing a short Greek tunic, squatted on his sandals gazing out at sea. Spread across his lap was a papyrus scroll, but the boy wasn't studying. He was watching for a ship with purple sails. Two weeks ago, he had seen the swift, fifty-oared galley, with a figurehead of Venus on its prow, glide out of the harbor by the Pharos lighthouse. When he saw it return, Cleopatra's son was ready to spring to his feet, dash down to the quay, and throw himself in her arms.

"Where is Tarsus?" Caesarion asked Populos, his Greek tutor, seated beside him. "Why did my mother go there? When is she coming back?"

"Tarsus is in Asia Minor, a long distance away, but the queen should be home any day now."

Carefully, Populos avoided the boy's question as to why Cleopatra had gone to Tarsus. The old man knew why—to meet Mark Antony—but should he tell the child? He was only six, would Caesarion understand if he explained to him that his mother had gone there to ask the Roman general to risk his career for the sake of Caesar's memory and Caesar's son?

61

Three years ago, when she had returned to Egypt to fight Arsinoe for the throne, Cleopatra had thought that, at least, she had Antony's backing. Raising a small force of supporters, Cleopatra had faced Arsinoe and her friends, and forced her sister to flee to Asia Minor, where she took refuge as a priestess in the temple of Artemis at Ephesus. Then, in B.C. 43, Octavian and Antony, who had been fighting each other for control of Italy, made up, to Cleopatra's consternation. United, they crossed to Macedonia, defeated Brutus and Cassius at Philippi, and, forming the second triumvirate, divided up the Roman world between themselves and M. Aemilius Lepidus, governor of Gaul. As his share, Lepidus took Africa; Octavian, Italy; and Antony, Asia Minor. That winter of 41, on a tour of his possessions, Antony had sent word to Cleopatra that she should sail across to Tarsus, in Cilicia (southern Turkey) where he was, and pay her respects to him.

Her first impulse had been to turn down his invitation. How dare Caesar's former cavalry officer order her to appear before him! Why didn't he come to her? Egypt was no client nation, like Syria or Judea, and Cleopatra intended to keep it that way, rich and independent of Rome. But in the end, she went to Tarsus. She was furious at Antony for becoming friendly with her enemy, Octavian, and signing a treaty of alliance with him. But Antony now ruled the eastern part of the empire, as far as the Euphrates River, and she wanted him on her side, if war with Octavian should come.

Populos remembered how he and Caesarion had watched Cleopatra's elegant ship, its slender hull ending in a poop shaped like a swan's neck, being made ready for the voyage to Cilicia, where the queen hoped to induce the Roman general to back her cause and that of her son. Since the boat had sailed out of the harbor two weeks ago, Populos had wondered, as had all Alexandria, what was happening in Tarsus. He was as eager for Cleopatra's return as Little Caesar. But the old scholar had been engaged to educate the next pharaoh, and he said to him sternly, 'Caesarion, get on with your lesson. What will your mother say, if she comes home and you haven't read that papyrus roll to me?'

The boy wasn't listening. "It's the ship! I see it!" Leaping to his feet, he raced out of the room and down the stairs.

Populos hurried after him, calling, "Don't go so fast! Wait for me!" What if all this excitement should bring on one of Little Caesar's epileptic fits? Greatly concerned, Populos caught up with his young pupil down on the quay before the palace, where a flock of people had gathered to watch the royal galley glide up to the wharf.

As Cleopatra came down the gangplank, Little Caesar darted through the crowd toward her. "Mama! Mama!" he cried. His mother bent and kissed him. Then she turned and Caesarion saw, to his surprise, that there was a big, smiling man with her. He tried to kiss Caesar's son. But, hiding his face in Cleopatra's mantle, the boy refused to be kissed.

"I'm Mark Antony," the curly-haired giant said. "When you left Italy, I saved your life by smuggling you aboard a ship. Don't you remember me?"

"No," replied Little Caesar, scowling.

"Why, Caesarion, don't be so rude!" his mother exclaimed. Then she turned to Antony. "Welcome to Alexandria!" Cleopatra said, looking up at him lovingly. And they walked away together, up the steps to the palace. Had they forgotten him? It seemed so. Caesarion ran after them, almost in tears.

Nothing would ever be the same for him again. Never!

* * * *

While Caesar was alive, Cleopatra had been faithful to him. In Rome, she and Antony had never been anything but good friends. But Caesar was dead now and, at Tarsus, Cleopatra set out to seduce her second Roman. She had sailed up the river Cydnus to Tarsus, where Antony was, in the silver-oared galley that Shakespeare made immortal, and the Roman general was enslaved. Now she had brought him back to Alexandria to see all the money, men, and ships she could lend him, if he were to lead an army against Octavian, and claim the throne for herself as Caesar's widow and for their son. So Cleopatra set out deliberately to charm Antony, as she had Caesar.

No two men were ever more different. Caesar had been a cold, aloof intellectual, disciplined, meticulous about his personal appearance. Antony was a hotheaded, impulsive, rather vulgar man, with a loud assertive manner, who liked practical jokes. Nor was he abstemious at table like Caesar, who seldom touched wine. Antony enjoyed good food and drink—in fact, too much. The banquets of Tarsus were repeated in Alexandria. Clad in transparent silk robes and fragrant with the heady perfumes of Arabia, Cleopatra lay on a dining couch by the side of her Roman guest night after night, entertaining him with acrobats, jugglers, and dancing girls.

All was not frivolity, however. Antony took Caesarion to watch camel-racing and swimming at the gymnasium, where the triumvir kept in trim, his muscular body the envy of all who saw him. He was trying hard to win over Cleopatra's son. It was no easy task. Lonely since Caesar's death, his young widow had lavished all her love on their son, and Little Caesar had become a spoiled boy, used to having things his own way. His praises were sung, his whims indulged. In the royal palace, as an only child, he ruled everyone, from lowest to highest.

Now, for the first time, Caesarion found himself having to compete with a rival for his mother's affection. He hated the big, jovial Roman. "When is Antony going away?" the boy kept asking.

An ardent fisherman, the triumvir liked to boast of the size of his catch. One time, when they were fishing on Lake

Mareotis, Cleopatra (writes Plutarch) secretly hired a diver to play a joke on him. When Antony pulled in his line, what did he find on his hook but a smoked herring! At the surprise on his face, how Caesarion laughed, until he nearly fell out of the boat. The triumvir longed to grab the boy and throw him into the water. He had endured enough from Cleopatra's beloved only child. Well, Antony knew how to fix that. He had good reason to believe that Little Caesar would not long be an only child.

Antony remained in Alexandria for a year, forgetting everything but Cleopatra, as Caesar had done. Then, in March B.C. 40, to Caesarion's delight, the triumvir was summoned to Greece by his wife. Wild with jealousy over Antony's affair with the Queen of Egypt, Fulvia had raised a few troops, with the help of his brother Lucius, and rashly attacked Octavian, hoping to force her husband to return to Italy. Defeated by Octavian, Fulvia and her sons by Antony, Antyllus (young Antony) and Julius, fled to Athens, where they begged him to join them.

Antony was angry with Fulvia for having attacked Octavian before he was ready. With Cleopatra's help, he had first intended to march against the Parthians, who lived in western Asia, southeast of the Caspian Sea. When he had made himself stronger by conquering them, and only then, would Antony pick a quarrel with Octavian—but not now.

"What a predicament I'm in!" he exclaimed to Cleopatra. "I can't break with Octavian at present. I'll have to go to Athens, talk with Fulvia, and try to patch things up."

Cleopatra agreed with Antony that it would be better for him to remain friendly with Octavian until he himself wanted war. But for him to leave Egypt at this time was hard on her, for she was pregnant.

Plutarch, who likes to draw a moral, states that the Queen of Egypt had recently rid herself of the last member of her family who stood in Caesarion's way by persuading Antony to send men to Asia Minor to murder her sister. It is true that Arsinoe was plotting at Ephesus with Serapion, the Egyptian governor of Cyprus, to oust Cleopatra from her throne. But Antony's cutthroats invaded the sacred temple of Artemis and stabbed Arsinoe to death on the altar steps, as she was offering a sacrifice to the goddess. For this ugly deed, Plutarch thinks Cleopatra deserved the cruel thing that Antony did to her after he left Egypt.

Arriving in Greece, Antony scolded his wife for attacking Octavian without first asking his consent. Fulvia crumpled and died, presumably of a broken heart. Antony wasted no time mourning her. Blaming everything that had happened on his late wife, he made up with Octavian and, at Brundisium (Brindisi) in the summer of 40, signed a new treaty with his former enemy.

That fall, Cleopatra, in Alexandria, was forced to endure the misery of childbirth alone. This time, there would be no loving Caesar to comfort her. With the queen were only her old doctor, Olympus, who had delivered Caesarion, and a few attendants.

September second, when Cleopatra's nine months of waiting were over, was also the festival of Artemis or Selene, as the Egyptians called the Greek moon goddess. Religious ceremonies took place that day in honor of the sister of Helios (the Sun), at her shrine on the tip of Lochias Point. Through the streets of Alexandria, the townspeople flocked out to the temple and the royal palace, whose grounds the queen always opened to the public at this time for their enjoyment. By noon, the noisy crowd had filled the gardens, shouting, singing, trodding down her lawn and lovely flower beds. In a room of the palace overlooking the island of Antirrhodus, its windows tightly sealed to shut out the noise, Cleopatra gave birth to twins.

"He is as handsome as Helios, the sun god," Olympus said,

when the first baby came. "She is as pretty as Selene, the moon goddess," he added, as a little girl followed her brother into the world.

Cleopatra turned her head weakly on the pillow. "That's what I shall call them," she whispered, "Helios and Selene."

The twins, officially named Alexander Helios and Cleopatra Selene, the Sun and the Moon, were born under favorable auspices—on the day of Artemis, the Greek goddess of childbirth and of all very young things. While Cleopatra was in labor, an eagle came to perch on the roof of the palace. The king of birds had never been seen before in Egypt, and the priests out at the temple of Isis, on Pharos Island, predicted it meant that one of the twins would someday rule over a great nation.

When she had recovered from their birth, and was on her feet again, Cleopatra began to wonder what had happened to their father. With the treaty signed with Octavian, the queen had naturally expected that Antony would return to Egypt, for she had been told of Fulvia's death. But weeks passed and nothing was heard from him.

Poor Cleopatra! Through her agents in Italy, she was to learn that another Roman had run out on her. For on October 15, B.C. 40, when Alexander Helios and Cleopatra Selene were six weeks old, their father had been married in Rome to Octavian's sister Octavia, left a widow two months before. To celebrate their wedding, Antony struck a coinage that made numismatic history, for it was the first time that a woman's portrait head appeared on a Roman coin. Remembering what had happened to their last treaty of friendship, it was Octavian who suggested the marriage. As he said to his friend Agrippa, "This will be a link with me that Antony will find it hard to break."

9

THE HEAVENLY TWINS

CLEOPATRA RULED EGYPT ALONE, and brought up her three fatherless children as best she could. She was told that Octavia had married Mark Antony to please her brother. It was the usual Roman marriage in aristocratic circles, purely political, but when a daughter, Antonia, was born to them, Cleopatra was sick with jealousy.

In despair, she turned to Caesarion for comfort, which was bad for the boy. He became prematurely adult, thrust at an early age into the role of confidante to his mother. Repeatedly, Cleopatra told him how his noble father had stood by her; how he had taken her to Rome and intended to make her the queen of a world empire. But that unreliable Antony! Why had she ever put her trust in him?

Once more, Little Caesar had his mother's complete attention. Cleopatra would hardly allow him out of her sight, while she left Alexander and Selene to the care of nurses. Her beloved Caesar was dead. But he seemed to live again in his son, whereas the sight of the twins evoked bitter memories of that mad year she had spent with their father. How she regretted it!

C L E O P A T R A

This is a cartouche—a name in hieroglyphics, with its English
equivalent.

Antony's defection to the enemy ruined Cleopatra's dream
of obtaining a vast empire for herself and for Caesar's son.
Instead, she settled down to the less ambitious task of training
him to rule Egypt. He was nine years old in B.C. 38 and, to
show the boy the country he would rule as Ptolemy Caesar
XIV, Cleopatra took him up the Nile to Dendera, where she
was having a temple built dedicated to Hathor, the Egyptian
goddess of love. Alighting from their thalamegus (houseboat),
they stood looking at a wall on which workmen were carving a bas-relief of the queen, wearing the disk-and-horn head-
dress of Isis. In front of her was Caesarion, chatting with the
gods.

"Is that me?" the boy asked. "Well, you'd never know it!"

Then back to Alexandria they went, and, after his holiday
on the Nile, Little Caesar settled down to his lessons with
Populos. Returning home one day from swimming off Pharos,
he found a courier in the hall, waiting to speak with his
mother. The boy walked past him into his room, little thinking
how this man would change his life, for he was a certain
Ponteius Capito, sent by Antony to ask Cleopatra to join him
in Syria.

* * * *

It was three years since Mark Antony had deserted her, and, in March of 37, he wanted a reconciliation with the Queen of Egypt for military reasons—although the saintly Octavia, with whom Antony was living in Athens, bored the lusty triumvir to death and he often thought wistfully of that year he had spent with Cleopatra. His relations with Octavian had grown steadily worse, and, if it had not been for Octavia, who tried to keep her husband and brother on friendly terms, the second triumvirate would have broken up long ago. It had become a farce, however, and Antony had decided to attempt the conquest of western Asia. If this was successful, he would be strong enough then to defy Octavian. But such an ambitious project could only be accomplished with the help of the Egyptian navy. So he had sent Ponteius Capito to ask Cleopatra, would she join her forces with his for an attack on the Parthians? Would she come to Antioch, in Syria, where he was, and discuss the matter?

"I never want to see that man again!" Cleopatra had been saying for years. But now, what choice had she? Lepidus was of no importance; Octavian and Antony ruled the Roman world. Obviously, she couldn't side with Octavian, her son's deadly enemy, while, through Antony, who controlled the eastern half of the empire, she might yet realize the dream of world conquest she had shared with Caesar. But what decided Cleopatra finally to accept his invitation? It was when Capito told her that Antony had sent his wife and their two-year-old daughter Antonia back to Rome (although Octavia was pregnant again), and he was alone. So, as Cleopatra had gone to Tarsus, in the end, she went to Antioch.

When Caesarion heard that his mother was going to Syria to join the man he hated, the boy flew into a jealous rage. "She can't go! I won't let her!" he shouted, bursting into tears.

Populos went over and shut the door into the next room. "What will your attendants think if they hear you acting like this?" he asked. "Caesarion, don't you know that your mother is going to Antoich for your sake? You loved your father very much, didn't you? Don't you want the queen to realize his dream and hers that someday you should rule over a great empire?"

"I'm sorry, Populos, I didn't understand."

"Well, you do now, I hope. Stop being so selfish and think of the twins. You lost your father, we can't do anything about that, but do you want Alexander and Selene to grow up without a father's love? Go to your mother and tell her that she is to go to Antioch."

When the boy did as his tutor asked him to do, Cleopatra was pleased, for she would have turned down Antony's invitation if Little Caesar had insisted. But she wisely decided to leave Caesar's son in Alexandria; he and Mark Antony had never been able to get along. So a week later, when Cleopatra left for Syria, with her were only Antony's children, the three-year-old twins.

As soon as he heard that the queen had arrived in Antioch, the triumvir, all eagerness, hurried out to the house that Cleopatra had rented overlooking the River Orontes, only to be told that she was resting from her journey and he should wait in the garden.

Not used to being snubbed, the Roman went to sulk on a bench. Presently, he saw a little girl, playing with a puppy. She was pretty, but dirty, and Antony took her to be the child of one of the servants. "What's your dog's name?" he asked. "*Shery* (Little One)," she replied, in Egyptian. They chatted for a while, then the girl ran back into the house.

Later, when Cleopatra deigned to see him, the same child came into the room, clean and properly dressed this time. To his delight, Antony discovered that she was his daughter. He also made the acquaintance of his small son, Alexander Helios. The blond, blue-eyed twins looked alike, but their dispositions were very different. Selene was as serious-minded as Cleopatra, while Alexander was happy-go-lucky, his father all over again.

Eventually, Cleopatra allowed the Roman to move into her house, and they settled down to a quiet family life. Antony found himself dealing with a different woman. There were no more drinking orgies. This time, Cleopatra named her terms. Knowing better than to trust Antony again, she insisted upon a formal military treaty between them and, for the sake of the twins, that he marry her. It would only be an Egyptian marriage. Since Cleopatra was a foreigner, this was, by Roman law, no marriage at all. But hadn't she been satisfied with that with Caesar?

Antony, infatuated with Cleopatra again, was willing to grant her slightest wish. As a wedding present, he gave his bride several countries he had conquered—Arabia, Cyprus, Cilicia, Crete, Galilee, the Phoenician coast, and part of Judea. Cleopatra tried to get him to give her all of Judea. This Antony refused to do. He had never forgotten how, when he went with Gabinius to Egypt to restore Ptolemy XI, it was thanks to Antipater of Idumea that his cavalry had been supplied with food and water as they crossed Palestine. When he could, Antony had made Antipater's son, Herod, the first King of Judea, and he was fond of him.

Antioch was situated on the caravan route heading east across Asia Minor, and when Antony and his army left in March of 36 B.C., to attack Parthia, Cleopatra and the twins started out with him. But, on arriving at the border of Armenia, the queen found, to her annoyance, that she was expecting another baby. So there was nothing for her to do but return to Egypt.

Traveling by way of Damascus, then south along the River Jordan, Cleopatra and her retinue came to the town of Jericho. There she was met by Herod, who had come to find out what part of his realm Antony had given her.

"Oh, not Jericho!" cried the Jewish king, when he heard that he had lost the richest part of Judea. Cleopatra agreed to let him farm the lush, warm valley of the Jordan for her, but she drove such a hard bargain, demanding an annual rent of 200 talents, that Herod was furious. He managed to hide his feelings, however, and invited the queen to continue her journey by way of Jerusalem. When she did, Herod was delighted, for, on the way, he planned to kill her.

The road from Jericho to Jerusalem wound up through a wild mountainous region and, at one point, passed through a narrow deep wadi, high above the Jordan River. Josephus tells in his *History of the Jews* how Herod intended to have Cleopatra ambushed there, and the murder of the queen, the twins, and all their attendants blamed on the highway robbers who infested those desolate heights. But his friends warned him not to risk Antony's anger. Afraid of Rome, Herod called off his "robbers." Instead, he gave Cleopatra some cuttings of the balm-of-Gilead tree, the fragrant *Balsamodendron Gileadense*, greatly esteemed in the East for its healing properties. Despite its name, it is not a native of Gilead, but indigenous to Arabia. It was used for making perfumed cosmetics, for which the balsam groves of Jericho were famous.

Having bestowed this parting gift, Herod escorted Cleopatra politely to the frontier fortress of Pelusium.

With deep regret, the Jewish king watched Cleopatra's cavalcade of horses, pack-mules, and wagons disappear safely along the coast road to Alexandria. When he had that woman in his power, what a fool he was to let her escape! Herod thought. Wasn't there some way by which he could still get even with her?

* * * *

On her return from Antioch, Cleopatra often thought of Rhodon of Damascus, a healer of whom Herod had told her.

He had cured the Jewish king of cataracts, but it seemed the Syrian could treat other ailments as well—dysentery, malaria, and smallpox. "Can he cast out demons?" Cleopatra had asked Herod. For in those days, epilepsy was not understood. It was thought that this nervous disease was caused by evil spirits who entered into a person.

Olympus had doctored Caesarion for years, and the boy's mother had consulted the priests of Isis at their temple on Pharos Island. They had tried, without success, all the remedies they knew. A *bulla* (locket) of gold with an amulet in it was hung about Little Caesar's neck. He was made to drink the nauseating, muddy water of the sacred Nile. Nothing did any good. His epileptic seizures came, not several months or weeks apart now, but every few days.

In desperation, Cleopatra thought of sending for this Rhodon of Damascus, but, for the present, other matters occupied her attention. The queen's fourth child, a boy whom she named Ptolemy Philadelphus, after his ancestor, the lighthouse builder, was born in the late autumn of 36 B.C. Her baby was only three months old when a courier arrived from Syria with the shocking news that Antony, defeated by the deadly archers of Parthia, had retreated to the Phoenician coast with less than a third of his army.

Cleopatra had never approved of Antony's campaign against the Parthians. Rome had been fighting these fierce Asiatic people for generations. And even Alexander the Great had never been able to conquer them entirely. So when Antony returned crestfallen to Alexandria, she hoped that, in the future, he would devote himself to opposing Octavian. He was now his only rival in the Roman Empire, for Octavian had forced Lepidus out of the second triumvirate, leaving him in entire control of the West.

But the conquest of Asia fascinated Antony, as it had Caesar. In 35, when the King of Media (now northwest Iran)

DEATH OF CLEOPATRA
by Guercino, Palazzo Rosso, Genoa, Italy

JULIUS CAESAR
Uffizi Gallery, Florence

Photograph: Alinari-Art Reference Bureau

MARK ANTONY
Vatican Museum, Rome

Photograph: Courtesy of the Metropolitan Museum of Art

CLEOPATRA AND HER SON CAESARION
Temple of Dendera, Egypt

M. VIPSANIUS AGRIPPA

Uffizi Gallery, Florence

Photograph: Alinari-Art Reference Bureau

POMPEY THE GREAT

Capitoline Museum, Rome

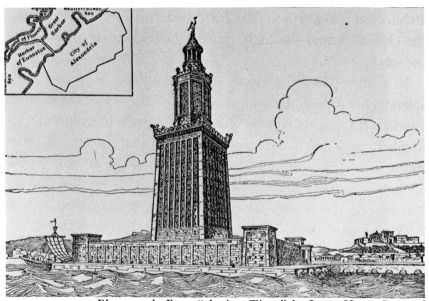

Photograph: From "Ancient Times" by James Henry Breasted

PHAROS LIGHTHOUSE
Alexandria, Egypt

Photograph: From "Caesar in Gaul" by D'Ooge and Eastman

ASSASSINATION OF CAESAR
by C. Rochegrosse

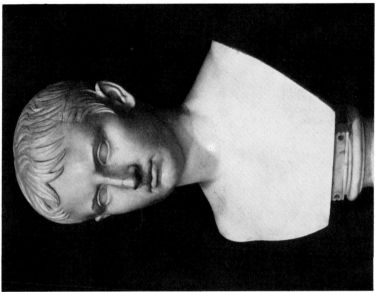

Photograph: *Alinari-Art Reference Bureau*

OCTAVIA
The Louvre, Paris

DRUSUS
Uffizi Gallery, Florence

TIBERIUS
Uffizi Gallery, Florence

Photograph: *The Bettmann Archive*

THE BATTLE OF ACTIUM, SEPTEMBER 2, 31 B.C.

Photograph: *The Bettmann Archive*

BLOODY SPORTS OF THE ARENA

Photograph: *Alinari-Art Reference Bureau*

ANTONIA MINOR
National Museum, Naples

Photograph: From "Caesar in Gaul" by D'Ooge and Eastman

A CHARIOT RACE IN THE CIRCUS MAXIMUS

OCTAVIAN

Uffizi Gallery, Florence

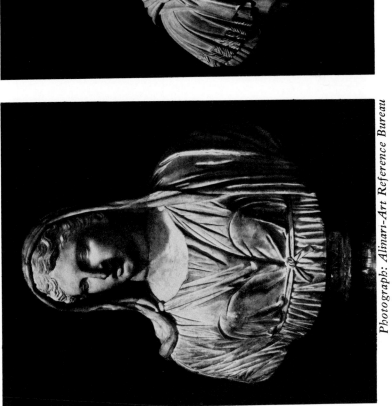

LIVIA

Uffizi Gallery, Florence

Photograph: From "*A History of the Ancient World*"
by George Willis Botsford

CAPITOLINE TEMPLE OF JUPITER

Photograph: *Ewing Galloway*

ANCIENT ROMAN FORUM

JULIA
Berlin Museum, Germany

A ROMAN BRIDE ARRIVES AT HER NEW HOME
by André Castaigne

proposed to him that they meet in Syria and discuss a joint attack on Parthia, Antony set out again. This time, Cleopatra insisted upon going with him. It was a good thing she did, for when they arrived in Syria, Antony was told that his Roman wife was in Athens, on her way to join him.

Octavia had been sent by her brother, Octavian, to test Antony's loyalty. Would he welcome his Roman wife? Or publicly reject her? Then the world would know where Mark Antony stood, with Rome or with Egypt. If the sweet, lovely Octavia had been allowed to reach Syria and tell Antony about the second little daughter she had born him (another Antonia), there is no knowing what might have happened. But Cleopatra was by her husband's side, determined that he should not abandon her again. She made Antony write to Octavia and tell her that he would refuse to see her if she came to Syria and she must return to Rome.

Cleopatra would have come to Syria, no matter what Antony said, and demanded to see him. But Octavia meekly returned to Italy. In triumph, Cleopatra brought her husband back to Alexandria, where they spent the winter of 35-34 B.C. By rejecting Octavian's sister, Antony had cut himself off from Rome. He was hers now, he could never leave her again.

Aligned with Cleopatra and the East against Octavian and the West, Mark Antony, not wanting an enemy at his back if he had to fight Rome, invaded Armenia in the spring of 34 and annexed it as a Roman province. Bringing King Artavasdes of Armenia back with him in chains, he returned to Alexandria to plan a wedding. In Syria, he had arranged for the marriage of the King of Media's daughter, the five-year-old Princess Iotapa, to his son Alexander Helios, now six.

So much has been written about Cleopatra's voluptuous nature and Antony's drunkenness, that it is hard to picture them as they were in B.C. 34—Antony forty-nine, and Cleopatra thirty-four and "putting on weight," Plutarch says.

They were no longer lovers, as much as parents of a large family of children. Still his mother's favorite, Caesarion must get along as best he could with his stepbrothers, Alexander and Ptolemy; his stepsister, Selene; and Antony's eldest son by Fulvia, Antyllus (young Antony), a boy of twelve, who had come to Alexandria to live with his father. Cleopatra had hoped that Antyllus, a year younger than Caesarion, would be a companion for him. Instead, a rough ill-mannered youth, he made fun of Little Caesar's fits. And the sensitive boy, ashamed of his attacks of epilepsy that made him feel "different" from other children, retreated into his shell.

Nor could the jovial Mark Antony, who liked to show off his courage by driving a pair of lions harnessed to a chariot in processions, understand a boy who spent his time reading Homer and playing the harp. But what mainly caused continual friction between them was Little Caesar's air of superiority. He was the great Julius Caesar's son, which, he felt, made him better than anyone else, and he never let his stepfather forget it.

Resenting this, Antony insisted one night that Antyllus (twelve) and Caesarion (thirteen) were old enough to attend a banquet he was giving for his officers. At the rowdy affair, Antyllus enjoyed himself, but Ptolemy Caesar (fastidious like his father) sat in stony disapproval, watching the drunken antics of Lucius Munatius Plancus, Antony's secretary and favorite drinking companion. As a seagod, the stout little Plancus was prancing about, his naked body painted blue, a crown of seaweed on his head, and a false fishtail tied to his waist.

The hours passed, the wine flowed, and Little Caesar, his head reeling, realized that his stepfather wanted him to get drunk and make a fool of himself. Springing up from his couch, he hurled his cup of wine on the floor. The guests stared in amazement, as, over the marble floor stained with split wine, the boy rushed from the room.

Antony was furious. Cleopatra's "precious son" thought himself better than his hard-fighting, hard-drinking cronies, and he had no right to, he was a stuck-up little prig.

Next morning, suffering from a hangover, the Roman stormed into Cleopatra's room to tell her that her prudish boy had insulted him and his guests. The sight that met Antony's eyes stopped his angry outburst, for Caesarion lay on the bed, limp after an epileptic fit. Olympus and his mother hovered anxiously over him. Also in the room, whispering among themselves, were several priests of Isis, just as useless as Olympus, and more frightened than Cleopatra.

His wife turned to Antony in despair. "See, what you've done! You upset him last night, and he's very ill. Oh, I don't know what to do!"

"Why don't you send for that healer Herod told you about?"

"I've tried everything else," Cleopatra sighed, "I think I will."

So the man entered Caesarion's life who was to completely dominate him. That Rhodon of Damascus was in the pay of Herod of Judea, sent by him to Alexandria to do all the harm he could, neither the boy nor his family would know until it was too late.

10

RHODON OF DAMASCUS

RHODON WAS ONE of those healers who, in Biblical times, roamed the shores of the Mediterranean, from village to village, driving ailments out of the sick. Cleopatra wrote to Herod to ask this man to come to Egypt and replace the aged Populos, who wanted to retire to a farm on the Nile. She was delighted when the Jewish king replied that the *Damascenus*, as the healer was called, from his birthplace, would be glad to become Caesarion's tutor and nurse.

When the queen first saw him, Rhodon was nothing to look at—an ugly little man, with a bald head. The only remarkable things about him were his piercing, dark eyes and his long fingers. On being presented to Cleopatra, Rhodon seized her hands in his and, staring fiercely, said, "You're worried about your son? Worry no more, the boy will be better as long as I'm with him. But you must have faith in me. Faith is everything." His extraordinary eyes held Cleopatra's and from this homely person there radiated a strange power. For the first time in years, she felt a sense of relief.

Rhodon knew the name of the evil spirit that had entered into Ptolemy Caesar and took his first attack calmly. "It's the

78

demon, Beelzebub, inside him," the healer told Caesarion's frantic mother when, gasping and panting, the boy uttered those frightful howls that always terrified her. "Don't be alarmed, I'll soon drive Beezlebub out."

Turning to the sick child, Rhodon stared into Little Caesar's eyes as if to hypnotize him and cried in a loud voice, "Be still, Beelzebub, and leave him!" It was miraculous. One minute, the boy was thrashing about, his body all distorted, then, in a remarkable short time, he was sitting up in bed, himself again.

Cleopatra's eyes filled with grateful tears. "Oh, Rhodon, how can I ever thank you! You must stay with my son always." The healer's mysterious power radiated from his long, slim fingers that he placed on Caesarion. His touch seemed to calm him.

Only Olympus was not impressed. Cleopatra's old doctor, advanced for his time in the study of medicine, thought that epilepsy might be a disease of the nerves, curable by rest and quiet. He considered the Syrian a quack, who sent for the queen when the crisis was passing and took credit for the boy's quick recovery. But as his fits came less often, Caesarion's mother soon had complete faith in this man who gave relief to her child and calmed her fears.

That Rhodon of Damascus was plotting to do her harm, instead of good, Cleopatra never for a moment suspected. Herod of Judea had sent the Damascan to Alexandria to make the boy utterly his tool. The Jewish king had been told that Cleopatra's son by Caesar was the most precious thing in the world to her. Through their child, Herod hoped to get his revenge on the Queen of Egypt for taking Jericho from him. He had given Rhodon his orders, and from the day of his arrival, the tutor lost no time in getting in his evil work.

When he undressed, Little Caesar had been in the habit of dropping his clothes on the floor—Populos picked them up.

But Rhodon said to him sternly, "Hang up your things." Caesarion gasped in surprise. No one had ever spoken to him in such a commanding voice. He ignored the remark. "Very well," his new tutor said, "your clothes will stay there until you do." They did, for two days, until the spoiled boy, realizing that he had met a will stronger than his own, picked them up.

A year passed and the new tutor had made himself indispensable, not only to Cleopatra, but to her entire household. In B.C. 33, when little Median princess, Iotapa, arrived in Egypt to marry seven-year-old Alexander Helios, it was Rhodon who planned their lavish wedding. The two children, richly dressed and hung with jewels, were married with all the Oriental pageantry that Antony, a frustrated actor fond of display, had grown to relish.

Rhodon had an even-more-splendid ceremony in mind. "After your magnificent victory over the Armenians, Imperator, you're entitled, like every Roman general, to hold a triumph," he said. "So why don't we have one?"

Antony enthusiatically agreed. He had succumbed to the East. He wore turbans and long flowing robes, and was always ready to take part in any affair where he could dress up as Hercules or Dionysus and show off.

Actually, Antony's conquest of Armenia had been an easy campaign. His troops had plundered an almost defenceless country. But, by the way he celebrated his Armenian victories with a mile-long parade through the streets of Alexandria, one would have thought that he had conquered Italy.

At the head of the procession marched a company of legionaries. Engraved on their shields, instead of the legions' insignia —S.P.Q.R. (*Senatus Populusque Romanus*) "Senate and People of Rome"—were the letters C (Cleopatra) and A (Antony) entwined. Behind his soldiers, in a golden chariot drawn by a pair of lions, rode Mark Antony, followed by King Artavasdes of Armenia in chains, long lines of Armenian prisoners, and wagons heaped with booty. Egyptian troops brought up the rear of the parade that moved slowly by Alexander's tomb, the law courts, and the university, to the temple of Serapis, the patron god of Alexandria. There, seated on a gold throne, dressed in Syrian silk, was Cleopatra, wearing the red-and-white double crown of Upper and Lower Egypt. Leading his Armenian captives up to the queen, her husband forced them to kneel in homage.

A month later, Antony's triumph was followed by a coronation—the confirmation of the gifts of the kingdoms that, in Antioch, he had promised to Cleopatra and her children. On the grounds of the gymnasium, Antony and Cleopatra sat on gold thrones. Below them were the four silver ones of the seven-year-old twins, three-year-old Ptolemy Philadelphus, and Caesarion, fourteen.

When the crowd had assembled, Mark Antony began giving away land recklessly. To Cleopatra went Egypt and Cyprus, and her son by Caesar was made co-regent. To his own son, Alexander Helios, Antony gave Armenia, Media, and Parthia (when it was conquered); and his twin, Cleopatra Selene, became Queen of Cyrenaica and Libya, lands on the North African coast, west of Egypt. Even small Ptolemy Philadelphus was not forgotten. He was made the ruler over Phoenicia, Syria, and Cilicia.

It was a proud day for Cleopatra. Antony had elevated her country to an importance Egypt had not had for centuries. She wished that Caesar could be alive to see his dark-haired, dignified son seated near her, wearing the sacred cobra on his brow and the false beard of a pharaoh. Rhodon had also dressed the new kings and queen in appropriate costumes and given them bodyguards from the countries over which they would rule. Selene, in the long veils of a North African princess, was surrounded by dark-skinned Lybians. Alexander and

Iotapa, dressed as Armenians in turbans, had their Persian escorts; while Ptolemy, with his Syrian retinue, resembled a chubby little Asiatic potentate, his crown askew on his auburn curls.

Rhodon, who had planned the affair, could hardly wait to write Herod how well he was carrying out his master's orders. By catering to Antony's vanity and Cleopatra's ambition for her children, the Damascan was encouraging the reckless pair to ruin themselves. Didn't they know that a Roman triumph could only be held in Rome? Antony's crowning sin, in the opinion of his countrymen, was to celebrate a victory of Roman arms in Rome's rival city—Cleopatra's Alexandria. From the day when the news of his Alexandrian triumph reached Italy, he ceased to be a Roman.

Nor could Rome forgive his bad treatment of the long-suffering Octavia. When Antony divorced her and announced his Egyptian marriage to Cleopatra, Octavian ordered his sister to leave the house of such a contemptible man. Octavia and her five children (three by C. Claudius Marcellus and two by Antony) came to live with her brother. With mounting anger, Octavian heard of Antony's gifts to his children by Cleopatra of strategic lands in the empire; and what was worse, that he had publicly declared Caesarion to be the legitimate son of Julius Caesar, and therefore his heir, which meant that Octavian was an imposter. Only war could wipe out such an insult.

Using as an excuse that Antony had no right to give his daughter Selene Cyrenaica and Libya (which, having taken them from Lepidus, Octavian considered his), the latter declared war. Standing before the temple of Bellona in the Campus Martius, he hurled a spear over an imaginary frontier into the land of the enemy. The gesture was to indicate to the Romans that this would be no civil war against Mark

Antony, whom many of them still liked, but against a foreign foe, Cleopatra of Egypt, whom they feared and hated.

Actually, it was against her fifteen-year-old son that Rome went to war. The late dictator's nephew was proudly calling himself Gaius Julius Caesar Octavian. Across the Mediterranean, there was another Caesar, Ptolemy, who had a better right to the name.

"Two Caesars are not good," M. Vipsanius Agrippa, Octavian's best friend and favorite general, said to him.

"Yes, the world is too small a place for both of us," Octavian replied. "Let's go after this other Caesar."

Like everything he did, the chase was very slow, very cautious, very carefully planned. A year passed before the East of the divided empire met the West, and the two Caesars fought it out in Greece.

11

ACTIUM:
A BOY'S FIRST BATTLE

WHENEVER HIS MOTHER HAD LEFT Alexandria previously, Caesarion had always been on the palace roof to wave good-by to her as the *Antonias* led the Egyptian fleet out of the harbor. But on the day, late in August of B.C. 31, when, after a year's preparation, Cleopatra sailed with sixty triremes (warships with three banks of oars) to join Antony and fight Octavian, Little Caesar was aboard the queen's flagship as it headed out into the Mediterranean. Cleopatra had wanted him to remain in Alexandria, but Antony insisted that his stepson come with her to Greece. Hadn't he broken with Rome and possibly ruined his career for the sake of Caesar's son? What did she expect him to do? Win an empire for the boy while he stayed home and played the harp?

"His first battle will be a glorious experience for Caesarion," Antony wrote his wife from Asia Minor, "and he won't be the only boy there. He'll have Antyllus for company." Antony doted on his eldest son by Fulvia, a sturdy, unimaginative youth, who was so like him. Antyllus had gone to Asia Minor with his father.

As a child, Little Caesar had never played with toy soldiers, the mere sight of blood made him ill, and here he was going to war. Wondering what lay ahead, the boy stood on the deck of the *Antonias* that August morning. Having passed the Pharos Light, the trireme began to pitch on reaching the open sea, and he walked aft to the cabin mounted on the poop, where his mother and Rhodon sat studying a map.

"Come, see where we're going," Cleopatra said.

Caesarion came to stand beside his mother. His head bent with hers over the map, as she pointed out several places on it. "Octavian and his army, having crossed the Adriatic from Italy, are coming down the west coast of Greece. By now, they should be about here . . ." Her finger came to rest on Actium, a promontory south of the island of Corfu. Then she touched another place on the map. "This is Ephesus, where your stepfather has been collecting men and ships. He is bringing them to join us in Greece and fight Octavian."

Caesarion knew that Antony, for a year now, had been in Asia Minor, assembling an army and navy from the client nations under his command. Added to Antony's thirty warships would be the sixty boats, loaded with 20,000 talents, men, munitions, and food, that Cleopatra was bringing to him from Egypt.

"Our combined strength will be the largest force ever assembled against the Romans," the Queen of Egypt proudly told her son. "We shall defeat Octavian easily."

*   *   *   *

A week later, Cleopatra's sixty triremes had joined Antony's smaller fleet assembled in the Ambracian Gulf, halfway down the west coast of Greece. His thirty boats lay at anchor in the narrow bay. The tents of his vast army (thirty legions) extended over the peninsula of Actium, that formed the southern shore of the inlet.

Octavian's forces, under the command of Agrippa, arrived several days later. His eight legions camped not a mile from Antony's forces, on the opposite, or northern, side of the bay. During the night, Octavian's forty ships moved into position before its narrow entrance.

The next morning, a council of war was held on board the *Antonias,* at which the Queen of Egypt insisted that Caesarion be present. Wasn't he the cause for this great mobilization? Wasn't it to place Caesar's son on the throne of the world that all these men from the nations under Antony's command had come to Actium? At least, she hoped so. The boy sat quietly and listened as Antony's generals, aware that the army consisted largely of his soldiers, while the better part of their navy were Egyptian ships, begged him to fight Octavian on land instead of at sea.

Cleopatra heard what they said with mounting anger. She knew that Egypt had supplied ships but few soldiers, and, since a land battle could be fought without her, his officers were hoping that Antony would send Cleopatra back to Egypt and defeat Octavian without her help. They didn't want him to enter Rome, even as a victor, with the hated Queen of Egypt at his side. And wasn't Antony capable of doing just that? Of going in triumph to Rome without her?

"No, we'll fight Octavian at sea," Cleopatra announced firmly.

As Antony hesitated, his wife reminded him of the 20,000 talents she had brought him from Egypt. Without her money, how was he going to pay his men? Antony turned to his generals. "It will be a sea battle."

With his great superiority over Octavian on land, had their commander lost his mind to fight him at sea, Antony's army officers wondered, as, on the 2nd of September, his fleet, followed by Cleopatra's ships, sailed out of the bay to where the enemy waited. Standing with his mother on the deck of the *Antonias*, Caesarion watched the two fleets maneuver into position.

At first, Octavian's boats could make little impression on Antony's larger warships, huge *quinqueremes* equipped with five tiers of oars and topheavy with catapults mounted on high wooden towers. But Agrippa managed to get Antony to stretch his lines. Then Octavian's smaller *liburnae*, swift little boats with only two banks of oars, and easy to handle, darted between Antony's big, cumbersome warships, setting one after another of them on fire.

Cleopatra and her son watched the battle with growing horror. Before long, a score of Antony's quinqueremes were aflame or drifting helplessly, and through the holes left in the line by his sunken or disabled men-of-war, Agrippa's fast little liburnae, with their deadly battering-rams, came after the Egyptian fleet. One of them managed to ram a hole in the side of the hemmed-in *Antonias* and start a leak. There was a rain of flaming arrows. The big purple sails caught on fire. Swords and shields in their hands, the Romans climbed on board, and the deck of the queen's flagship became a mass of fighting men.

Through the smoke and confusion, Cleopatra saw some of Octavian's soldiers coming toward Caesarion. She almost fainted from fright. Had they been sent to capture the boy? That had been Octavian's intention, his mother knew, ever since those frightful weeks in Rome after Caesar's death. Oh, why had she let Antony persuade her to bring Little Caesar with her to Greece and risk his precious life!

"Rhodon!" the queen screamed.

As the Syrian came running from the cabin, an officer stepped between Caesarion and the Romans who had boarded the ship. There was the clash of sword on sword, while the gallant fellow held off Octavian's soldiers, until Rhodon could whisk the boy away.

Cleopatra came to a quick decision. What did she care about Antony? The battle was all but over, he would be killed or taken prisoner, and she was not going to stand by him and risk Caesarion's life.

"Hoist the signal to assemble our scattered ships," the queen ordered the captain of her fleet. "We're sailing for Egypt."

As the *Antonias* took flight and, followed by the whole Egyptian navy, sailed past his crippled flagship, Antony could hardly believe his eyes. Why didn't Cleopatra come to his rescue? Was she deserting him? Furious at his wife, Antony got into a *celoce* (a small boat built for speed) with his son Antyllus, abandoning his fleet and all the loyal men who were fighting and dying for him, and chased after the fleeing Cleopatra.

His celoce finally overtook the *Antonias*, as the galley sailed south, away from the coast of Greece. Antony and his son climbed aboard. Striding aft to the queen's cabin, her husband burst in on her.

Tenderly stroking her son's forehead, Cleopatra sat by Caesarion, lying on the berth. She looked up at Antony with a frown. "Be quiet," she said softly. "He has dropped off to sleep."

"I'll not be quiet. You ruined my last hope of victory," her husband shouted at her. "It was your idea, this naval battle. I wanted to fight Octavian on land. Why did you run away?"

"So that Caesarion should not be captured. As it is, being in all that dreadful noise and confusion has upset the boy emotionally. I should never have brought him."

Antony was no longer the handsome, curly-haired giant, the darling of his troops, with whom Cleopatra had been infatuated. He had become an alcoholic, insufferable when drunk, and not much better when he was sober. Ignoring the loudmouthed braggart, she had grown to despise, Cleopatra turned her back on him, to hover over her child. This made her husband all the more furious.

"Caesarion . . . Caesarion . . . that's . . . that's all you ever think about, your precious Caesarion . . ." he stammered in his rage. "During the battle, when I was fighting for my . . . my very life . . . didn't you wonder what would happen . . . to me?"

"I no longer care."

Antony's face flushed. He lifted his fist to strike her. Then, unable to do so, the red-faced, bloated Roman began angrily pacing about the cabin, stopping now and then to hurl a curse at his wife. Cleopatra stood this as long as she could. Then, sickened beyond endurance by the sight of this dirty, disheveled wreck of a man, the queen sprang to her feet and pointed to the door. "Get out!" she ordered.

Meekly, Antony left her and walked, as in a trance, to the bow of the ship, where he seated himself and buried his face in his hands. He sat there for three days. Hour after hour, as the Egyptian fleet sailed toward Alexandria, the defeated Roman general stared out over the water in despair. Antyllus brought his father food. Antony hardly touched it. He knew now that Cleopatra no longer loved him—if she ever really had—all she cared about was Caesarion. She had merely used him to get what she wanted for herself and for Caesar's son.

12

ONE CAESAR TOO MANY

THE *Antonias* was badly damaged at Actium, but, when the trireme returned to Alexandria, all traces of fighting on board her had vanished. With pennants flying, Cleopatra's flagship sailed proudly home at the head of the Egyptian fleet, as if returning after a great victory. But where was Antony? Before reaching Alexandria, the *Antonias* had stopped at the desert outpost of Paraetonium (now Matruh), and, to Caesarion's astonishment, he saw Antony and his son, Antyllus, being rowed ashore.

"Your stepfather is tired after the battle," Little Caesar's mother told him. "He wishes to stay at Paraetonium for a while and rest."

That was the explanation Cleopatra also gave when the twins and Ptolemy asked where their father was. Nor would she admit that Octavian had won the battle of Actium. Hadn't the Egyptian fleet returned home without a ship damaged? The queen couldn't prevent her sailors from talking in the taverns, but by the time the people of Alexandria learned the truth about the disaster in Greece—that, after Antony's flight, his fleet was sunk and most of his army surrendered—Cleopatra had pulled herself together. Actium seemed like a bad dream.

The new master of the Mediterranean world had gone back to Italy to recoup his forces. All Rome demanded that he march against Egypt, and Octavian was only too eager to do so, for in Alexandria was the only person whom Caesar's adopted son now had reason to fear—Caesar's real son. But Cleopatra made good use of the winter months ahead, during which the Romans could not safely cross the Mediterranean. The Egyptian treasury being low, because of the help given Antony, she raised taxes, plundered the temples of their gold, and transported part of the Egyptian fleet on wheels across the Isthmus of Suez to the Red Sea, so that, if Octavian came in the spring, he could not capture all of her ships.

Helping his mother in these preparations for war was Caesarion. Almost seventeen, he attended all of her cabinet meetings, and Cleopatra's heart swelled with pride as she looked at the tall, earnest boy, so like his famous father. Why worry? If Octavian came to Egypt, didn't she have a grown son to help her? She hoped that, in Paraetonium, Antony would plunge a sword into his breast, as it was customary for a defeated Roman general to do. She no longer had the slightest need of him as an ally or as a husband. He had merely become a nuisance. Wasn't Caesarion worth a dozen Antonys?

* * * *

In spite of his faults, Mark Antony had been a good father, never too busy fighting and carousing to play with his children. They missed him, especially Selene. Their mutual love of animals had made Antony and his nine-year-old daughter very congenial. From a small child, Selene's idea of a good time was not playing with dolls, but riding out into the desert with her father to capture wild beasts. She had a menagerie of pets—gazelles, monkeys, lion cubs, snakes, dogs and cats.

When Antony had been at Paraetonium for two months, Selene came into Cleopatra's room one November day, carrying a young leopard. He was purring contentedly. Had anyone else touched the animal, he would have lost a hand!

"When is Papa coming home?" the girl asked, only to be put off by her mother with the usual evasive answer.

That afternoon, Selene and her Greek tutor, Euphronius, started off for a picnic on Pharos. Crossing the harbor in her skiff, Selene thought of the beach house Antony had built near the lighthouse for his children and of the happy times they had shared there. Arriving at the island, she jumped out of the boat, hurried ahead of Euphronius up the path—and stopped short in surprise. A man was sitting on the porch of the cottage. Who could he be? Coming closer, Selene cried out in delight. It was her father. She ran up to the steps of the shack. "Papa, what are you doing here?"

His daughter was horrified at the change in him. Disheveled and bloated, the once-handsome Mark Antony sat slumped in a chair, wishing he was dead. Selene, whose tender heart ached for any man or beast in misery, knelt and put her arms around him.

Tears of self-pity rolled down Antony's sagging cheeks. "I knew you'd come, Selene. I knew you wouldn't forget me."

"But, Papa, Mama told us that you were in Paraetonium. How long have you been here?"

"About a week," said a voice, and Antyllus came out onto the porch. "We had to leave, the mosquitos were eating us alive."

"Why didn't you come home?"

"We couldn't. Your mother put us ashore on that barren coast and said never to come near her again."

Selene listened, shocked, while Antyllus told her of the

two ghastly months they had spent at Paraetonium, a desert oasis a hundred miles west of Alexandria, consisting in those days of a border fort, some mud huts, and a few palm trees. On hearing of the loss of his army and navy in Greece, Mark Antony had tried to kill himself, but Antyllus had snatched the dagger from his father's hand and hidden it. The mosquitos, finally, drove them to Alexandria. Afraid to approach his wife, Antony had crept back to live like a hermit on Pharos, in the cottage he remembered from happier days.

"Antyllus, what do you do for food?" Selene asked.

"Row over and buy it at the market. But Papa doesn't like me to, he's afraid your mother will find out we're here."

"Don't go again, I'll bring you some. What else do you need?"

"Blankets, it's chilly at night, and ask Olympus to give you some medicine for Papa's cold."

Selene eagerly agreed to help. For several days, she and Euphronius made regular trips across the harbor. "Don't tell your mother," Antony cautioned his daughter, but it was inevitable that Cleopatra should find out, with all Alexandria talking—and laughing—about the queen's consort being banished to a shack on the beach. People were going out in boats to row by the island, hoping to catch a glimpse of the "hermit," seated on the sand, feeling sorry for himself.

Cleopatra realized that this absurd situation should not continue. Meeting Selene and her Greek tutor one morning, carrying boxes out to a boat, she spoke tartly to her daughter. "I suppose those things are for your father. Well, tell him to come home, and stop making a fool of himself."

So Antony and Antyllus returned to Lochias Point; and, within a week, the queen's husband was his old self again and back in the taverns. As boastful as ever, Mark Antony was telling everyone that he would have won at Actium, if his wife had not abandoned him. Cleopatra let him talk. Octavian had left Italy and begun his march on Egypt, and she was too busy worrying over her country's defenses to care about what her husband did or said. Cleopatra celebrated Antony's fifty-second birthday with a banquet—taking no notice of the day when she reached thirty-seven—and tried her best to restore his reputation. Otherwise, she ignored him.

By December B.C. 31, Octavian was in Greece, on his way to Egypt through Asia Minor. Allies for Egypt who would stop him must be won there. Antony had placed the kings of Media, Cappadocia, Pontos, Phoenicia, and Judea on their thrones, and the Queen of Egypt wrote to remind these client nations of their obligation to her husband. One monarch Cleopatra felt she could count on was Iotapa's father. Alexander Helios and his child-wife were sent off across the Euphrates, to the King of Media, loaded down with presents.

Naturally, the rulers of Asia Minor preferred to side with the victor of Actium. The only response to Cleopatra's appeal for help came from Herod of Judea, who appeared late in December, ostensibly to negotiate a treaty of alliance with Egypt—but actually to check up on Rhodon.

Herod's hatred of Cleopatra still rankled. Antony had given Syria to Ptolemy Philadelphus, making the Queen of Egypt, through her child, too close a neighbor to please him. More than ever, Herod regretted not having murdered the woman years ago, when she passed through Judea on her way home from Antioch. So, on arriving in Alexandria, the shifty-eyed, little man of forty-two closeted himself with Rhodon in earnest conversation. He had sent the Damascan to Cleopatra's court to do her all the harm possible. So far, what had happened?

"Just be patient," Rhodon told him. "The queen's dearest love is her son by Caesar. Behind his haughty manner, Caesarion is an exceptionally timid boy, and I have gained complete mastery over him—especially, during his epileptic fits. If something should happen to him then, it would break his mother's heart."

Not satisfied with this, later, when Herod was alone with Antony, he tried to hurry matters. "Do you want me to give you some advice?" Herod said. "If Octavian comes, do you know how you can save your neck? All you have to do is get rid of Cleopatra—"

Antony sprang to his feet. "You miserable creature! What are you suggesting? That I poison my wife!" His huge fist shot out and the big Roman sent the little Judean king hurling backward against the wall.

That was the end of their friendship. As Antipater had backed Caesar, and his son had supported Antony, for their own selfish interests, now Herod was eager to save his throne by siding with the winner. He scrambled to his feet and fled to Rhodes, where Octavian was, and told him how many soldiers and ships Cleopatra had, and how strong were her defenses.

Since he was now able to count upon Herod's support, Octavian crossed into Asia Minor with the intention of marching to Egypt by way of Syria—that is, when he could get money enough to pay his troops. Antony's thirty legions, who had surrendered after Actium and were at present under Octavian's command, were being more of a liability to him than an asset. The historian Dion Cassius says that, unable to pay his huge army, Octavian was forced to return to Italy in February B.C. 30 and remain there for two months.

Cleopatra made the most of this precious respite. Caesarion had been born in July of 47, but eighty days having been added to the calendar, his seventeenth birthday would come in the middle of April. She decided to celebrate it with a public announcement that the heir to the throne had reached his majority. Her people should know that, if Octavian came, the Egyptian army would have a grown man, a son of the

great Julius Caesar, to lead them. She also had Antyllus, sixteen, declared of age, which pleased his father, and the birth-
days of the two youths were celebrated by athletic games that
lasted several days.

Now there was nothing to do but wait for the Romans to
come after them. This happened in April, soon after Caesarion's birthday. Having raised sufficient money, thanks to a
boyhood friend, the rich Gaius Cilnius Maecenas, Octavian
was able again to march against Egypt. By May, he had
reached Syria. Alexandria was in a panic.

The thought of flight never occurred to Cleopatra, but her
children must be sent away. Alexander Helios was safe in
Media. It was Caesarion who was in the greatest danger, and
his mother reconciled herself to the fact that she would have
to part with him, for the boy must be put beyond Octavian's
reach. Why not in India, bound to Egypt by years of trade?
Surely, India was far enough away so that her precious child
would be safe there.

Little Caesar must not suspect that he was being shipped
overseas to save his life. So Cleopatra told him about his
journey, casually, one day. "Caesarion, we're short of troops.
I want you to go to India and get me more soldiers. . . . No,
don't say you won't, I've made all the arrangements. You and
Rhodon are leaving tomorrow. You're to travel up the Nile
to Coptos, then across the Arabian desert to Berenice, on the
Red Sea. From there, you'll sail with the merchant ships going to India at this season. The Indian princes are good cus-
tomers of ours. It won't be hard for you to get them to help
us."

"To India . . . ?" Little Caesar gasped. He longed to help
his mother, but to travel across the ocean, to a land so far
away, could he do it?

Of course he could, Cleopatra assured him, and when she
explained that she would not be able to hold out long against

Rome without his help, her son agreed to go. But his flight must be kept secret. Caesarion and Rhodon mounted a pair of horses the next night, galloped out of Alexandria in the dark, and rode to the banks of the Nile, where a boat was waiting.

Several days later, they were far up the river. No one knew they had gone but Cleopatra and—unfortunately—one other person. Before leaving Alexandria, Rhodon had managed to send word to Octavian who, having taken Syria, had advanced down the coast to Pelusium, that Caesar's son had escaped and just where he and his traitorous companion were going.

But could the Romans catch him? The felucca on which Little Caesar and his tutor were traveling, pushed rapidly upstream by the prevailing winds, glided by the pyramids at Giza and then moved further up the Nile, past the temple of Dendera. Caesarion remembered the bas-relief there of himself and his mother. He would have liked to have seen it again, but there wasn't time to stop. The ship reached Coptos, and Cleopatra's son and his tutor left it to mount camels for the long ride across the Arabian desert.

They reached the Red Sea early in July and found the port of Berenice crowded with Arab dhows, waiting to take advantage of the summer monsoon and sail to Muziris in India (now Calcutta). The predominant winds reverse themselves with the calendar in the Indian Ocean. It is a phenomenon that exists nowhere else in the world. As has been pointed out, in the winter they blow west, then the winds turn and, from May to September, travel clockwise over the sea, driving the sailing ships east at seven knots from Africa to India.

But, for a week now, the monsoon had failed to blow. The sharp-prowed dhows, loaded with copal, ivory, tortoise-shell, hides, hippopotamus teeth, rhinoceros horn, and Egyptian linen, rode at anchor in the Sinus Immundus (Foul Bay), unable to sail. Their crews sat gloomily in the bazaar. The long calm pleased no one but Rhodon. Each day without a breeze gave the Syrian fresh hope. Every few hours, he climbed to the flat roof of the inn, and looked out over the desert, to see if galloping horsemen were approaching.

To his distress, in the middle of July, the monsoon winds began again. What could Rhodon do to stop their departure? The dhow they had chartered was loaded and ready to sail. If Octavian's men didn't come soon, he and Caesarion would have to be off to India. That, the Syrian knew, must not happen or his life wouldn't be worth much. Where could he hide from Herod's anger and Octavian's revenge, if he let Cleopatra's son escape?

Frantically trying to keep Little Caesar in Berenice, until the Romans could catch up with him, his tutor played on the boy's superstitious fears. "We cannot sail now," he said to him. "The stars predict that you must beware of a sea voyage in July." And he sought the help of the local augurs, who told fortunes by the flight of a bird or by examining the entrails of a sheep.

"The sacred chickens refuse to eat," Rhodon returned from the temple to report. "That's a sure sign we'll be captured by pirates. Just remember that, if your father, the great Julius Caesar, had listened to the soothsayer's warning on the Ides of March, and not gone to the senate, he would be alive today."

Caesarion listened, impressed. Perhaps they should do as his tutor said, not sail, but how could he fail his mother? Rhodon's mention of his father brought back to the boy all the nightmare scenes of his childhood. He remembered his panic when, with Cleopatra, he had fled from Italy after Caesar's death. That had brought on his first epileptic fit. Ever since, he had feared boats and the sea.

Afraid to sail, Caesarion was even more terrified to remain in Berenice. Why? He didn't know. But he didn't like being shut up in this tavern room with Rhodon. The man was no longer respectful. There was something evil and sinister about him. "I must escape to India alone," Little Caesar thought. But how? He knew it was impossible. Feeling himself in great danger and helpless, so far from his mother, Cleopatra's son collapsed under the strain. One morning, Rhodon found him on his bed, writhing and foaming at the mouth. An epileptic fit! The tutor looked at the sick boy with delight. He was saved.

Sitting down by Caesarion's bed, the Syrian stared fixedly into his eyes, but this time he didn't make the usual ritual gestures of exorcism and order the evil spirit to leave the boy entrusted to his care. He let Little Caesar's howls, his agonizing moans, and convulsive gyrations go on and on, until he was utterly exhausted. It was then that Rhodon, a student of hypnotism, could do anything he wanted with him.

Twenty minutes later, the room was quiet. Ptolemy Caesar lay limp, as though in a trance. Leaning over the semiconscious boy, the Damascan said to him in a commanding voice, "You're not going to sail. Some men are coming from Pelusium to get you. And you're going back with them. Do you understand?"

Caesarion saw his tutor gazing at him intently, with that dreadful hypnotic stare that always terrified him. "Yes . . ." he murmured.

"You will do exactly as I say? Promise!"

The Syrian rose from his chair and went to the window. What was his joy to see, down in the courtyard, some of Octavian's soldiers dismounting. He hurried back to Little Caesar's side.

"Get up," Rhodon ordered. "The men have come for you."

13

A SWORD BIGGER THAN
A BOY

It HAD BROKEN Cleopatra's heart to part with Caesarion, but, happy to know that he was on his way to India, she thought of the safety of her other children. She had planned to send Selene to Cyrenaica. Hadn't Antony made his daughter the queen of that North Africa country? And Ptolemy was to be hidden in his kingdom of Syria. But it was too late. By July B.C. 30, Syria was lost and Octavian was in Pelusium, the fortress guarding the eastern entrance to Egypt. Nor could Selene go to Cyrenaica. A Roman army under Cornelius Gallus had captured Paraetonium, the corresponding fort to Pelusium on the west.

The enemy were closing in on Alexandria from both sides. But Octavian, in camp at Pelusium, had first to settle an old grudge. The Roman Caesar's long chase after the only person who could dispute his right to rule the world was over. The Egyptian Caesar had been brought back from Berenice in chains. Caesarion must die. But how? By the knife? By poison? Or, as Seleucus (one of Octavian's aides) suggested, by dropping him into a vat of live snakes? Such a horrible end shocked even Octavian. He gave a more humane order, and Julius Caesar's son, who was to have inherited the earth, died like a common criminal, strangled in his cell.

That left the next heir to the throne to be disposed of, and emissaries were sent to Media to assure Alexander Helios, that, if he returned to Egypt, he would be made joint ruler with his mother, his half-brother Caesarion "having unfortunately died." Octavian had no intention of doing any such thing, but the ten-year-old Alexander was guillible enough to believe him. The boy started back and vanished on the way.

Octavian also sent Cleopatra word that, if she wished to remain queen of Egypt, she had only to get rid of Antony. Her husband was now of little use to her, but did Octavian think she would be so disloyal to the father of her three children? Cleopatra replied scornfully, "If you want Antony's head, come and get it!"

That was just what the Romans intended to do. Octavian came from the east, Gallus from the west, and the two armies pitched their tents outside the walls of Alexandria, beyond the Canopic gate, near the race track. The city could not stand a long siege. Cleopatra and Antony decided to fight Octavian in the morning (August first), on land and at sea.

Shortly after dawn, Selene and Ptolemy watched as their father put on his battle armor. What the children most wanted to see was when Eros, Antony's shield bearer, helped their father to buckle on his big sword. Engraved along the blade with scenes from Homer, the magnificent weapon had been made for Mark Antony in Damascus, a city noted for its steel. The sword was almost as long as little Ptolemy and very heavy. "Only a man as strong as I am could handle it," his father liked to boast.

Generally it was Antyllus, his son by Fulvia, who had the honor of taking Antony's sword down from the wall and giving it to him. But this time, as the older boy reached for it, Ptolemy asked, "Papa, can I hold the sword?" Antony turned to his youngest child, looking down into his round chubby face. "Yes, and I'll show you how to swing it." When he handed him the sword, it was so heavy the five-year-old boy could hardly hold it.

Then, as though Antony's aides were not waiting impatiently outside, sitting their horses and holding his mare, he bent down to show Ptolemy how a warrior handles such a big sword in battle.

"I'd like to run this through Octavian," her husband said to Cleopatra, over Ptolemy's head. "Well, I may do it, when, in an hour or so, I lead the land attack. At the same time, our fleet will sail out to meet Octavian's ships. From the roof of the palace, you and the children should get a fine view of the sea fight."

Now Eros was handing to Antony his shield and bronze helmet. Selene's heart ached with love and pride in her father. He was sober this morning and looked so manly and brave, dressed for the battle. "Give me a kiss . . ." Antony took Cleopatra in his arms and kissed her hard on the mouth. Selene and Ptolemy watched their parents, fascinated. Faced with the possible approach of death, they had become lovers again. Their children had not seen them kiss like this for a long time.

"Hurry, Father," Antyllus said, "you promised to be with the army at dawn. We're late already."

"Coming . . ." Hurriedly kissing Selene and Ptolemy, Antony dashed out of the room and down the stairs. Cleopatra and her children rushed to the window to see him gallop away.

"Can we go up on the roof, Mama?" Selene asked.

"Later, when you've done your lessons. You heard what your father said, nothing will happen for several hours."

It was hard to act as if this was just an ordinary morning. Selene sat down to study with her Greek tutor, Euphronius.

Ptolemy played with his toy soldiers. The queen's maids, Charmian and Iras, went about their usual tasks. But everyone was nervous and jumpy. From the window, they could see the Egyptian fleet at anchor in the harbor. But what was happening out by the race course?

"Mama, can we go to the Tomb?" Ptolemy asked. The Soma being overcrowded with buried Ptolemies, Cleopatra was building herself a mausoleum on the end of Lochias Point, near the temple of Artemis. Her children liked to play in the half-finished building.

"No, Ptolemy, I want you and your sister with me this morning, where I can keep an eye on you." Cleopatra was peering anxiously out of the window again. After a while, Selene asked, "Are you afraid, Mama?"

"I don't think so. Your father would send us word if we were in any danger. Come, children, let's go up on the roof."

They climbed the stairs, Selene and Ptolemy chattering gaily all the way. From the flat roof, converted into a garden with flower beds and trees, where Cleopatra liked to lie basking in the sun and her children played during the winter months, one could see far out over the harbor.

"Oh, there go the ships!" Selene cried.

It was thrilling to see the Egyptian fleet sail out beyond the Pharos Light to meet the Roman ships . . . but not so pleasant a sight when they all came rowing back together into the harbor, the Roman triremes leading the captured Egyptians. Ptolemy, too young to realize that they had surrendered to the enemy, waved at the home fleet as they passed. But Selene kept watching her mother's white face. She knew now that she was afraid.

Nor was it any comfort for them to look in the other direction. An ominous column of smoke was rising over the housetops to the east. "What is it, Mama?" the children asked.

"I don't know."

"It's a big fire, isn't it, out by the race course?"

"It looks so." Cleopatra made her voice sound calm. "Come, children, it's time to go down. When your father comes back, he'll want to find us waiting for him."

They went downstairs and walked through the long, echoing corridors of the palace. How empty they suddenly were! Not a person there. "Euphronius!" Cleopatra called. Where had Selene's tutor gone? He must have fled, as had most of the other servants. Only the faithful Charmian and Iras, tears in their eyes, waited in the queen's apartment for their mistress.

"Madame, someone has come from the battlefield," Charmian announced. It was Pelucas, Antony's chief-of-staff. Cleopatra went into the next room, and shut the door behind her, so the children would not hear what he said.

She almost fainted when Pelucas told her that Mark Antony, sitting his horse on a hill by the Canopic gate, had seen the entire Egyptian army ride over to join the enemy, as the Egyptian navy had, and for the same reason. Octavian's forces were largely composed of Antony's soldiers and sailors, who had surrendered after Actium, and the Egyptians refused to fight their former allies. "The Romans are pouring into the city," Pelucas warned the queen. "They'll be here any minute to capture you."

What had become of Antony? Pelucas didn't know. Cleopatra realized that it was up to her to save herself and the children. They must hide. But where? Ptolemy's asking to be allowed to play in her mausoleum gave his mother an idea. In her tomb, of course! Octavian's men would hardly look for them there.

Going back to Selene and her little brother, Cleopatra said to them, as casually as she could, "Your father won't be home for some time. So why don't we all go out to my tomb? On this hot day, it will be cool there by the sea." Then, telling Charmian and Iras in a low voice of their danger, the queen ordered her maids to pack her jewels, also clothing and food enough for several days.

While they did this, Cleopatra went again to the window and looked out. It was then that she saw the Roman soldiers down in the courtyard.

14

WHAT SNAKE IS THAT?

FIVE OF OCTAVIAN's soldiers—big, burly fellows, with cruel faces—were getting off their horses. Cleopatra's heart began to race. But she must not lose her head. No use pretending any longer that they were not in danger, so she said, "Children, we must get into my tomb as fast as we can and hide. Some bad men are coming to hurt us. Hurry!"

Their mother led Selene and Ptolemy quickly down the stairs and through the empty corridors of the palace. Charmian and Iras followed, carrying the jewels, the clothing and food. They could hear the men breaking down the front door, as the three frightened women and two terrified children slipped out the back way. Then they ran for the mausoleum. Cleopatra tried to make a game of it. "Let's see which one of us can get there first!"

Selene was a good runner. But she had never before run as fast as this. When Ptolemy fell down and burst out crying, Iras had to hand over the major part of her burden to Cleopatra and Selene and pick up the little boy and carry him. Fortunately, the tomb was near by. Reaching the two-storied building, the women and children rushed into a dimly-lit hall, where a sarcophagus stood ready to receive the Queen's body. They shut and bolted the heavy door behind them.

Quickly, they climbed a flight of stairs to a suite of rooms on the upper floor, to be used by the priests who would guard the tomb when it was completed and some day watch over Cleopatra's remains. In the small apartment, simply furnished with beds, tables, and a few chairs, the fugitives flung themselves down, exhausted and panting. What a narrow escape!

After they had been in the mausoleum about an hour, they were startled to hear shouts outside. Selene ran to a back window. "Mama, come quick!" she called. "Oh, it's terrible! Papa's lying below, on a stretcher, covered with blood."

Some workmen had left a ladder by the wall, and as the three excited women rushed to look out, the helmeted-head of an aide of Antony's named Diomedes (one of the four Egyptians who had carried the defeated Roman general over from the palace) appeared at the top of the ladder.

"What has happened?" demanded Cleopatra.

"Your husband is dying," Diomedes told her. "We came back with him from the battlefield to find the palace empty. Thinking that you and the children had been captured by Octavian, Antony wept and cried out that he no longer wanted to live. Shortly after, when we had gone to get him some food and drink, he took advantage of our absence to plunge his great Damascus sword into his stomach. On our return, we found him lying on the floor, bleeding to death."

Cleopatra listened in anguish while Diomedes told her how he had sent two soldiers to search the palace grounds, hoping to find Antony's wife and children still alive. Hiding in the stables, his men had discovered an old groom, too crippled with rheumatism to flee with the other servants, who admitted, when threatened with torture, that he had seen the Queen, her children and two maids, running from the house to hide in the tomb from some Roman soldiers who had come (so the groom imagined) to capture them. He had watched the men searching everywhere, and not finding the royal family, finally ride away.

"Rushing to Antony's side, we told him that you and the children were safe, hiding in your mausoleum. He was sinking rapidly, and had just strength enough left to beg us to bring him here, so he could die in your arms. But we can't get him into the tomb unless you come down and unlock the door."

Cleopatra had never trusted Diomedes. Afraid that to get a reward, the Egyptian would seize her and take her to Octavian if she went down to open the door, the Queen replied, "No, carry my husband up the ladder."

The men somehow succeeded in following her orders, and Cleopatra and her two maids, with great effort, managed to drag the limp, two-hundred-pound Roman in through the window. They placed him on a bed, where, at the sight of Antony's sufferings, Cleopatra knelt in tears and covered his face with kisses. Charmian and Iras led young Selene and Ptolemy away, so they would not see their father die.

Octavian was determined to capture the Queen of Egypt and her children. Antony was hardly dead before more Roman soldiers—a dozen of them this time, sent by Cleopatra's deadly enemy with orders to bring her to him or lose their heads—rode in through the gate. The palace appeared to the men to be empty. But noticing some activity out on Lochias Point, about the Queen's tomb, and suspecting that this might be where she had taken refuge, they made for the mausoleum as fast as possible.

On arriving there, the Romans divided into two groups. Six of them hurried around to the back of the building. Diomedes and his friends were still at the foot of the ladder, quarreling over some coins that Cleopatra had tossed out to them. On his knees, the trembling Diomedes tried to save his life by revealing the Queen's hiding place. The Romans listened, with contempt. Then, leaving two of their men to disarm and guard the Egyptians, the four remaining soldiers started up the ladder.

Meanwhile, the other six Romans were around, at the front of the tomb, breaking open the door. They ran up the stairs just as their companions jumped into the room, through the window, and took the weeping Queen, her frightened children, and two maids by surprise. Cleopatra snatched a dagger from her belt. But she didn't have time to use it. She was forced to stand with her hands held high above her head, while the soldiers searched everywhere for hidden weapons or poison. The Queen must not find a way to commit suicide.

While all this was going on, Octavian had been making his entrance into Alexandria with his victorious army. He hoped to convince the Egyptians that he was a kindly man, whose quarrel with Antony and Cleopatra had been forced upon him. So any looting was forbidden, as was the killing of all but a few people. Among these unfortunates was Antyllus, Antony's son, who had fled after the battle and hidden himself in a shrine built by Cleopatra in memory of Caesar. He was dragged out and the executioner cut off the young captive's head on the same day that Octavian buried the boy's father in the Soma, the cemetery of the Ptolemies.

Cleopatra asked but one favor of Octavian. Could she attend her husband's funeral? He granted it. Escorted by their old physician, Olympus, his widow and two children followed Antony's remains to the grave.

* * * *

Octavian commandeered the Ptolemies' palace on Lochias Point for his residence, as Julius Caesar had installed himself there, on conquering Egypt, eighteen years before. After his crushing defeat of Antony's forces, there were many urgent matters to occupy the Roman conqueror's attention. So, now in possession of Egypt and its riches, and with Cleopatra too well guarded to escape, he was in no hurry to visit his captive in her prison-tomb. It was early on the morning of August 28th, three weeks after Antony's funeral, before her jailer came to see her.

He found Cleopatra still in bed. She sat up, startled to see Octavian standing, looking down at her. The sight of the forlorn little widow, a woman only thirty-eight, her hair hanging loose, her robe slipping from her bare shoulders, as she faced him trembling, would have touched the heart of most men, but not this cold-eyed young man. Octavian was no susceptible Caesar or Antony whom Cleopatra could charm. Very much in love with his second wife, Livia, the older woman did not attract him. He was only interested in her gold.

The Roman general—short, blond, and thirty-two—sat down beside the bed and listened politely while Cleopatra begged him not to take the throne of Egypt from her son. "If you will bring Caesarion back from India and be merciful to him, to the twins, and to little Ptolemy, I will do anything—anything—" she pleaded. "All I care about are my children."

Octavian, knowing that both Caesarion and Alexander Helios were dead, assured their mother that Egypt would remain independent of Rome and be ruled over by Caesar's son. He was willing to promise his prisoner all she asked to prevent her from committing suicide, for the ambition of the lowborn Octavian, great-grandson of a humble ropemaker, was to parade Cleopatra of Egypt, the descendant of a long line of pharaohs, as his captive through the streets of Rome. So, assuring the boy's mother that he would bring Caesarion back from India, the Roman left, believing he had deceived her.

But Cleopatra wasn't fooled. By his manner, she was certain

that Octavian intended to take her to Rome and exhibit her in his triumph, as she had watched her sister Arsinoe being forced to walk past the jeering crowds, chained hand and foot, by Caesar. Then, thoroughly humiliated, Cleopatra would be dragged back to prison and strangled. "I couldn't imagine a more degrading death," thought the proud queen. "Somehow, I must rob Octavian of that day of glory."

While the Romans were advancing on Alexandria, Cleopatra, foreseeing possible defeat, had experimented with various snake poisons by trying them out on condemned criminals. The puff adder's was slow, she found, but the venom of an asp, the Egyptian cobra *(naja haje)*, was rapidly absorbed in the blood. It was one of the most lethal of serpents. The bite of an asp could cause death in a half hour. Cleopatra had decided, if she must, to commit suicide in this manner. She would not die shamefully but have a royal death. The sacred cobra, emblem of Lower Egypt and messenger of the gods, would come and take her to live immortal by Ammon's side.

At Antony's funeral, Cleopatra had managed to have a few whispered words with Olympus. "Will you get an asp and have the snake ready, in case I need it?" she asked him. The Queen had hoped then to be able to win over Octavian, as she had charmed Caesar and Antony. Now she knew this was impossible. But who could bring her the cobra? The prisoners were heavily guarded. Octavian was making certain that, when he sailed for Rome, he would be able to take the Queen of Egypt and her children with him. Her maids, Charmian and Iras, were as closely watched as she was. Ptolemy was too young to help her. There was only one person on whom she could count.

"Selene, you're a brave girl, would you be afraid to go to the temple of Artemis and get from Olympus a basket of figs?"

"No, but will the soldiers let me out?"

"I'll fix that—" Her mother walked over and threw Selene's doll out of the window. "Now run down and tell the guard on duty that your toy was dropped. Ask him if you can go out on the rocks and pick it up. If he lets you, run as fast as you can to the temple. You know where Olympus lives there? Get him to give you those figs I spoke to him about. Then bring them to me. Do you understand?"

"Yes, Mama," Selene replied eagerly.

Cleopatra looked at her nine-year-old daughter, thinking how young she was to have such an important thing to do. "Dear, listen carefully to me. Under those figs, there will be a snake. It won't be like the harmless ones you see at the temple of Isis, handled by the priests at the altar, with their fangs removed. This will be a deadly cobra, fresh from the desert. Be careful not to let it bite you." Leaning down, she put her arms around her daughter and kissed her. "My brave child!"

Selene stood ready to go. She looked small and white and frightened. "What do you do?" her mother asked. The girl repeated her instructions carefully and accurately.

"I'm having you do this because you're not afraid of snakes," Cleopatra said to her. "Do you remember Ula, that pet you had? Well, this asp won't be tame and gentle like Ula."

"I'll remember." Selene's voice shook. "Why do you want the snake, Mama?"

"So it will bite me and I'll die. I want to, Selene. The soldiers are trying to keep me from dying, because Octavian plans to take me with him to Rome and humiliate me, but you mustn't let him. If you love me, Selene, promise me that you'll help me die."

Cleopatra kissed her daughter again and watched her start down the stairs. "Mama is proud of you," she called after her.

Then the Queen went back to her room, and told Charmian and Iras how she hoped to end her life. Weeping bitterly, the two women begged to die with Cleopatra rather than be sold in a Roman slave market. She granted their request and ordered them to dress her, for death, in the royal robes of Egypt they had brought with them from the palace. While the maids did so, perfuming their mistress and decking her in silk and jewels, Cleopatra's thoughts were with her daughter. Had she sent the girl, she wondered, on an errand too dangerous for a child of nine to undertake?

Meanwhile, at the bottom of the stairs, Selene had explained to the soldier on duty that her doll had been dropped from the window. Luckily for her, Cornelius Dolabella was a kindly fellow. The Queen's little daughter reminded him of his own blue-eyed, blonde child, back in Italy, so he said, "All right, run out and get your doll, but don't be gone long." Selene raced off as fast as her legs would carry her.

In a short time, she was back, carrying a basket of figs—very gingerly. "Look out for your fingers," Olympus had warned. "Don't touch the fruit or the leaves, the asp may strike at you."

"What have you there?" Dolabella asked. "I thought you went for your toy."

"My doll was broken, so I left her. A nice man gave me these figs for my mother's supper."

"Say, they look good! How about giving me one?" Dolabella reached out an eager hand. "Look out! You'll get bitten!" Selene cried. Clutching the basket tight, she darted up the stairs. The soldier thought of going after the girl, but, the August day being hot, he sat down instead, put his feet up and took a drink of beer.

As he did so, there was a change of guards. The next sentry was not so easygoing. He was shocked to learn that Dolabella had allowed the Queen's daughter to bring in a basket of figs for Cleopatra without first inspecting it. When the soldier hurried up the stairs to the top floor, his worse fears were confirmed—the Queen lay on her bed as though asleep, dressed in her royal robes and jewels, the cobra-and-vulture crown of Egypt on her head. At her feet were Charmian and Iras, dead.

Octavian was sent for immediately. He rushed over from the palace, furious about what had happened. Cleopatra had not yet died. She was in a coma. It was possible that, if snake doctors came, and they knew what poison was in the Queen's veins and used the proper magic, they could still revive her.

"Selene!" Octavian turned on the girl, who was standing with her arms around little Ptolemy, trying to comfort him. "Where are those figs you brought your mother? Who gave them to you?"

"A man—" was all that Selene would reply.

The basket, empty, was found by the bed. Had the fruit been poisoned? Or had a small snake been smuggled in to the Queen, hidden under the leaves? Octavian decided that this was what had happened, for the guard Dolabella had finally admitted that, when he had tried to take a fig, Selene cried, "Look out! You'll get bitten!" Cleopatra had probably teased the reptile until she made it strike, first Charmian and Iras, and then herself. On examining their bodies, Octavian found two tiny marks on an arm of each of the three women that could have been caused by the bite of a snake. A search was made, but only a faint track across the floor was found, to indicate where the serpent might have crawled away.

Octavian sent at once for some snake charmers, belonging to a North African tribe, the Psylli—wild-eyed, long-haired men from the Sahara Desert, who roamed the streets of Alexandria, entertaining the crowds. Luckily, several of them were encamped close by, on Lochias Point, having put on a show at the palace the night before for Octavian and his officers.

Used to handling dangerous serpents, and being sometimes bitten themselves, the Psylli treated their victims of snake-bite by means of "magic charms," accompanied by chants and frantic dancing—a "cure," unfortunately, that seldom worked.

However, sending for the Psylli was all that Octavian could think of doing, at the moment. Cleopatra was still breathing when they arrived. He hoped that, if not a moment were lost, it would be possible for these men of the Sahara to save the Queen's life by using a miraculous "snake stone" they had brought with them. Her death would be slower than that of her maids. Octavian believed that Cleopatra had provoked the reptile to first strike at Charmian and Iras. So its fangs were not as full of venom, its bite not as quick and deadly, when the Queen lay down and took the tired serpent in her arms.

But the Psylli were perplexed. "What kind of a snake was it?" the tribesmen asked Octavian. "We must know. Otherwise, how can we tell the proper remedies to use?"

"Selene!" Octavian turned on the trembling girl. "You brought in that snake, was it a puff adder? A horned viper? An asp?"

"I don't know."

"Well, the man does who gave you that basket of figs! Who was he? Where can we find him?" Octavian grabbed Cleopatra's daughter by the shoulders and shook her. If the girl would only tell them, there might still be time to rush to this man and force an answer from him.

"I don't know."

Since that was all the reply that Octavian could get out of Selene, the Psylli, not knowing what species of snake had bitten Cleopatra, and therefore the proper words to chant and the correct steps to dance, did what little they could. They rubbed the Queen's wound with their magic "snake stone," and tried to suck out the poison, but they were too late. The deadly venom was already racing through her veins. So, Cleopatra died while still in her thirties, but, thanks to her young daughter, as she had wanted to die—royally, with a smile of triumph on her lips.

Her death would deprive Rome of a great sight—the hated Queen of Egypt in chains. Octavian, sick with disappointment, sank down by the bed and covered his face in his hands. Who would have thought it possible? The ruler of the Roman world outwitted by a child of nine!

15

TO MAKE A ROMAN HOLIDAY

CLEOPATRA WAS BURIED beside Antony in the Soma, the cemetery of the Ptolemies that also contained the remains of Alexander the Great. Octavian did not attend her funeral. He had
more important things on his mind. Rich Egypt, the greatest
Roman conquest since Carthage, was his at last. In the future,
Octavian would have ample funds, for he took the huge annual revenues of Egypt for himself, as the successor of the
Ptolemies. Caesar had been recognized there as Cleopatra's
husband. And wasn't he Caesar's adopted son and heir? What
if the dead queen had left two children who had a stronger
claim to the wealth and throne of Egypt? Octavian wasn't
afraid of them. He intended to keep Cleopatra Selene and
Ptolemy Philadelphus alive to walk in his triumphal procession.

When would it take place? With the Roman empire at his
feet, Octavian was in no hurry. It was a preliminary triumphal
march the world-conqueror made in the spring of B.C. 29, the
year following the death of Cleopatra, as he returned home
through Palestine, Syria, and Asia Minor. Everywhere, the
kings of the countries now to be governed from Italy rushed
to pay him homage. Among the first of them was the fawning

Herod of Judea, always eager to ingratiate himself with Rome.

Back in Italy by July, Octavian settled down in his home on Palatine Hill, overlooking the Forum, to enjoy the honors showered upon him. The senate was planning a triple triumph on three successive days, for his Balkan conquests, for Actium, and for Egypt.

The first of these, which took place on August 13th, was followed the next day by the celebration for Actium. This was chiefly a parade in honor of M. Vipsanius Agrippa, who had won for Octavian that decisive naval battle. There were wild cheers as Agrippa rode through the Forum, followed by a display of naval trophies and a huge painting, showing Cleopatra's ships running away.

These processions were only a minor prelude to the third celebration. Held on August 15th, the day for Egypt was the finest triumph Rome had ever seen. Shops and schools were closed; the streets were lined with excited people. Everyone who could possibly do so hurried to the Forum, to crowd into the raised seats along the Via Sacra and wait impatiently for the parade to begin.

"It won't be long in coming," people kept saying. "The Vestal Virgins have gone out to the Campus Martius, where the procession is being formed, to escort Octavian into the city. What an unprecedented honor! But then, what other triumphs can compare with this one? Rome need never fear Egypt again."

Seated in the crowded Forum, as eager as everyone in the reviewing stands to hear the martial music, thrill at the lines of marching soldiers, and gaze in awe at the succession of wagons heaped with all the fabulous loot the Roman ships had brought back from the East, was a tall, brown-skinned young man of twenty-three. He was Juba, son of King Juba I of Numidia, who had walked in a similar triumph, seventeen years ago, when Caesar had conquered his father's North African kingdom.

"Here they come!" someone shouted, as the procession was seen approaching along the Via Sacra. Led by priests and a *popa*, who carried the sacrificial axe over his shoulder, twenty white oxen crowned with flowers, to be sacrificed as a thank-offering to Jupiter, walked to their death. The treasure from Egypt followed. There were delighted "Oh-h-s" from the spectators, as the long line of carts, heaped with shields, armor, javelins, and swords captured from the enemy, passed by. These were followed by four columns of men, carrying urns filled with gold and jewels. But what pleased the Romans even more was knowing that the grain ships from Alexandria were once more arriving at the port of Ostia, for Rome consumed twenty million bushels of Egyptian wheat a year.

"Bread will be plentiful again," a woman, seated beside Juba, said to him. "Now nobody will be hungry."

Next came floats showing the conquered countries—Syria, Armenia, Phoenicia, and Egypt—and two caged animals as new to the Romans as the giraffe and the camel had been at Caesar's triumph, a rhinoceros and a hippopotamus. They were followed by companies of marching soldiers who had won the East for Rome, carrying their battle standards. Finally, bringing up the rear of the parade, came the senators, the lictors, and what everyone was eagerly waiting for—Octavian and his prisoners. All heads turned to look as the victor's chariot, followed by his captives in chains, came into view.

A hush of awe fell over the cheering crowd at the sight of the world-conqueror, dressed in purple embroidered with gold, standing in a gilded chariot drawn by four white horses. Clasped in Octavian's right hand was a branch of laurel. Like the crown on his head, it had come from the laurel grove Octavian's wife Livia had planted at her villa on the Via

Flaminia. His eyes sought hers as he passed the reviewing stand.

Two boys rode spirited horses on either side of the chariot in which Octavian stood. On his right was his nephew, the fourteen-year-old Marcellus, son of his sister Octavia, while to his left was his stepson Tiberius, thirteen, Livia's boy by a former husband. Behind them walked Cleopatra's two children, tied to the conqueror's chariot by gold chains that were wound about their necks. Then came Cleopatra herself! Octavian had promised the Romans to bring her back from Egypt for his triumph. Hadn't he done so? A huge wax figure of the queen had been made, with a snake coiled about her arm to show how she had died. The crowd took a savage delight in shouting obscene epithets and spitting at the hated "Serpent of the Nile," as she was carried by.

Their rude jeers at a fallen foe shocked Juba. "How cruel the Romans are!" he thought. It reminded him of the time when he had walked in Caesar's triumph between such lines of hostile people. A bewildered, frightened boy, brought from Africa, Juba of Numidia had been about the age then of these poor children of Cleopatra's. Selene was stumbling along, biting her lips to fight back the tears; Ptolemy was crying. Both children were dusty, hot, and exhausted, from their long walk under the August sun.

The procession came to a halt before the Basilica Aemilia. Trumpets sounded and Tiberius' horse, frightened by the shrill noise, backed into the two children. Selene screamed and put her arms about her little brother.

This was too much! Seeing their terror, Juba sprang to his feet and ran down from the stands onto the Via Sacra. Lifting up the sobbing Ptolemy, the African prince set the Egyptian boy on his shoulder, speaking to him words of comfort. The confusion was soon over. Tiberius controlled his horse.

The procession moved on again, Juba carrying little Ptolemy and leading the trembling Selene by the hand.

At the foot of Capitoline Hill, the parade stopped again. The vanquished kings, their wives and sons—all those brave people who had dared to fight Rome—were led away from here to be strangled or starved to death. Juba remembered how, at Caesar's triumph, he had been taken back to his cell in the Mamertine prison. A terrified, helpless child, he would have died down in that ghastly dungeon, twelve feet underground, if Octavian had not rescued him.

Such a fate was not in store for Cleopatra's children. Brought from Egypt a week ago, they were to live with Octavian's sister, Octavia. "But what will I do with them now?" Juba thought. Looking at their tear-stained faces, he realized that Selene and Ptolemy could not walk much further. Their little legs had given out. Octavian had descended from his chariot and, followed by the senators, was climbing to the temple of Jupiter, to offer thanks for his victory over their parents. Did Selene and Ptolemy have to follow him up those long flights of steps and listen to that? Hadn't they endured enough?

As Juba was wondering how he could spare Cleopatra's weary children this last humiliation, Tiberius came up to them. "I'm sorry my horse backed into you," he said to Selene. "I couldn't help it."

She answered him with a scowl. It was obvious that Cleopatra's daughter hated every Roman in sight, for the spiteful things the crowd had shouted at the statue of her mother. Juba could hardly blame the girl.

Still, Selene would have to learn to live with these people, as he had. So when Tiberius went to join his stepfather, Juba said to her, "Why don't you smile and hold up your head? I did, when I walked in Caesar's triumph. My father killed himself, like your mother did, rather than be led in chains through the Forum. Caesar brought me from Africa to be exhibited in my father's place, as Octavian has brought you. I know what you're going through. Selene, I was younger than you are, only six, but I didn't let the Romans know that I was afraid. You can smile too, if you try."

"After Caesar's triumph, they didn't kill you?"

"No, Octavian rescued me from prison. He educated me and has been good to me. He isn't going to kill you, either. So hold up your chin and show your contempt of these Romans, as your mother would have done."

The procession moved on again, following Octavian up the steps to the temple of Jupiter. Juba was wondering whether he could carry both Selene and Ptolemy, when he saw a sweet-faced, middle-aged woman coming toward him through the crowd. It was Octavia. Juba had never been so glad to see her.

"Give me those children," Octavian's sister said. "This is barbaric! I'm taking the poor things home. I won't have them tortured any further." Summoning her litter, she took Selene and Ptolemy away with her, to Juba's relief, up to her home on Palatine Hill overlooking the Forum.

Octavian had promised the Romans a series of events to follow his triumphs. The next day, an African big-game hunt was to be staged in the Circus Maximus. Protected by a water-filled ditch, the spectators would watch lions and elephants fight one another. The arena would then be flooded and, the following day, a sea battle would be fought. For a week, Rome would enjoy a continual holiday, paid for out of the plunder of the conquered cities of the East, most of it coming from Alexandria.

The night of his Egyptian triumph, Octavian gave a banquet for the senators, his principal army officers and their wives, in the temple of Flora. Octavia was to attend the feast. But before leaving for the affair, she went to say good night to Selene and Ptolemy, who had been put to bed. Worn out by his exhausting day, Ptolemy was sound asleep. Octavia kissed him and went on into the room where Selene lay, looking up at her with resentful eyes.

"Go away," the girl muttered. "I hate you. What has happened to Caesarion and Alexander Helios? Nobody will tell me. Are they dead? Then your brother is a murderer! Why didn't Octavian kill me, too? Why did he bring me to Rome? I don't want to live with you or have anything to do with you." And she burst into tears.

Trying to appear calm, Octavia sat down by the bed, but she could feel her heart pounding. Octavia thought she could handle Ptolemy. But how was she going to get along with his rebellious sister? It was absurd to be frightened of a child of ten, but Octavia was afraid of Selene.

"I know you hate us and have good reason to," she said gently. "But I hope that, in time, I can make you feel differently. Now, Selene, you've had a hard day. It's all over now. So go to sleep and try to forget it. Good night, my dear."

Not daring to kiss the little girl, as she had kissed her brother, Octavia hurried to the door and closed it softly behind her. In the next room, she sank into a chair and put her hands over her face. Having Cleopatra's children to bring up was going to be even worse than Octavia had feared! She had not wanted them. It was Octavian who had insisted that she take the orphans. He was posing as Cleopatra's legal heir and not a foreign usurper, and he wished to ingratiate himself with the Egyptians. Since they might resent the execution of the last of the Ptolemies, Octavian thought it would look well if his sister took into her home these children (illegitimate, in Roman eyes) of her faithless husband.

Octavia loved her younger brother dearly. She never refused him anything. So, always meek and dutiful, she had agreed to the arrangement. But Octavian did not know how much he was asking of her, for, having married Mark Antony to please her brother, Octavia had fallen in love with him. Nobody knew how deeply hurt Antony's discarded wife had been when she had gone to join her husband in Syria and he had ordered her back to Rome. Now to have "that woman's" children by Antony to bring up! For the first time in her life, Octavia felt that her brother demanded too much of her.

Ptolemy, chubby and red-haired, resembled Antony at the age of six. Octavia loved him already. But Selene, with those big blue eyes and that mass of blonde hair, was the living image of Cleopatra. "How can I bear to look at her every day?" Octavia thought, in despair.

16

GETTING TO KNOW THE ROMANS

AN ENTIRELY NEW LIFE began for Selene and Ptolemy. In Octavia's home, the Egyptian orphans were brought up with six Romans their own age. There were the three children Octavia had by her first husband, C. Claudius Marcellus—one son, M. Claudius Marcellus (fourteen), and two daughters named Claudia Marcella (thirteen and twelve). Then there were two girls (ten and seven), both called Antonia, Octavia had by Mark Antony. The sixth child was an orphan—Julius Antonius (thirteen), Antony's son by Fulvia—a younger brother of the murdered Antyllus. While, near by, living with Octavian and his wife Livia, were Julia (ten), his daughter by a former wife, Scribonia; and Tiberius Claudius Nero (thirteen) and Drusus Claudius Nero (nine), Livia's children by T. Claudius Nero.

Both houses were situated on Palatine Hill, where Romulus and the early kings had lived. Born there in humble quarters, Octavian, after Actium, had bought the home of Cicero's friend, Quintus Hortensius, overlooking the Circus Maximus,

TH

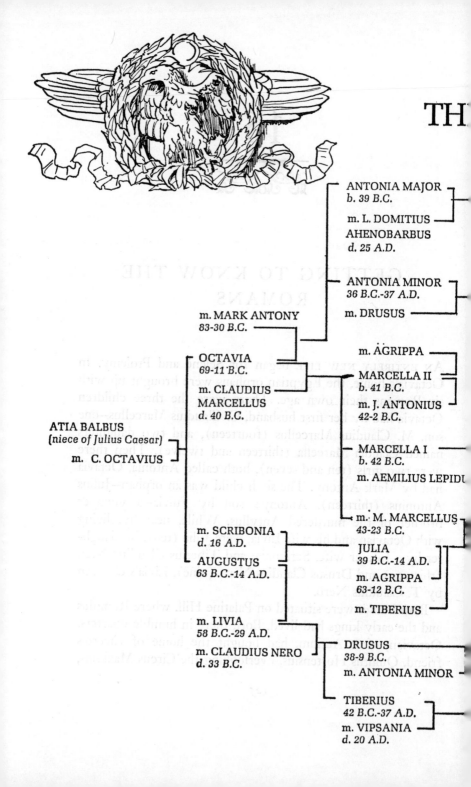

ANTONIA MAJOR
b. 39 B.C.

m. L. DOMITIUS
AHENOBARBUS
d. 25 A.D.

ANTONIA MINOR
36 B.C.-37 A.D.

m. DRUSUS

m. MARK ANTONY
83-30 B.C.

m. AGRIPPA

OCTAVIA
69-11 B.C.

MARCELLA II
b. 41 B.C.

m. CLAUDIUS
MARCELLUS
d. 40 B.C.

m. J. ANTONIUS
42-2 B.C.

ATIA BALBUS
(niece of Julius Caesar)
m. C. OCTAVIUS

MARCELLA I
b. 42 B.C.

m. AEMILIUS LEPIDU

m. M. MARCELLUS
43-23 B.C.

m. SCRIBONIA
d. 16 A.D.

JULIA
39 B.C.-14 A.D.

AUGUSTUS
63 B.C.-14 A.D.

m. AGRIPPA
63-12 B.C.

m. TIBERIUS

m. LIVIA
58 B.C.-29 A.D.

DRUSUS
38-9 B.C.

m. CLAUDIUS NERO
d. 33 B.C.

m. ANTONIA MINOR

TIBERIUS
42 B.C.-37 A.D.

m. VIPSANIA
d. 20 A.D.

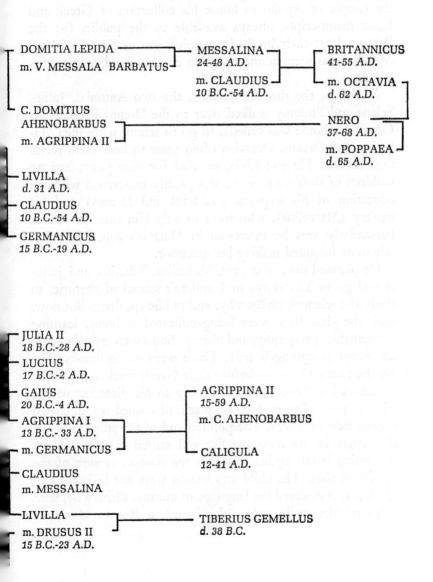

DOMITIA LEPIDA
m. V. MESSALA BARBATUS

MESSALINA
24-48 A.D.
m. CLAUDIUS
10 B.C.-54 A.D.

BRITANNICUS
41-55 A.D.
m. OCTAVIA
d. 62 A.D.

C. DOMITIUS
AHENOBARBUS
m. AGRIPPINA II

NERO
37-68 A.D.
m. POPPAEA
d. 65 A.D.

LIVILLA
d. 31 A.D.

CLAUDIUS
10 B.C.-54 A.D.

GERMANICUS
15 B.C.-19 A.D.

JULIA II
18 B.C.-28 A.D.

LUCIUS
17 B.C.-2 A.D.

GAIUS
20 B.C.-4 A.D.

AGRIPPINA I
13 B.C.- 33 A.D.
m. GERMANICUS

AGRIPPINA II
15-59 A.D.
m. C. AHENOBARBUS

CALIGULA
12-41 A.D.

CLAUDIUS
m. MESSALINA

LIVILLA
m. DRUSUS II
15 B.C.-23 A.D.

TIBERIUS GEMELLUS
d. 38 B.C.

and also a house for his sister Octavia. Modest, simply-furnished buildings, Suetonius describes them scornfully as "homes scarcely fit for a private citizen." But on the grounds between them, shaded by cypress trees, Octavian had built the temple of Apollo to house his collection of Greek and Latin manuscripts, always available to the public, for the Romans kept their books in temples, just as libraries in the Middle Ages were connected with churches and religious institutions.

Mornings, the three Marcellaes, the two Antonias, Julius, Selene and Ptolemy walked over to the Domus Palatina (as Octavian's home was called), to go to school with Julia, Tiberius, and Drusus. Octavian often came to hear them recite their lessons. He and Livia, married for nine years, had no children of their own, so he was greatly concerned with the education of his stepsons (Tiberius and Drusus) and his nephey (Marcellus), who were to help him rule the world. Particularly was he interested in Octavia's son, Marcellus, whom he intended making his successor.

He planned that, next year, Marcellus, Tiberius, and Julius should go to Theodorus of Gandara's school of rhetoric, to study the sciences, philosophy, and public speaking. But now, with the girls, they were being educated at home, learning mathematics, geography, and history. Sums were calculated on an *abacus* (counting-board). There were no textbooks. The children sat on benches before their Greek teacher, repeating in turn what Areus said, or writing to his dictation with a stilus (a pointed metal rod) on pieces of framed wood, coated on one side with wax. The pointed end of the stilus indented the letters in the wax; the flat end served as an eraser by smoothing it out again. This was the Roman version of the American slate. The children's lessons were not in Latin, but in Greek, considered the language of culture. Otherwise, with maps on the walls and a blackboard, a Roman classroom would have resembled a modern one. When they were tired of reciting long passages from Homer, the older boys, Marcellus, Julius and Tiberius, were apt to just idle and yawn, while the elder Antonia and Julia chatted in a whisper, and Drusus swatted at the flies.

Physical training was considered necessary to toughen Roman boys for war. So, afternoons, Marcellus, Tiberius, Drusus, and Julius went to the Campus Martius, an athletic field and drill ground for the army located outside the city walls, to do gymnastic exercises, while the girls had music lessons or spun wool.

In spite of a houseful of slaves, Octavian's capable, twenty-nine-year-old wife Livia directed all of the spinning and weaving. In olden times, the making of clothes for her husband and children was a Roman matron's chief occupation; and Octavian, who wanted to revive the old strict ways of the republic, which were dying out, would wear only homemade togas. Julia, already a pert, spoiled child at ten, hated these rough homespun garments her father forced his family to wear.

Octavia usually came over to help her sister-in-law with the work. Both women loved Octavian, but Selene detected a secret antagonism between them. People were saying that Livia wanted her eldest son, Tiberius, to replace Marcellus as Octavian's successor. Her husband wouldn't hear of it, for Tiberius was a Claudian, with not a drop of the great Julius Caesar's blood in his veins.

Listening to the gossip of the slaves, Selene learned a great deal about these Romans with whom she was living. It seemed that, while he was married to Scribonia (Julia's mother), a woman older than himself, the usually cautious Octavian had shocked Rome by falling so madly in love with the pregnant, twenty-year-old Livia Drusilla, wife of T. Claudius Nero, that he couldn't wait to marry her—not even for three months, until after the birth of her second child, Drusus. He rid himself of Scribonia, on the day that Julia was born. He forced Livia's husband to divorce her. On January 17, B.C. 38, Octavian and Livia were married.

Livia's eldest son, Tiberius, was a tall, robust fellow, with a small mouth, big eyes, and a bad complexion. Being shortsighted, he looked at people frowning, so few liked him—but Selene did. After school, the reserved, moody Tiberius walked home with her, while his outgoing, attractive brother, Drusus, escorted Antonia Minor. When they went to the *venationes*, the two young couples usually sat together.

These spectacles that Octavia took the children to see were (like today's circus) chiefly shows of wild animals that had been tamed. Little Ptolemy shouted with glee at the sights down in the arena—panthers harnessed to a chariot, tigers performing at the order of a ringmaster, and "educated" elephants who wrote with their trunks in the sand. Marcellus, Tiberius, Drusus and Julius being older, were occasionally allowed to go Rome's huge open-air ampitheater by the Tiber, to watch fights between wild animals or gladiators pitted against lions, leopards, and bears trained to feed on human flesh. But Octavia never let the girls and Ptolemy see this ugly side of Roman life.

At the *Circus Maximus* (Big Circus), lying between the Palatine and Aventine Hills, where the chariot races were held, Selene and Ptolemy sat with Octavian's family in the principal box over the entrance. And the conqueror of the world cheered as loudly as anyone when the horses galloped neck and neck to the finishing post. It was then, when he relaxed and enjoyed himself, that Selene grew to like him better.

A short, blond man with a limp, due to a weak left hip, Octavian wore high heels to add a few inches to his height. Otherwise, there was no vanity in him. He led a frugal life, slept on an army cot, and, except on gala occasions, wore a toga as plain as the average citizen's. Nor were the *convivia* (dinners) he and Livia gave for the aristocracy of Rome very lavish. Liking plain meals of fish, coarse bread, cheese and a few figs, Octavian usually ate before his guests arrived. His chief concern was his health. He suffered from bladder trouble, which often caused him great embarrassment while he was delivering a speech; and, being subject to colds, he wore heavy woolen garments under his toga, even in summer. Octavian was also tormented by a constant itch. Because of this distressing skin disease, he never went out in the sun without wearing a hat.

It amazed Selene that such a sickly invalid should have the power of life and death over three-quarters of the people in the world. But she admired the man's courage. Octavian never let the Romans see his weak side. Before the public, he behaved like a god, while in the privacy of his home, Livia wrapped her husband in a flannel stomacher, and slaves oiled his itching back. Octavian was also afraid of thunderstorms. At the first flash of lightning, he rushed to hide in an underground vault.

If she suspected that Octavian knew more about the mysterious disappearance of Caesarion and Alexander Helios than he would admit, Selene learned to keep her thoughts to herself. "Since you're at his mercy, you'd better forgive and forget," Julius advised his half-sister. "Didn't your mother have your Aunt Arsinoe murdered? And probably your Uncle Ptolemy? Well, Octavian killed my brother Antyllus, but, like Juba, I'm one of his greatest admirers."

Selene often thought of the African prince who had been kind to her on Octavian's day for Egypt. They had much in common. Both were exiles who had walked, a captive, in a Roman triumph. Where was he now? "Juba has been sent to Numidia, his father's old kingdom, to get us some marble," Julius told her.

"I found the city of brick and will leave it marble," Octa-

vian often said. Rebuilding Rome to make it a capital worthy
of the empire, he was tearing down blocks of insulae (walkup
apartments), widening streets, and erecting temples and government offices. The new buildings, made possible by a Roman invention, concrete, were faced with white marble. Most
of it came from quarries in Tuscany. But for the temple of
Vesta he was building on the Palatine, Octavian wanted Numidian rose marble. So he had sent the twenty-three-year-old
Juba, who spoke the native Punic language, to North Africa
to get it.

After that, the African prince went to help the Romans
fight the Cantabri, a rebellious Spanish tribe on the Bay of
Biscay. He was away from Italy for two years. In B.C. 27,
when Octavian had become the Emperor Augustus (the
Romans' Sextilis—the month of August in today's calendar—
is named after him), and Selene was thirteen, Juba returned
to Rome. Glad his military service was over, he settled down
to the work he loved, as a research scholar in Greek manuscripts at the *Atrium Libertatis* (Hall of the Goddess Liberty),
the public library that Asinius Pollio had opened in 39, the
first in Rome.

On a shopping tour in the Forum with the two Antonias,
Cleopatra Selene ran into him. "You've grown so, I hardly
knew you!" exclaimed the young African, at the sight of the
three pretty girls.

After that, Selene saw Juba often, for he left Pollio's library
and became an assistant to the head librarian, Gaius Julius
Hegenus, at the temple of Apollo, that Augustus (as we must
call Octavian now) had built on the site of his birthplace
on the Palatine, as a thank-offering for his victory over Antony and Cleopatra.

Constructed of Carrara marble, this public library, the second in Rome, was stocked with Greek as well as Latin works.
These books (long scrolls of rolled-up papyri) were kept in

wall cupboards. There were catalogs, but no printing presses. It was very different from today, with thousands of copies of the same book in circulation. In Roman times, it took many rolls to make one book, and every roll must be laboriously transcribed by hand. Slave-copyists were to ancient literature what the printing press is to modern publishing. Juba was in charge of a group of Greek prisoners-of-war called *servi literati*—educated men, skilled at reproducing manuscripts. They copied or wrote under his dictation, using abbreviations for speed, which were known as *notae tironianae*, after M. Tullius Tiro, Cicero's secretary, who invented the first shorthand.

Evenings, Juba frequented the *tabernae* (shops) along the Vicus Sandalarius, where there were on sale the rolls their copiers produced. These *bibliopolae* (book dealers) were really literary clubs. At the Sosii Brothers, Rome's leading *scriptoria* (publishing house), which brought out Horace's poems, book lovers met to discuss the firm's newest publications, or to listen to the reading of new works by their authors before copies were made.

Besides these public readings, private ones (an author reading his manuscript to a wealthy patron) were popular. Many an evening Virgil read passages from his work-in-progress, the *Aeneid*, to the Emperor Augustus. Juba often attended these literary gatherings at the Domus Palatina, in the company of such successful authors as Virgil, Horace, Livy and Ovid. There he became acquainted with Agrippa (who had won Augustus' battles for him) and rich Maecenas (who financed the emperor's campaigns). The Empress Livia, a cold, stately beauty, presided graciously at these affairs. Usually, Octavia was there with the Marcellaes, the Antonias, Julius, and Cleopatra Selene.

Looking at Selene one evening across the crowded room, Juba was startled to see that, at thirteen, she was no longer a child. Her blonde hair was braided tonight into a coronet entwined with flowers on the top of her head. It changed her amazingly. Tiberius, also looking at Selene, saw Juba's eyes on her and didn't like it. It seemed to him that, since the African prince's return from Spain, Selene went to the temple of Apollo pretty often. Several days later, meeting the girl coming out of the library with two papyri rolls under arm, Tiberius asked crossly, "More books? Why do you want to know so much?"

"Because I'm not the emperor's heiress like Julia; I haven't gorgeous red hair like the younger Marcella; or a lovely figure like Antonia Major. So I'll have to be smart, if I want to get ahead in the world. And I do!"

"Oh, I wouldn't be so sure about not being pretty." Tiberius looked at Cleopatra's daughter critically. "Your eyes are lovely. I've never seen such a heavenly blue. Did your mother have eyes like yours? No wonder Caesar and Antony fell in love with her."

Selene bristled, defensively. She always did at any mention of her mother. The gold statue of Cleopatra, set up by Caesar in the Forum, had been dragged out of the temple of Venus by the Romans and shattered into fragments. No woman in history was subjected to such a campaign of vilification as Cleopatra. Nor had her death ended the Romans' spite. Malicious stories were still being circulated about the "Siren of the Nile," part courtesan and part witch, who had seduced Caesar and, by persuading Antony to turn traitor, had brought on his ruin and death. Selene suffered from them. No one let her forget that she was Cleopatra's daughter.

Some months later, Octavia, sewing in her bedroom, heard the voices of Selene and the two Antonias out in the garden. The girls were making chains of flowers. Suddenly, Selene jumped up, scattered the blossoms in her lap, and advanced on the elder Antonia with clenched fists. "Don't you ever say that again!" she shouted.

"I will so! Because it's true. Julius told me, and he knows."

"It's not, it's a lie!" Selene grabbed her half-sister and shook her. Antonia shrieked. "Stop it! You're tearing my new stola. I'll tell Mama on you—" And she gave Selene a hard slap. Upon which, Selene caught hold of Antonia's long back curls and pulled. The next minute, the girls were down on the grass, rolling over and over, kicking and screaming. The younger Antonia, running over to them, added her shrill cries to theirs.

In the portico beside the garden, Marcellus was practicing on his lyre. Disturbed by the noise, he hurried out, angrily pulled the combatants apart and marched them into the house to where Octavia was seated.

"Girls of twelve and thirteen fighting, aren't you ashamed of yourselves?" she asked.

"No!" Antonia, in tears, looked down at the rips in her stola. "Selene has ruined my best dress. I hate her."

"I hate you, too!" Her half-sister turned on her fiercely. "When I'm big, I'm going to kill you, for what you said about my mother."

In despair, Octavia looked from one red-faced girl to the other. "I'm sure that Antonia didn't mean it, Selene," she said gently. "How can you grow up to be dignified young ladies, if you act like hoodlums? That wasn't nice of you, Selene, to pull Antonia's hair. Nor of you, Antonia, to slap Selene. Now I want both of you to say that you're sorry."

Antonia hung her head. It was hard for her to do it, but she finally blurted out, "I'm sorry—" Octavia turned to Selene. "And now you, dear." When Selene spoke it was through clenched teeth and very fast. "I'm—not—sorry—but—I'll—say —I—am—because—I—must—will—that—do?"

Octavia sighed. "I suppose so."

Later that night, when the girls were in bed, the younger Antonia, a gentle, sweet-faced girl, came over in the dark, and, sitting down beside Selene, put her arms around her. "I'm sorry about what Antonia said," she whispered.

Selene hugged her. How different her sisters were! One loved her, the other was jealous of her, and Selene would never feel the same toward Julius after what he had said to Antonia Major about her mother.

17

TIBERIUS DISCOVERS CAPRI

In ROMAN FAMILIES, childhood engagements were common. Babies were promised from birth. At twelve a girl, and a boy at fourteen, were considered ready for marriage. They were expected to accept without question their parents' choice of a husband or wife. Since Roman marriages usually had a political or financial purpose, the young people's wishes were seldom consulted.

This was especially true in the imperial family. Reconciled to never having a child by Livia, the emperor began to marry off his nephew and nieces to the best advantage. The first to leave Octavia's household were the two Claudia Marcellas. Marcella I was married in 28 B.C. to Aemilius Lepidus; Marcella II to Augustus' boyhood friend, M. Vipsanius Agrippa, a widower of thirty-five, more than twenty years her senior. The next girl to go (in December of 26) was the elder Antonia, who became the wife of the wealthy Lucius Domitus Ahenobarbus. But what set Rome agog was the engagement of the emperor's only child, Julia, to her cousin Marcellus, the heir apparent.

Marcella I (sixteen), Marcella II (fifteen), Julia (thirteen), and Antonia I (thirteen) were all about Selene's age (four-teen), and Cleopatra's daughter began to think "What about me?" and wonder whom Augustus would select for her. An urge to be grownup and become someone of importance surged within her. Julia, married to Marcellus, would be empress of Rome someday. The night their engagement was announced, Selene, jealous through and through, looked at herself in a mirror. "You'd make a better looking empress than Julia," she told the pretty girl she saw there. "Still, we'll be next in importance to Marcellus and Julia, Tiberius and I, for the emperor will never allow me to marry outside the imperial family."

The thought consoled Selene. Who else was there for her but Tiberius? Drusus loved the younger Antonia. And al-though Tiberius had been pledged by his mother to marry Vipsania, the daughter of Agrippa by his first wife, their en-gagement did not worry Selene. Livia had betrothed her eld-est son to Agrippa's daughter, when Vipsania was one year old. Since then, Tiberius had hardly seen the child.

* * * *

When Rome grew uncomfortably hot, it was to the Sabine Hills or Campania that well-to-do Romans hurried in the summer months. The imperial family was always to be found at Baiae, near the little hamlet of Neapolis (Naples), the most fashionable of the seaside resorts. With its hillsides covered with villas and gardens, as Amalfi and Sorrento are today, Baiae was noted for its mineral springs. Briefly back in Italy, Augustus came there in March of B.C. 25 with his family and the household of his sister Octavia. The emperor's physician, Antonius Musa, hoped that the hot, healing waters of Baiae might relieve his itch, before he had to rejoin the army fight-ing in Spain.

Besides the baths and convalescent homes for the sick, Baiae had plenty of amusements for those in good health. The Romans rarely went into the ocean (mixed bathing, like dancing, being considered improper), but there was sailing and fishing. A kiss now and then was all that had happened between Selene and Tiberius. But, one day, stepping out of a boat, she slipped and landed in his arms. Then and there Tiberius knew, holding Selene close, that he would never love anyone else.

That night, alone in his room, Livia's eldest son talked to himself sternly. What if he was engaged to Vipsania? She was only ten now, his junior by seven years—a homely little girl, too shy to speak, who had blushed and giggled incessantly, the few times he had seen her. His mother couldn't force him into such a distasteful marriage. It was Selene that Tiberius loved and wanted for his wife. He would go right to the empress, this minute, and tell her . . . Tell her what? That he wished to marry Cleopatra's illegitimate daughter? Tiberius knew only too well what Livia would say. He shuddered. He had always been afraid of his domineering mother.

"I'll go tomorrow," Tiberius promised himself. But, the next morning, the empress had a headache. He thought it better not to upset her. So he put off having a quarrel with his mother for several days. Then a chance remark from Julius informed everybody.

A Roman lady went shopping for clothing and jewelry, but never for food. The purchasing of supplies for the household was done by her slaves. But she was expected to discuss with her cook every morning the dishes to be served at the evening *cena* (dinner), the principal meal of the day, that came at sundown, after her husband returned from the *thermae* (public baths). Octavia was making out her menus, several mornings later, when she heard Julius leaving the house to go to the barber.

At one time, the Romans all wore beards. The Greeks cut off theirs, following the example of Alexander the Great. Now, imitating the Greeks, the Romans were mostly clean-shaven, but they never shaved at home. A Roman dandy went daily to the *tonsor* (hairdresser) to be shaved, and to have his hair cut, curled and perfumed. A boy's first shave was as important an occassion as his sixteenth birthday, when he was old enough to discard his child's toga with a purple hem and put on the completely white *toga virilis* (of manhood). This spring Julius, seventeen, was submitting his face for the first time to the barber's razor.

"Julius, will you be home tonight for dinner?" Octavia asked. "If you are, I'll get some oysters. I know you like them."

"Could you get them tomorrow, instead? Antonia, Drusus and I are going to the chariot races in Puteoli (Pozzuoli). We won't be back for dinner."

"What about Selene?"

"She won't be home, either. She's going out with Tiberius to Capreae (Capri) for a picnic. Tiberius has fallen in love with that deserted island. He says it's a paradise. I'd like to see Capreae some day, but Tiberius never takes anyone out there in his sailboat but Selene. Those lovers always want to be off by themselves."

Octavia repeated, incredulously, "Those lovers?"

"Didn't you know?"

"Know what?"

"That Tiberius is in love with Selene and wants to marry her." Julius, delighted that he had created a sensation, looked at Octavia's stricken face with a pleased grin. "Well, if you didn't know, everyone else does."

It was incredible! Long after Julius left her, Octavia, trembling from the shock, sat wondering what to do. What a blind fool she had been! Suddenly, she sprang to her feet and summoned her litter. "I'll go and talk it over with Livia," she thought. "She always knows how to handle her sons."

A half hour later, Octavia was entering her sister-in-law's pink stucco villa, perched on the rocks by the sea. She found Livia seated in her boudoir, her maids exchanging frightened looks as they dressed her. Twice the hairdresser had been compelled to begin the empress' complicated hair-do all over again. The make-up women could do nothing right. Livia was in such a bad humor that Octavia knew she had been told.

"I was just coming to see you," her sister-in-law greeted her. "Oh, Octavia, I've had the most frightful scene with Tiberius—"

"I know about what, Julius told me."

"He did! Then everybody knew about this but us?"

Octavia, seating herself, tried to speak cheerfully. "Tiberius can't be serious. It's just a flirtation."

"No, he wants to marry the girl. Imagine! Cleopatra's illegitimate daughter. A penniless exile, besides. Tiberius must be out of his mind. He knows that he is to marry Vipsania."

The two women looked at each other in despair. Vipsania Agrippina, daughter of the plebian Agrippa, was the grandchild of Cicero's rich publisher, T. Pompenius Atticus, who had died leaving the baby of his daughter Pomponia a huge fortune. Of course, the bride that Livia would have preferred for her son was Julia, but Augustus had never liked his stepson—the morose Tiberius. So Livia had been forced to content herself with the child-heiress, Vipsania Agrippina, for a daughter-in-law. She was only ten, but Tiberius seventeen, could wait.

"I blame myself for this, Livia," Octavia sighed. "I have brought up Selene like one of my own children."

"Yes, it has gone to her head. That she should dream of marrying Tiberius! For of course it was Selene who seduced him."

"I wouldn't doubt it. She's ambitious, like her mother."

"And a witch!" The empress rose and put on her stola, which fell in elegant pleats down to her red leather slippers. She was going to pay some morning calls. Roman women never wore hats. Two maids stood waiting, one carrying Livia's hooded palla with which she would cover her head on getting into her *basterna* (a litter carried by mules), the other girl holding a purse and a fan.

"Now go home, Octavia, and don't worry," the empress said, as the two women walked through the *atrium* (reception hall) to their litters. "Leave everything to me. I'll see that this affair is broken off. Selene must be married to a man who will take her far away, where Tiberius will never see her again. Who? Well, I don't know now, but I'll think of someone."

The "someone" Livia thought of, after she left Octavia, was Juba, the African prince. He was twenty-seven and Augustus had told her that he was thinking of sending him out to his native Numidia, to replace the Roman governor there. Juba, as a husband, seemed ideal. With Selene living in far-off Africa, Tiberius would forget her.

That night, Livia could hardly wait to talk with her husband, but there were guests to dinner, and it was bedtime before the imperial couple were alone. When she had undressed and dismissed her maids, Livia told him—and Augustus was surprised and displeased! He had grown very fond of Selene. She was not only pretty, but smart. He would never forget how the girl had outwitted him at Cleopatra's death. "Of course, she knew what kind of a snake it was," he often thought, with a chuckle.

But the emperor didn't like the idea of Selene marrying Tiberius, for it would upset Livia, and he didn't want any quarrels with his wife just now. Augustus had been indulging lately in some mild philandering, but always discreetly. He never allowed his private recreations to disturb his public image of being a model of virtue and abstinence. Still, he thought that Livia suspected him. So, anxious to keep her in a good humor, Augustus was glad to give in to his wife on what he considered a minor matter—whom Selene should marry.

It was quickly arranged, Livia saw to that. Juba was appointed proconsul (governor) of Numidia and told that he was to wed Cleopatra Selene. Tiberius was also given his orders. He would leave with Augustus, when his stepfather returned to Spain.

Tiberius didn't go willingly. Burning with hot resentment, the heartbroken young man lived over and over the times he and Selene had been out to Capri together. When had he ever done what he liked? Or had what he wanted? As he angrily paced his room in the Domus Palatina, it seemed to the unhappy Tiberius that all he had done in life was please his mother.

Livia finally took pity on his anguish, and told her son that he could see Selene once more and say good-by to her, before he left for Spain. Tiberius kissed his love for the last time, his throat too thick for speech, and Selene held back her tears until he had left the house. Then she flung herself into the younger Antonia's arms. "I wanted him terribly," she sobbed.

Her sister consoled Selene as best she could and, within a week or so, the girl's broken heart ceased to ache so much. Common sense told her that Tiberius, second in line to the throne, would never be allowed to marry Cleopatra's daughter.

If she couldn't have Tiberius, Selene was glad they had chosen Juba for her. His broad nose and thick lips proclaimed his mixture of Numidian and Negro blood (Juba's mother had been a Congo slave in his father's harem), and he was tall. She liked tall men. He had soft dark eyes, curly black hair, and when Juba smiled, his teeth were very white against his brown skin. He had a lovely smile. "And we both have royal blood," Selene reminded herself, proudly.

18

THE BRIDE WORE ORANGE

ALL THE SHORES of the Mediterranean now belonged to Rome, but parts of the empire were in different states of subjection. Greece, Syria, and Egypt were firmly in Roman hands; Judea was ruled by a client king; but Spain (which included modern Portugal) still resisted; and although Caesar had conquered Gaul (France, Holland, and Belgium), the "invincible" legions had not been able to crush those barbarians (the *"Germani"*) who lived beyond the Rhine.

In North Africa, to the west of Egypt, were the Roman provinces of Africa, Numidia, and Mauretania. They were hardly more than a narrow strip along the coast. South of them extended the boundless (for all the Romans could tell) Sahara Desert. The Numidians had been hard to subdue. Under Jugurtha, a former king, they had fought savage wars with Rome. In 46 B.C., Caesar conquered them and Numidia (modern eastern Algeria) now lay, apparently quiet, under a Roman proconsul. It was an undeveloped land. The Romans had never dared penetrate far into the interior of Africa.

This was the country that the son of Juba I, last king of Numidia, was being sent out to rule for Rome. He heard what was expected of him with mixed feelings. That he, a deposed African prince, was to be given the daughter of the great Cleopatra of Egypt for a wife! Juba could scarcely believe his good fortune. He had always admired Selene, but he wasn't in love with her. The serious-minded young custodian of the emperor's collection of books was in love with Rome and its literary life.

Juba had come to Italy as a child, had been educated there, and he thought of himself as a Roman now. He had seen enough of his native Numidia on that brief trip he had made for Augustus, when he went to North Africa to get the marble. A scholar, not a soldier or an administrator, Juba had hated his term of duty in Spain with the army. Nor did he care for politics. He wanted to be a writer. Now to be told that he must leave the work he loved at the temple of Apollo and the company of his literary friends and go out to Numidia, even with Selene as his bride, made him sick at heart.

Greatly upset, Juba went to talk over the matter with C. Cilnius Maecenas, who was like a father to him. Immensely rich and fond of the arts, Maecenas was using his wealth to help deserving writers. Thanks to him, P. Vergilius Maro (Virgil), made financially independent, had written his *Georgics* in praise of country life and was now at work on the *Aeneid;* and Q. Horatius Flaccus (Horace) had been freed from money troubles to compose poems. So good was the rich Etruscan to struggling authors that ever since, the expression "a Maecenas" has been a synonym for any generous patron of the arts.

Seated in his magnificent home on Esquiline Hill, Maecenas listened with sympathy to Juba's troubles. They had often discussed a history of Rome that the young Numidian wanted to write, and Maecenas had told Juba that he would buy him a Sabine farm, like the one he had bought for Horace, to which he could retire and have the leisure to begin his book.

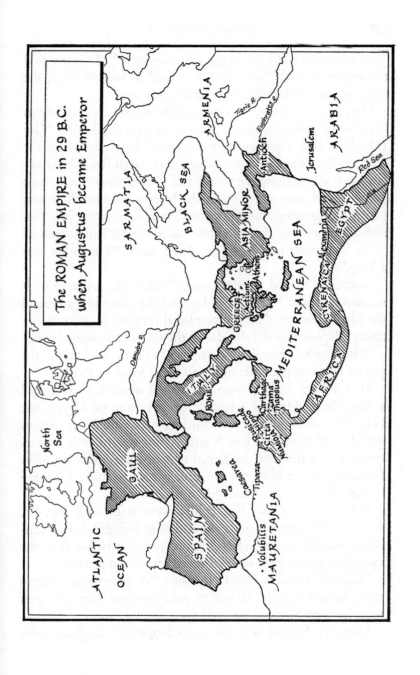

The ROMAN EMPIRE in 29 B.C.
when Augustus became Emperor

"But now you must do as the emperor says," Maecenas told the unhappy young man, and he talked to him of duty, the necessity of self-sacrifice and serving the empire.

Maecenas, however, didn't forget the matter. Several nights later, while Juba was seated in a tavern with P. Ovidius Naso (Ovid), a rich, eighteen-year-old friend from Sulmo, in the Abruzzi Mountains of Italy, who had come to Rome to study law and was writing verse on the side, a discussion about Juba's future was going on in the Domus Palatina. The emperor was agreeing that the young Numidian might, just possibly, be worthy of the high rank that Maecenas had suggested.

"A king, why not?" Empress Livia asked. "His father was a king."

Maecenas turned to Augustus. "After all, what does it amount to? Like Herod in Judea, and the other kings around the Mediterranean that you've placed on the throne, you can always depose him if Juba shows the slightest independence."

"He won't," promised Agrippa. "I've never known the prince of a conquered country to be so loyal to Rome."

Had it been Egypt, Augustus would never have tolerated a king there. He had selected for governor of Egypt one Gaius Petronius, a humble centurion, who would not dare to get ideas of grandeur. But North Africa was of little importance. It was the least developed part of the empire. So, after frowning deliberation, the emperor agreed to make Juba and Cleopatra Selene king and queen of Numidia.

When Octavia told her, Selene went wild with joy. "A queen!" Any secret regrets she had over losing Tiberius vanished, and life was wonderful again. Jumping to her feet, the excited fourteen-year-old girl raced out to the garden.

"Selene!" Octavia called after her. "A queen must always carry herself royally. If you're going to rule Numidia, you must learn to conduct yourself with dignity."

Octavia's lecture was lost on Cleopatra's daughter, who

was dancing around a rosebush. I'll be almost as important as Julia, Selene thought. An empress? Who wants to be empress?

* * * *

The betrothal ceremony took place in Octavia's home, before a roomful of relatives and friends. Gifts were exchanged, and Juba slipped onto the third finger of Selene's left hand a plain circle of gold. Engagement and wedding rings are still worn on this finger in many countries of the world. The Romans chose it because they believed that a nerve ran directly from this finger to the heart.

That night, everyone at Octavia's house was discussing the wedding of the new King and Queen of Numidia, which would take place in May. "In May? But the dead are at large then!" Octavia had exclaimed, when Livia announced the date, for a Roman wedding day was carefully chosen for good luck. Only the foolhardy invited trouble by marrying in May, when, on the festival of *Lemuria*, which corresponded to America's Halloween, the Latins believed the ghosts of the dead returned. The Romans had a saying, "Wed in May and rue the day." But Livia did not want the marriage of Selene and Juba to conflict with that of the heirs-apparent. Julia and Marcellus had selected the month of June, named from Juno, wife of Jupiter, the special protectress of marriage. The luckiest month in the Roman calendar, June is still a popular wedding time.

With the great day only a few weeks off, Selene went with Octavia to the dress shops along the Vicus Tuscus, to select her trousseau. Cleopatra had shocked Rome by being the first woman in Italy to wear silk—sheer, clinging gowns that revealed only too well her lovely figure. Now, in the stores, Cleopatra's daughter lingered longingly over the silken stolas and pallas. Then, seeing Octavia frown, she chose instead thick, practical woolens, for Augustus wished the imperial family to dress modestly and simply and set a good example to the Roman people.

Meanwhile, Juba was visiting his old literary haunts, possibly, the young man thought sadly, for the last time. He still regretted leaving Rome, but, to his surprise, he began to discover a change in his heart. Juba's blood leaped whenever he looked at Selene. He was in love. Even when he thought of the little farm that Maecenas had promised to buy for him in the Sabine hills, Juba couldn't imagine living there happily now without Selene. Then he caught himself up short. What of Tiberius? Hadn't she been, always, very fond of him?

"Oh, that's all over—" Selene assured her betrothed. Tiberius seemed to her now very dull in comparison with Juba. The Numidian prince was thirteen years Selene's senior (yet not middle-aged like Marcella's Agrippa), and he was frightfully learned. He knew all about botany, history, zoology, and philosophy, and spoke three languages—Latin, Greek, and Punic. Selene, who admired brains, always felt young and stupid with Juba, as she certainly didn't with Tiberius, who seldom "unrolled" a book.

The wedding presents began to arrive. And all Rome was wondering what *dos* (dowry) the emperor had given his ward. Selene could have told them. Nothing! By rights entitled to all the riches of Egypt, Cleopatra's daughter did not have so much as a *sestertius* (5 cents) to bring her husband. The bride's dowry was an important part of a Roman marriage, as it still is in many European countries, but Augustus had apparently gone off to Spain without signing Selene's *tabulae nuptiales* (marriage contract). She was humiliated.

Roman weddings always took place at night. Full of tenderness over losing the girl she had grown to love, Octavia came into Selene's room one evening in May to dress the *nova nupta* (bride) for her wedding. It was to take place in the Domus Palatina, across the garden.

Selene sat at her dressing table, a bit frightened, as Octavia helped her to get ready. First of all, her hair. Octavia divided it into six braids and wound them with ribbons on the top of Selene's head in the shape of a cone. This strange hair-do was worn by Roman brides only on their wedding day. Then Octavia helped the girl put on her wedding dress, a long white muslin tunic, fastened around the waist with a band of wool, which was tied in the knot of Hercules (the guardian of wedded life). This marriage girdle only her husband was privileged to untie.

Julius and Ptolemy were waiting in the atrium to escort their sister to the imperial palace, as Octavia draped over Selene's head the *flammeum*, a veil of bright orange that matched her shoes. On top of the veil, she placed a wreath of sweet-scented marjoram.

"My beautiful sister!" Julius exclaimed, when he saw her. Proudly, he offered his arm and they started across the garden, Selene and Julius leading the way, Octavia following with Antonia and Ptolemy.

On approaching the Domus Palatina, they heard music and Juba stood in the doorway to greet them. Behind him, the house, lighted by torches and decorated with flowers, was filled with guests who were admiring the wedding gifts on display. Julia, Drusus, and Marcellus rushed up to kiss the bride. There were gay greetings and laughter, and when Juba led Selene by the hand through the rooms, everyone cried out in admiration because she looked so lovely and her face under the flowing orange veil had the freshness of a rose.

The *augur* (soothsayer) had already "read" the young couple's future in the entrails of a slaughtered sheep—it was good, with a promise of many children and a happy old age— so Empress Livia said that the ceremony could begin. Selene was led by her *pronuba* (bridesmaid), the younger Antonia, to the altar. There, joining hands with Juba, she declared herself his wife with the words, *"Ubi tu Gaius, ego Gaia."* This did not mean that she adopted his name, for her name did not change. It meant: "To whatever family you belong, I also belong." Congratulations followed, the guests all wishing the young couple, *"Epagatho!"* (good luck).

The moment had come for witnesses to sign the *tabulae nuptiales* (marriage contract), which should contain a list of the bride's real estate, her slaves, clothing and jewels. Selene flushed with shame. Now everyone would know that she had nothing to bring her husband—not even the huge British pearls that Caesar had hung on the gold statue of Cleopatra!

To the girl's amazement, the Empress Livia came and put an arm around her. "Selene, my dear, we have a surprise for you—" She turned to Agrippa, who rose and unfolded a roll of papyrus. "Read to her what the emperor has given the Queen of Numidia for a wedding present," Livia said.

The bride gasped when Agrippa announced that Augustus had left instructions that his beloved ward, Cleopatra Selene, was to become Queen of Mauretania, a section of North Africa now western Algeria and Morocco. And it was to be her very own country. In the usual Roman marriage contract, the bride's dowry became part of her husband's fortune, but not in Selene's case. She was to be the sole ruler of Mauretania, the only reigning queen in the entire Roman empire—at fourteen!

"What a dowry I have to bring Juba!" the bride thought, proudly. She remembered how the priests of Isis had prophesied, at the birth of Cleopatra's twins, that one of them would someday rule over a vast kingdom. How right they were!

By this time, everyone was hungry and ready for the wedding feast. Livia had brought out her best gold dishes for the occasion. Servants passed them to the guests, who dined reclining on couches. Julius became a bit drunk. Drusus and Antonia held hands. And Ptolemy choked on an olive. But they all enjoyed themselves, although the wine was diluted and the food simple. Shocked at the amount of money the Romans were spending on weddings, Augustus had limited their cost by law to a thousand sesterces ($50). The marriage of Julia and Marcellus would not be any more lavish.

The meal ended with the distribution to the guests of pieces of wedding cake, as is often done today, and the time had come for the bride to be escorted to the groom's house. She must appear frightened and take refuge in her mother's arms, from which her new husband should pretend to take her by force. Juba had no great trouble in doing so. Octavia tenderly kissed the bride good-by, and smiling happily, Selene took her place beside Juba at the head of the bridal procession, which would walk through the city to the groom's humble lodgings. It set out, headed by torchbearers and flute players.

As they marched through the dark streets of Rome, singing songs composed for the occasion by Ovid, Juba's *auspex* (best man), people waved at the bridal party and shouted *"Talasio!"* (best wishes). In return, Drusus and Ptolemy scattered nuts, candy, and small coins to the crowd. There is a similar custom today of throwing rice after the bride and groom.

When the wedding guests reached the insula, where Juba had a small ground-floor apartment, Marcellus and Ovid carried the bride over the threshold, for it was bad luck if she stumbled on entering her new home. On the hearth, wood was ready for a fire. Selene kindled it with a torch, lit on Octavia's hearth, that Ptolemy had carried in the procession. Her brother then tossed the bundle of burned-out sticks to the bridal party (as, today, the bride throws away her bouquet). There was a merry scramble to catch it, for its possession gave promise of a long life.

So ended a wedding held two thousand years ago, which, except for the taking of the auspices and the orange bridal veil, was similar to our modern weddings, for the Christian church took over almost entirely the Roman nuptial rite. Everything is the same, down to the guests taking home pieces of wedding cake. Selene and Juba felt just like any young married couple does now, thrilled but a bit frightened and apprehensive, when their relatives and friends discreetly left the house and they were alone at last.

Juba came to where Selene was sitting on the bed. His heart was beating wildly. No other girl had ever given him this feeling of tenderness. He sat down beside his *uxor* (wife) and, stretching out his hands, with reverent fingers untied the knot of Hercules that fastened her marriage girdle.

19

WED IN MAY AND RUE THE DAY

IN SPITE OF the humiliation Antony caused her, Octavia, to
please her brother, had taken in her husband's children by
another woman and raised them with her own. All Rome admired her for it. Only Octavia knew how hard it had been for
her, at times. But now she found herself sorry to be losing
Selene. Rebellious at first, the girl had become sweet and
obedient; Octavia grew to love her. So it was a sad-faced
family group who stood before her house on the Palatine a
week later, to bid good-by to Selene and Juba when they set
out for Africa. With Octavia were Julia, the two Antonias
and Marcellus, the future emperor. Julius and Ptolemy were
going as far as Ostia with their sister.

Octavia clung to Selene. "You'll write often, dear? You'll
come back and see us?" It had been Octavia who, with Livia,
had arranged this marriage. Selene must be separated from Tiberius. In Spain, so his family heard, the unhappy young man
was drowning his sorrow in drink. Still, now that the parting
had come, Octavia broke down and wept.

Juba stood waiting to help his wife into a litter. "Come,
Selene, we must be going." he said. There were more kisses,

some tears, and the cortege started off. It seemed as though all Rome had turned out to wave farewell. Well-wishers lined the way to catch a glimpse of the blonde queen and her brown-skinned king. Many of them were the same people who had stood in the Forum four years ago, mocking Cleopatra's daughter as she stumbled along in the dust behind Octavian's chariot. Now Selene passed between cheering crowds.

The streets of Rome were so narrow that market carts brought in their produce at night. Wheeled vehicles were not allowed in the walled city from sunrise to sunset. People walked or rode in litters and sedan chairs. But a long procession of carriages and wagons, piled high with chests containing the clothing and household utensils that Selene and Juba were taking to Numidia, were waiting for them when they reached the Porta Trigemina, the gate of Rome opening onto the Via Ostiensis.

Here, the four bearers who had carried the curtained basterna (litter) in which the royal couple rode were replaced by mules, put between the shafts—one before and one behind. Then the vehicles moved out along the well-paved road that led to Ostia and the sea. Julius and Ptolemy followed in a *carruca*, a canvas-covered carriage resembling an American Conestoga wagon, furnished with a bed, for the Romans, not having saddles, found it uncomfortable to ride horseback any great distance. Behind them came four-wheeled *carri* filled with servants. Then a line of *petoritums* (baggage carts), drawn by six horses, piled with luggage.

Their fifteen-mile drive to the coast would take Selene and Juba three hours, but it would not be an uncomfortable journey. The Romans who traveled by land two thousand years ago fared better than American travelers did at the time of the Revolution. The dirty inns of the Romans, crawling with bedbugs, were avoided by respectable people, but their horses and carriages were as good as those of Colonial America, and their roads surpassed any built until recent times.

Only an accident on the highway would have driven a wealthy Roman to spend a night in one of their roadside taverns, that had painted signs over the door displaying an elephant, an eagle, or some other symbol, as inns in England still do. Maecenas had lent Juba his villa in Ostia, one of eight estates he had scattered over Italy. Since there were no decent hostels, a traveler usually stayed in a private house—his own or that of a friend—when he left Rome for any reason.

So Selene spent several days at the mouth of the Tiber River, as her mother had done, but not like Cleopatra, in hiding. At Maecenas' luxurious seaside villa she visited with her brothers, while Juba saw to the loading of the *Scylla*, the sailing ship he had chartered to take them to Africa, and looked over the instructions Agrippa had given him. He was to map Numidia and Mauretania, to build roads and aqueducts. As he read, the new King of Numidia realized fully what an uncongenial burden he had undertaken.

His depressed feelings were beyond Selene's understanding. She was glad to be leaving Rome where, an object of charity in Octavia's household for four years, Cleopatra's daughter had never been very happy. Her only regret was at leaving Ptolemy. He was all that was left of Selene's immediate family. "I shall worry about him," she thought.

Now ten, Ptolemy Philadelphus, red-haired and freckled, was not much of a student, but intensely interested in sports. Having no competitive sports such as baseball, football or cricket, the Romans excelled in what today we call track athletics. Ptolemy spent most of his time on the Campus Martius, foot racing, jumping, and trying to throw the discus. Selene disliked some friends her brother had made there.

Four years ago, King Herod of Judea had murdered his

second wife, the beautiful Hasmonean princess, Mariamme, in a jealous rage. Alexander and Aristobulus, Mariamme's sons, had been sent to Rome by their father to be educated. And it was these two princes who had introduced Ptolemy to his newest enthusiasm, chariot racing. On race days, the three boys were usually to be found at the Circus Maximus, the hippodrome shaped like a narrow U, located south of the Palatine. Like the other spectators, they sat tense in their seats, hoping to see a chariot upset at the *spina*, the sharp turn between the legs of the U, when a charioteer tried to squeeze his rivals against the wall.

"When I'm older, I'm going to drive in the races," boasted young Ptolemy, as he walked with Selene and Julius in Maecenas' *hortus* (garden), laid out in geometrical flower beds edged with boxwood.

"Ptolemy, don't talk such nonsense!" his sister exclaimed, for a high-class Roman never drove his own racing chariots. He had slaves to do that. Chariot-racing, however, was not considered a low sport by the Jews. Herod of Judea, to show how thoroughly Romanized he was, had built an open-air theater and a hippodrome at Jerusalem, and Alexander and Aristobulus had driven in the races held there. "No sport can compare with it," they told Ptolemy.

Selene did not know that Herod was responsible for Caesarion's death. But she knew that, after his quarrel with her father, the Jewish king had fled to Octavian at Rhodes, and betrayed Cleopatra and Antony by telling the Romans exactly how strong their defenses were—one of the reasons why the invaders were able to conquer Egypt so easily. Consequently, Selene was sorry that her brother had become intimate with Herod's sons.

"We've never been separated before, you'll look after Ptolemy, won't you?" she asked Julius. He was seventeen and studying to be a lawyer, for in Roman times, just as today, the practice of law often led to a successful political career.

Julius promised her that he would, but was this handsome, blond man-about-Rome the proper guardian for such a young boy? Julius wrote poetry (even the great Horace thought he had talent), but he was overly fond of the theater and gambling. "I'm glad that Ptolemy will have Octavia to watch over him," Selene thought. Since she had stood by the dying Cleopatra, her arms about Ptolemy to comfort him, Selene had felt responsible for her young brother.

To Ostia, ships brought grain from Egypt, tin from Britain, wine and honey from Greece, glass and leather from Asia Minor, and salt from Spain. Along the water front were the branch offices of traders from all over the empire. After unloading his cargo, a foreign merchant could find his local agent by the colored mosaic design—a mermaid, lighthouse, or dolphin—on the sidewalk before his office door.

Beyond the *horrea* (warehouses), stacked with *amphorae* (large two-handled jars) full of African olive oil bound for Rome, the *Scylla* was berthed, among a forest of masts, beside a wharf of the Porta Marina from where Cleopatra had fled to Egypt.

The hour of departure came, the royal couple and their suite went on board. "Will I ever see Ptolemy and Julius again?" Selene wondered, as she kissed her brothers good-by.

Standing in the stern of the ship, the young Queen of Numidia waved to them until the *Scylla* was well out into the harbor, escorted by a flight of seagulls that abandoned the boat only when she was far from land. Then Selene went to her cabin, a cramped cubbyhole under the poop, but luxury compared to what the other passengers had. They slept mostly on deck.

Unlike their warships, Roman merchantmen were usually propelled by sails instead of oars. And, of course, they had an eye painted on each side of the prow to see where they were going, as eyes are painted today on boats in the Mediterranean. Up on the poop, the *kubernetes* (helmsman), already on the lookout for pirates, was operating the two oar-shaped rudders that trailed in the ship's wake, as slowly the Italian coast receded, and the *Scylla* found herself alone on the blue expanse of water.

Almost in tears, Juba had stood at the stern of the ship, watching Italy sink out of sight over the horizon. He amazed Selene. "What ails you?" she asked him. "Here we are, going to Numidia, to rule your father's old kingdom, and you act as though you were being led away to prison." Before them lay a wonderful future, Selene was sure, for she was returning to her beloved Africa.

* * * *

So began a sea voyage which, in 25 B.C., was no worse than what all seafarers had to endure before steamships were invented. The sailing season, in Roman times, was only between March and October. Navigators steered by the sun and the stars, and the lack of a compass compelled them to follow the coast. This increased the length of a voyage. Their sturdy, beaked-nosed cargo ships, propelled by big square sails, covered about seventy miles a day, depending on the wind. They sailed only during the daylight hours. At night, captains anchored in some sheltered cove. This made travel by water slow, and, disliking being cooped up for weeks in a foul-smelling galley, the Romans avoided a trip by boat whenever possible.

But Juba loved the sea. He soon regained his good humor and enjoyed the voyage. It was on the whole uneventful, except for a day of frustrating calm, when the sails hung limp and the ship couldn't move. But brisk winds arrived to move them forward once more. As they neared the African coast, the waves subsided and the pilot headed the *Scylla* into the harbor of Rusicade (now Philippeville), the port for Cirta, capital of Numidia, fifty miles inland.

Wearing her best palla draped becomingly over her head, so that it framed her face like a hood, Selene stood by Juba's side as the crew tied up the ship to the wharf. The new King and Queen of Numidia searched the shore with eager eyes. Where was the reception committee? Only a few loiterers were on the dock.

With a feeling of apprehension, Selene looked at the ugly little town, strung along the rocky coast under a towering wall of mountains. Where was Marcus Fabius who, in the name of the Roman senate, had been governing Numidia? Juba had notified him as to the approximate date of their arrival.

"Proconsul Fabius will come down from Cirta, with a delegation of important people, to meet us," Juba had told his wife.

As the royal party stepped ashore, the heat was stifling. Juba, who had expected that, by now, he would be replying to laudatory speeches with one of his own (he had written it out in both Latin and Punic), had to occupy himself instead with the menial task of getting the horses and carriages they had brought from Rome off the boat. A few Numidians gathered on the dock to watch. They were (dark-skinned, ferocious looking men, naked except for a piece of dirty sackcloth tied around the waist), and they stared at the strangers with a hostility in their eyes that chilled Selene and Juba. Was this their royal welcome to Africa?

Selene had thought how she would smile at the cheering crowds and, with a queenlike gesture, graciously wave to her new subjects. But when she and her husband took their seats in one of the carriages and drove through the forlorn seaside town of Rusicade and out the Porta Stora toward Cirta, they passed through almost deserted streets. Only a few people came out of their houses to gaze at the newcomers.

Juba looked so dejected that Selene, her heart aching for him, reached over and took his hand. "Fabius is probably ill," she said consolingly.

The road to Cirta led up through a hilly region, with an occasional cork-tree plantation. After they passed Mount Skikda it grew worse, and finally became hardly more than a path along the banks of the swift-flowing Ampsaga River. As the procession of carriages and baggage wagons climbed, cork trees gave way to pines and cedars. Finally, a high plateau with hardly a shrub, only a few farm-forts behind thick walls, was all they saw. It grew colder and Selene, shivering, was glad of her woolen palla that had been too hot for her in Rusicade.

Still their road led up and up, into the mountains, where the rushing Ampsaga foamed in a chasm beneath them. They had climbed so rapidly from the hot, humid coast to these chilly heights that Selene was breathless from the altitude— 2,113 feet. So was Juba. "What is he thinking?" his wife wondered. He had been very quiet all day.

"This is the road by which Caesar brought me down from Cirta in chains, when I was a boy," Juba finally said. And Selene knew that he had been reliving every moment of that ghastly journey.

There were no villas in Numidia, belonging to hospitable Roman friends, where the travelers could rest and break their uncomfortable drive—not even an unsavory inn. All during the fifty-mile drive up from the coast they hardly saw a human being. At nightfall, the procession of carriages stopped, and the royal couple and their suite slept as best they could on the hard beds in their traveling coaches, drawn up by the side of the road. The trail was so steep that the trip inland took them two days. By sunset on the second day, when they drew near Cirta, an escort of soldiers from the III *Legio Au-*

gusta, the only Roman troops stationed in Africa, came out to greet them. Proconsul Fabius joined them too, full of excuses, at the gates of the city. Selene was barely civil to him.

For protection from the wind on this high barren plateau, Cirta had been built down in the ravine of the Ampsaga. The steep streets rose in steps up the rocky sides of the gorge, so it was necessary for the royal party to descend from their carriages and walk. Glad to do so after their long ride, Selene and Juba set out, escorted by the Roman governor, for the ancient palace of the Numidian kings which was to be their home.

From its windows, there was a fine view down the gorge of the Ampsaga. Otherwise, it was an impossible dwelling. No one had occupied the big, drafty building since the time of King Hiempsal, Juba's grandfather. His father, Juba I, had preferred to live in Zama. But after his death, Caesar transferred the capital of Numidia back to Cirta. Selene's heart sank as they entered the shabby, gloomy building, one wing of which the Third Augusta used as a barracks. There was something sinister about the place. Fabius had refused to live in it. He occupied a flat down the street.

Selene was tired. She was dirty. She longed, more than ever in her entire life, for a bath. But the pipes of the old, decaying palace had been allowed to rot away. There wasn't even running water (a *must* for a Roman). Instead, there were rats in the walls, filth and vermin everywhere. As she was undressing, Selene let out a scream. A scorpion had run over her foot.

Their beds were crawling with fleas. The Queen of Numidia sat up all night in a chair, while the King walked the floor or stretched out for brief naps on a table.

Wrapped, shivering, in her palla, Selene stared despondently before her. "Oh, Juba, what fools we were!" she sighed. "To marry and come out to Africa in May, the most unlucky month in the Roman calendar!"

20

AN AFRICAN NIGHTMARE

MASINISSA WAS THE first king to reign (from 201-148 B.C.) over a united Numidia. But his grandson Jugurtha, who ruled from 118-104, was the national hero. A bearded barbarian, who liked to tame wild horses, drink and carouse with his soldiers, the people idolized him. Jugurtha had the utmost contempt for Rome. In one battle, he captured an entire Roman army and passed it under the yoke.

Jugurtha, handsome and able, had boldly seized the throne. At the death of Masinissa, Numidia was divided between his three sons, Micipsa, Gulussa and Mastanabal. An illegitimate son of Mastanabal, Jugurtha had no right to share in the inheritance, but he was so popular with the people that, at his death in B.C. 118, Micipsa, who had outlived his brothers and become king of all Numidia, left his nephew Jugurtha a third of the kingdom, and the rest of it to his sons, Hiempsal and Adherbal.

Jealousy developed between the three kings. Jugurtha murdered Hiempsal (Juba's great-grandfather), and then attacked Adherbal, who called upon Rome for help. Several armies came to North Africa to try to defeat Jugurtha, but he killed

KINGS OF NUMIDIA

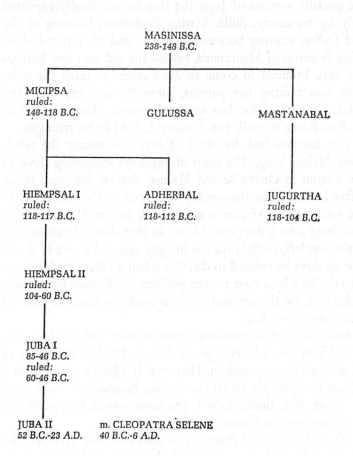

MASINISSA
238-148 B.C.

MICIPSA
ruled:
148-118 B.C.

GULUSSA

MASTANABAL

HIEMPSAL I
ruled:
118-117 B.C.

ADHERBAL
ruled:
118-112 B.C.

JUGURTHA
ruled:
118-104 B.C.

HIEMPSAL II
ruled:
104-60 B.C.

JUBA I
85-46 B.C.
ruled:
60-46 B.C.

JUBA II
52 B.C.-23 A.D.

m. **CLEOPATRA SELENE**
40 B.C.-6 A.D.

off Adherbal and alone ruled Numidia, outwitting a succession of incompetent Roman generals.

By B.C. 107, Rome had endured all it would take from the arrogant Numidian king. The senate sent an army under C. Marius (married to Julia, Caesar's aunt) with orders to seize Jugurtha. It took him three years to do it. So successful was the guerilla warfare of Jugurtha that he was finally captured only by treachery. Sulla, Marius' lieutenant, learning of the bad feeling existing between Jugurtha and his father-in-law, King Bocchus of Mauretania, bribed the old man into betraying him. Induced to come to Mauretania to fetch his wife, who was visiting her parents, Jugurtha was captured and handed over by Bocchus to the Romans. Marius took him back to Rome to walk (on January 1, 104) in his triumph.

The Romans had despaired of ever conquering the rebellious African king. The sight of Jugurtha staggering through the Forum in chains behind Marius' chariot delighted them. After he had been thoroughly exhibited to the jeering mob, the once-proud African was led back to the Mamertine jail and flung into a dungeon. Down in that slimy darkness Jugurtha was left, to fight off the hungry rats and starve to death. For six days he refused to die. But when a jailer was let down into the hole by a rope to strangle him, the Roman found only a skeleton, for the rats had done his work for him, the prisoner had been eaten alive.

Shocked by the gruesome death of their national hero, the Numidians vowed revenge on Rome. During the reign of Masinissa's great-grandson, Hiempsal II (Juba's grandfather), whom Pompey placed on the throne, Numidia was too weak to revolt. But, under Juba I, the natives took Pompey's side in his war against Caesar.

After the death of Pompey, his sons and their African ally, Juba I, who had succeeded his father Hiempsal II in B.C. 60, still resisted; and Caesar came to Numidia to fight them. King

Juba had a superb army of archers, cavalry mounted on swift Numidian ponies, forty camels, and a herd of war elephants. But he was attacked in the rear by Caesar's friend, the same treacherous old Bocchus of Mauretania who had betrayed Jugurtha. Defeated by the Romans at Thapsus, Juba fled to his capital city of Zama. Rather than be captured by the enemy, he ordered a slave to kill him, and Numidia became a Roman province.

Since then, ruled by proconsuls sent out by the senate, the high taxes and abuse the Numidians had endured made them hate the Romans even more. For his help to Caesar at Thapsus, Gaius Sallustius Crispus (Sallust) became the first Roman governor of Numidia. His term in office was a scandal. Amassing a huge fortune by extortion while in Cirta, Sallust returned to Rome to build himself a fine mansion on the Quirinal and write, among other works, a book on Rome's war against Jugurtha *(Bellum Jugurthinum)*, leaving bitterness behind him.

But in 25 B.C., the hopes of the Numidians soared. Augustus had restored the throne and they heard that a king, the son of Juba I, was being sent to reign over them. Juba II would be a bearded barbarian, coarse and illiterate like his father, the Numidians imagined, who would help them drive out the Romans. When they saw him—a gentle, scholarly man, wearing a toga and clean-shaven like the hated Romans, who talked to them not of fighting Rome but of building aqueducts and roads—the Numidians felt cheated. This wasn't the fierce leader they had expected. This was just another Roman like Sallust and the other governors who had oppressed them.

Nor could the Numidians respect a man who had only one wife. Juba II was a direct descendant of Masinissa, who, when he died in 148 B.C., at the age of ninety, had not only helped Rome crush Hannibal at Zama but had produced fifty-four sons. The Numidians liked to boast about that, and of their new king's lusty, bearded old father, who had maintained a harem of eight wives and forty concubines. They revered Juba I as a bitter enemy of Rome, but more so, as a great lover. Could this be his son?

Poor well-meaning Juba! He was so anxious to rule well, to help the poor, and grant his people all the freedom that Rome would allow him to give them. In return, he expected the Numidians to be grateful and love him. Fabius could have told Juba that it is easier to conquer a country than it is to rule it afterwards, but knowing what a tough job had been handed the young king, the proconsul left for Rome as quickly as he could get away.

Only Selene was any help. She read Sallust's *Bellum Jug-urthinum* and tried to learn Punic. A teacher came to the palace every morning. Madly in love with her husband by now, Selene had but one desire, to be a good wife and assist Juba in every way she could. Like any young bride, she began by first creating a nice home for him. Nearly every day the queen went to the native market to buy furniture, textiles and pottery, for she was cleaning and redecorating the palace, ridding it of rats and years of accumulated filth. It was so exciting to have her own house. In Rome, Octavia had managed everything.

Remembering Livia's afternoon classes, Selene invited the daughters of the *aguellids* (tribal chiefs) to the palace to learn to spin and weave. She turned a wing of the building into a small imitation of the temple of Aesculapius, the hospital at Rome. But the native tribesmen refused to allow their daughters to come to "the Roman's." Boycotting the clinic, they continued to doctor themselves. Finally, Gnaeus Metius, *primus pilus* (brigade commander) of the III Augusta in Cirta, warned the queen that, due to the unrest in Numidia, it would be dangerous to go to the market again without soldiers to protect her.

"Protect me from what? My own subjects!" Selene exclaimed indignantly. If she couldn't go out among the Numidians, how were they going to get to know and love her?

Virtually prisoners in their big, gloomy home overlooking the gorge of the Ampsaga, only a few rooms of which Selene could make livable, Rome was no help to the royal couple. All Juba's pleas for a more humane rule in Numidia were ignored by the senate. He had been sent to North Africa to be a handsome figurehead, and he was kept that way. The senate never asked the young king's advice. They simply sent him his orders by the official couriers who arrived in Cirta every month, and expected him to carry them out without question, as the other client kings in the empire were doing.

His most urgent job, Agrippa wrote Juba, was to build roads. In the Forum at Rome there was a golden milestone. From it radiated the network of *viae* (roads)—more than 80,000 miles of them—that the Romans had built to link Italy with their most remote provinces. Over these superb highways passed merchants, officials, and diplomats on business, as well as armies to conquer distant lands, but seldom a family bound on a holiday, for the Romans never traveled for pleasure. There were no tourists in those days.

The first of these roads, built three centuries before Christ, was the *Via Appia,* which went across Italy to Brundusium (Brindisi). Other routes followed: the *Ostiensis* to Ostia; the *Clodia* to Etruria; the *Flaminia* to the Adriatic; the *Egnatia* to the Balkans; and the *Aurelia* into Gaul. But North Africa had only dirt Punic paths. Agrippa wanted the III Legio Augusta to construct a paved highway west of Numidia, leading into Mauretania. The legionaries were just as much roadbuilders as they were soldiers. As in every army sent out from Rome, along with the infantry and cavalry of the Third Augusta had come a corp of engineers. A legionary felt himself an exile in North Africa and far from home, but he didn't have much time to feel sorry for himself. When he wasn't fighting, a Roman *miles* (foot soldier) was kept busy building forts and digging wells.

So after he had been in Numidia a few months, and Cirta seemed fairly quiet, Juba felt that he could safely leave Selene and to go to Tebessa, the camp where the III Legio Augusta was stationed, and talk to them about the road that Agrippa wanted built.

Juba was cordially welcomed by Julius Pollux, the legion's *legatus* (commanding officer), who put on an exhibition of army training for him. The king understood how the *centurions* and their hundred men could march with a full pack fifteen miles a day, or twenty if necessary, when he saw them being put through strenuous exercises, for a Roman soldier must keep himself in fine physical condition. But when Juba mentioned a road to Mauretania, he aroused little interest. On arriving in Africa, the III Augusta had built one highway inland to Tebessa, and they had had enough of road building in Africa.

A road in Britain, Italy, Spain and Gaul, was laid down under the direction of Roman engineers by prisoners of war or soldiers between campaigns. Upon a layer of crushed stone, concrete was poured; and over that, stone blocks were placed. Road building in Europe and Asia Minor was relatively easy, but along the coast of North Africa, there was no firm road-bed on which stone paving blocks could be laid.

"The land is mostly sand," Legatus Pollux informed Juba. "Even if we lay down a gravel road to Mauretania, the fierce sirocco from the Sahara will blow it away."

This was bad news. What would Juba write to Agrippa, who expected his orders to be carried out? All he managed to get from Pollux was a vague promise, for the senate was finding better use for its armies elsewhere. Britain, a tiny province, had four legions stationed there, while North Africa, the size

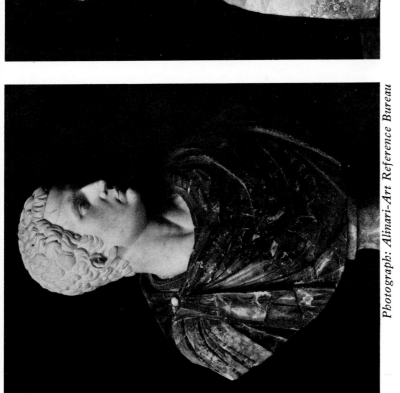

Photograph: Alinari-Art Reference Bureau

JUBA I OF NUMIDIA
National Museum, Naples

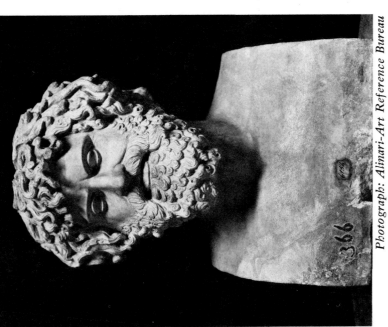

Photograph: Alinari-Art Reference Bureau

THE EMPEROR AUGUSTUS
National Museum, Naples

Photograph: The Bettmann Archive

CIRCUS MAXIMUS RESTORED

Photograph: The Bettmann Archive

BATTLE OF THAPSUS, APRIL 46 B.C.

GENEALOGICAL TREE OF THE
JULIO-CLAUDIAN FAMILY

CIRTA, THE FIRST HOME OF SELENE AND JUBA IN AFRICA,
NOW CONSTANTINE, ALGERIA

KING JUBA II
Rabat Museum, Morocco

QUEEN CLEOPATRA SELENE
Cherchel Museum, Algeria

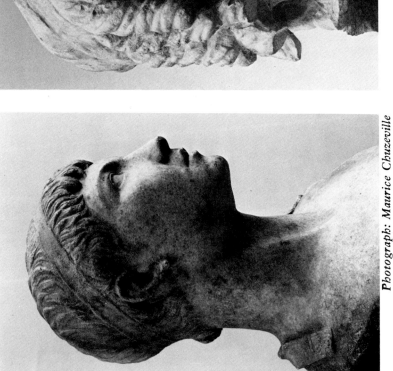

DRUSILLA OF MAURETANIA (?)

The Louvre, Paris

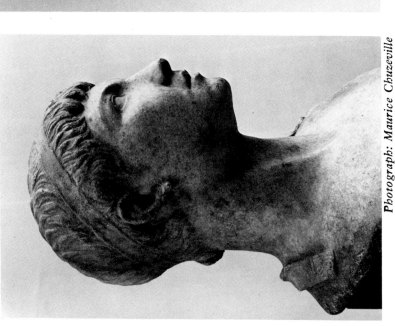

PTOLEMY OF MAURETANIA

The Louvre, Paris

COINS MINTED BY JUBA II AND QUEEN CLEOPATRA SELENE

CLEOPATRA SELENE
Cherchel Museum, Algeria

JUBA II
Cherchel Museum, Algeria

Photograph: Emmanuel Boudot-Lamotte

STATUE OF AUGUSTUS

Cherchel Museum, Algeria

Photograph: Emmanuel Boudot-Lamotte

AQUEDUCT BUILT BY JUBA II

Cherchel (Caesarea), Algeria

Photograph: P. A. Février

CLEOPATRA SELENE
Cherchel Museum, Algeria

Photograph: Emmanuel Boudot-Lamotte

TOMB OF KING JUBA II AND QUEEN CLEOPATRA SELENE
Tipaza, Algeria

PTOLEMY OF MAURETANIA
The Louvre, Paris

Photograph: Alinari-Art Reference Bureau

CLAUDIUS
Uffizi Gallery, Florence

Photograph: Anderson-Art Reference Bureau

AGRIPPINA MINOR (*Nero's Mother*)
National Museum, Naples

ROMAN FORUM TODAY
Showing the Palatine Hill in the Background

MAUSOLEUM OF AUGUSTUS, ROME

CALIGULA
Uffizi Gallery, Florence

NERO
Uffizi Gallery, Florence

Photograph: Anderson-Art Reference Bureau
RUINS OF THE PALACES OF THE CAESARS, PALATINE HILL, ROME

Photograph: Alinari-Art Reference Bureau
RELIEF ON THE ARA PACIS, ROME
Left to right: Antonia Minor, Octavia, Drusus, Livia, Antonia Major, and Lucius Ahenobarbus. Children in the foreground: Germanicus, Gnaeus and Domitia Ahenobarbus.

of the whole of Western Europe, was policed by but a single legion, and Pollux was short of men. "Any road will have to be gravel," he insisted. And so it was. During Roman times, outside of the cities, there was never a paved road in Africa.

Juba left Tebessa discouraged, and a visit to his father's old capital of Zama, where Scipio had defeated Hannibal and the Second Punic War ended, depressed him still more, for it brought back scenes of his childhood. Juba remembered how his father had used elephants, captured in the nearby Atlas Mountains, in the battle of Thapsus against the Romans. He had found them to be effective, at first. Their flanks protected by armor and with bells hung around their necks to excite them, the huge beasts charged into the ranks of the advancing Romans, trampling down foot soldiers and stampeding the cavalry's horses. All went well, until the Romans thought of a simple defense. Capturing an elephant, they tied a burning torch to his tail and sent him thundering back into Juba's ranks, throwing the rest of the herd into a panic.

Juba II remembered clinging to the mahout on a galloping elephant's back, as they fled from the battlefield. With his father and the Pompeian general, Marcus Petreius, the six-year-old boy had then moved from city to city, trying to escape from the Romans. Even Numidia's capital city refused to open its gates to them, because Juba I had sworn that, if defeated, he would make Zama his funeral pyre, burning the town down with everyone, including himself, in it.

So in his tent outside the city walls, Juba I of Numidia, defeated by the Romans and rejected by his own people, decided to end it all by fighting a duel with Petreius to the death. "Such an end is better than being crucified, our probable fate if Caesar catches us alive," he told him. Juba killed Petreius first, then, before his small son's horrified eyes, the survivor (his father) was finished off by a slave.

All this had happened over twenty years ago, but to Juba II, now a grown man, it still seemed like yesterday. He often said to himself, "That scene in the tent outside of Zama is one I shall never forget!"

21

ROME AWAY FROM ROME

JUBA TRAVELED for three months through Numidia, talking with the people and being disappointed, nearly everywhere, at the reception he received. When their king told the Numidians of the benefits that cooperation with the Romans would bring them—courts of law, with an equal standard of justice for all, as well as aqueducts, baths, and circus arenas, he met with indifference or actual hostility. The Numidians wanted no part of Rome. Juba realized how they hated the Romans. Exhausted and heartsick, he returned to Cirta.

Selene was frightened when she saw how depressed her husband had become during his absence. I should have gone with him, she reproached herself. I must always be by his side to help and comfort him. Juba was suffering from a nervous breakdown. As he lay recuperating, his wife sat by his couch and read to him from the *Diurna*, trying to find in the news-bulletin from Rome some amusing gossip about Juba's literary friends—Virgil, Horace, or Ovid—to divert him.

The ancestor our modern newspapers, the *Acta Diurna* (Daily Doings), founded in 59 B.C., by Julius Caesar, was posted each day in the Forum, where people could read it and make copies to send to subscribers in the provinces. It was through this news-sheet that Juba and Selene kept in touch with events in Rome. Besides lists of births, marriages, and deaths, the erection of new buildings, and an account of festivals, a column of court items told of the activities of the imperial family. In the *Diurna*, soon after their arrival in Africa, Juba and Selene read of the wedding of Marcellus and Julia.

In B.C. 23, two years after this marriage, came shocking news. First, it was the Emperor who was ill. That didn't surprise them. Delicate from birth, Augustus was often sick and his doctor, Antonias Musa, cured him by cold baths. Then, a few months later, the *Diurna* reported that there was an epidemic in Rome and Marcellus was gravely ill. This time, Musa's cold baths did no good, Octavia's only son died at twenty, leaving Julia a childless widow of sixteen.

The death of the heir to the throne was a national calamity. The *Diurna* told how Augustus spoke the funeral oration, Virgil wrote an elegy, and all Italy mourned. "Oh, Juba, if only a letter would come from Ptolemy or Antonia!" Selene exclaimed. She wanted to know so much more than the news-sheet told them. For instance, how was Octavia bearing up in her grief?

It would be nearly a month before Selene could hope to hear from her family. The Romans had no public postal service. Local mail was delivered by one's servants and letters sent long distances, such as overseas, were entrusted to a ship's captain or to a friend going in the right direction, as they were elsewhere in the world, up to the first part of the 19th century. Mail sent from Rome to North Africa took about twenty-one days in transit.

Local letters were written on two *tabellae* (writing tablets), like the slates Roman children used in school. They were placed with their wax surfaces together, tied with a string, and sealed. The *cera* (wax) could be smoothed out and the tablets used again, often for a reply to the letter itself. But they made too bulky a package to be sent far. Then "paper" (papyrus) was better.

So when Selene finally heard from Ptolemy, she hastily broke the wax seal and unwound the cord tied around the rolled-up sheet of papyrus, eager to see what her brother had written. For fear that the friend to whom he had entrusted his letter would open and read it, Ptolemy had used a cipher code invented by Julius Caesar, Suetonius says, substituting for each letter the one three places further on in the alphabet (for instance, D for A, E for B, etc.).

On puzzling out her brother's letter, Selene learned that, dressed in a *stola pulla*, black mourning garments that Marcellus' mother would wear as long as she lived, Octavia wept and refused to be comforted. Her grief at losing the son she had dearly loved, and expected to see become emperor, was more than Octavia could bear. She was building a library in Marcellus' memory, and Augustus was erecting a memorial theater. (Its ruins are still standing by the Tiber today.)

Shortly, another letter arrived, from the younger Antonia, who wrote, "We're all wondering who will be Julia's next husband." It seemed that the Emperor was already looking for a suitable father for the grandchildren he wanted so badly. The old rivalry between Octavia and Livia, Antonia said, had flared up again. Livia wanted Tiberius to jilt Vipsania and marry the widowed Julia, so he would be the next emperor, and Octavia was determined that Livia's Tiberius should not get the throne her Marcellus had been promised.

"Oh, Juba, if only Ptolemy or Antonia would come to Numidia for a visit! I've so much I want to ask them," Selene looked up from Antonia's letter to say. There was little chance of that. Once in a lifetime, a wealthy Roman might visit Greece or spend a few years abroad on the staff of a general or governor. Otherwise, nothing could induce him to leave Rome and his Italian country estates.

So without even the prospect of a visit from their family or Roman friends to break the monotony, the months dragged by in the old palace at Cirta. The letters he received from P. Ovidius Naso only added to Juba's feeling of exile. To the disappointment of his wealthy father, Ovid had given up the idea of a law career and was devoting himself to poetry. He went everywhere, knew everybody of importance in Rome, and regaled Juba with the latest literary gossip: "Strabo is writing a history of Rome and may do a geography . . . Virgil is still working on his *Aeneid*, after eleven years. Will he live to finish it? My tragedy *Medea* was performed, and I hope to get my *Amores* (Love Poems) published. That is, if they aren't censored. . . ." Ovid always ended his letters by telling Juba how much his Roman literary friends missed him. Was he doing any writing?

No, Juba wasn't. He had not written a line since coming to Numidia. Even if he had the time, which the King of Numidia hadn't, occupied as he was with uncongenial tasks, what was there to write about in Africa?

These were bad days for Selene, too. "Perhaps, in a few years, when I get Numidia better organized, we can go back to Rome for a visit," her husband said. Selene's heart sank. Go home and face Augustus' cold, appraising stare? What had they accomplished in Numidia? Very little. She knew he had expected more from them.

Lonely and bored, they were often ill, for the climate of Cirta was frightful, cold and damp. In summer, the sirocco, the hot dust-laden wind from the Sahara, blew continuously. And the banks of the Ampsaga were malarious from June to October. Still, Juba, grim and discouraged, sat at his desk day after day, trying to rule Numidia according to Agrippa's wishes, while Selene occupied herself with household tasks.

But, after a few months, the novelty of having her own home had worn off.

"If we could only have a child," Selene often thought. "Even Cirta might be bearable then."

In May B.C., 23 they had been married two years, and although she had built a shrine to Isis and sacrificed regularly to the Egyptian goddess of fertility, Selene still was not pregnant. How she and Juba longed for a child! Even the dreary old palace in Cirta might become a more cheerful, happy place, if the laughter of romping children echoed through its rooms. Selene grew so despondent that she could hardly endure Numidia any longer. But she refused to go back to Italy, even for a brief visit, without Juba. And he couldn't get away.

The situation had grown steadily worse. No matter how hard he tried, Juba II represented Rome in the eyes of the Numidians and they hated him. All the more so, since, being the son of that bitter enemy of Rome, Juba I, they considered their half-Roman king a traitor. This upset Selene's kindly husband, who wanted everybody to like him.

How much his subjects resented Roman rule Juba realized one day when he was to dedicate a new circus arena. Primus Pilus Metius, commander of the Third Augusta brigade stationed in Cirta, advised Numidia's king not to attend the ceremony. "They'll murder you both," he warned, for there was a rumor that assassins would be lying in wait for the royal couple that afternoon.

"No matter, I must go," replied Juba. He meant alone. He wasn't going to allow Selene to risk her life. But she laughed when he told her. "How ridiculous, of course I'm going! Do you think I'm afraid?"

"No, not of man or beast," her husband replied, admiringly. Hadn't she brought that deadly asp to Cleopatra?

So, with only unarmed outriders escorting their *pilentum* (state coach), King Juba and Queen Cleopatra Selene drove that afternoon to the arena. The crowd pressed close about them, as they entered the royal box. Their guards stood helpless, unable to keep the people back, but no attempt at murder was made.

Still, it was like living on a volcano about to erupt. Rome, wanting more revenue, increased Numidia's taxes, and Juba was compelled to enfore the unpopular law. After that, there were several attempts on his life. He didn't tell Selene. It made him heartsick to be misunderstood. Didn't the Numidians realize that he didn't want to oppress them? But he must carry out his orders from Rome. How tired he was, Juba thought, of ruling these unfriendly people! If he could only escape from them for a while, go away on a boat with Selene, drift over the water in the sunshine and just be happy.

"A boat! That's what I need, why didn't I think of it before?" Juba said to himself. He and Selene had a good excuse for exploring the North African coast. As yet, they had not visited her kingdom of Mauretania. From a boy, Juba had loved to sail. A few weeks at sea and, he was sure, all his troubles would vanish.

So, leaving their problems behind in Cirta, Selene and Juba set off from Rusicade one day in the fall of B.C. 23, to cruise west to Mauretania. The white hot beaches, the palm trees, and the blue backdrop of the Atlas Mountains, that had seemed ugly to them on coming from Italy, were beautiful now after the bleak highlands. Juba, who hated cold weather, basked in the warm sunshine. He and Selene lay on deck all day, exclaiming over the scenery. "Why, Mauretania's lovely! And it's mine, my own kingdom!" she would say repeatedly, as the boat slipped along.

One night, they anchored in a cove near the site of the ancient Phoenician colony of Iol. Coming out on deck from her cabin the next morning, Selene caught sight of an island. What did it remind her of? Why, the island of Pharos in

Egypt! This little bay looked like the Eunostos (Harbor of the Happy Return) might have appeared to Alexander the Great, when he first sailed into it and decided to found a city there. The thought came to Selene—why not leave Cirta that they hated and start a new town here in Mauretania?

When she told him, Juba was aghast. "What will the Emperor say? Do you want me to leave Cirta and admit that I've been a failure?"

"Yes, Numidia is ungovernable. Give your father's old kingdom back to the senate to rule, and let's devote ourselves to developing Mauretania. If we start fresh here, I'm sure we can make a success of it. Anyhow, please, Juba darling, ask Augustus if we can."

To the amazement of everyone, Selene included, the Emperor liked the idea. For some time, Agrippa had been saying to him, "We sent the wrong man to Numidia. The country needs someone tougher than Juba to rule it." And the senate was anxious to develop Numidia's neighbor, Mauretania, still in a semi-wild state. The population of Italy was growing, more wheat was needed, and Egypt could no longer fill the demand. Experiments in raising grain in Mauretania had been most encouraging, for it was a country similar in many respects to Egypt. "If we had a good port along the coast, from which wheat could be shipped to Ostia, it would help to ease the food shortage in Italy," experts told the Emperor.

So the senate voted to rule Numidia again as a province, with a proconsul. That left Juba and his wife free to move to Selene's Mauretania. On the site of the old Phoenician settlement of Iol, sixty miles west of the tiny hamlet of Icosium (modern Algiers), they began to build the beautiful white marble city of Caesarea, overlooking the blue Mediterranean, that was to become one of the most famous places in the Roman empire.

22

STRUGGLES OF A CLASSIC AUTHOR

CAESAREA, capital city of Mauretania, was named by Juba in honor of the man who had rescued him from prison, educated him, and made him a king—the Emperor Augustus. During the next eight years, the cove that he and Selene discovered was transformed into a busy port, crowded with ships loading cargoes brought in from the wheat farms, the olive groves, and the vineyards that sprang up behind the town they built between the sea and the Atlas Mountains.

Selene had dreamed of a city like Alexandria. The architects brought from Rome erected a similar town in Mauretania under her supervision. Streets lined by buildings with Greek columns led to the Forum, where there were temples to Apollo, to Saturn, and to Isis. Selene saw to it that her favorite diety, the Egyptian goddess, had her shrine. There was also the inevitable triumphal arch, a *basilica* (law court), and public baths.

These *thermae* served the same social purpose as community centers do now. By paying a small copper coin, ordinary citizens could spend the day relaxing in rooms heated to different degrees of temperature. There were exercise courts, a bowling alley, and a pool enclosed by colonnades, where the bathers sat after their swim. Making all this possible was the water piped in from the Atlas Mountains. An abundance of free water was one of the blessings the Romans brought to their conquered provinces. It was especially welcome in arid Mauretania. Suspended over a valley on entering the city, Caesarea's aqueduct, the longest in Africa, mounted in a series of arches than ran far back into the High Atlas.

The Greeks never cared for the bloody sports of the arena, but they were to the Romans what rugby is to the English and baseball to Americans. Since Agrippa wanted Caesarea to be "a little Rome in Africa," Selene and Juba built an oval circus, and, being fond of Greek dramas, an open-air theater on a hillside overlooking the town. But their chief interest was in the royal palace, perched on a rock by the Mediterranean. Selene and Juba were so eager to escape from Cirta that they moved into a wing of it while the rest of the building was being completed.

Juba loved to create. Superintending the workmen, he was in his element, for no builder ever had finer material with which to work. Numidia was noted for its rose marble. Ships also brought him Carrara marble from Italy and alabaster from Egypt, while Mauretania had an abundance of citron-wood (*callistris quadrivalis*), the African arbor vitae. But the chief beauty of the palace was its mosaic floors, made of pieces of colored glass, arranged to resemble a series of pictures. Juba saw to their installation himself.

Next, he turned his attention to the grounds. One of Juba's many interests was botany. He imported umbrella pines from Italy and cypresses from Crete to frame his gleaming white marble palace and laid out *horti* (gardens), bright with tropical flowers. The preservation of a garden in the highlands of

Numidia had been a constant struggle. In Mauretania, everything grew riotously. Their new home was perfection, Selene thought. But what made her happiest was Juba's delight in it.

"Come and look at this, darling," her husband would call, and when Selene came to join him on the terrace, she was shown a horticultural zoo filled with green animals. Out of privet hedges, trimmed continually by hand, Juba had fashioned for her dozens of fantastic creatures—from a lion and a camel to a prancing horse. Still popular in Italy today, topiary work was first invented by Roman gardeners.

Juba loved beautiful things. And he spent money like water. At first his wife worried. What would Augustus think? The imperial family lived simply on the Palatine. The Emperor wore homespun togas, ate fish instead of meat, and frowned on any extravagances. But Juba laughed at her fears. A great builder himself, Agrippa had written him, "If Caesarea will attract colonists to North Africa, don't count the cost, go ahead and give Mauretania a fine capital."

Soon Selene, too, lost all sense of caution. Decorating the inside of the palace, she was spending money as lavishly as Juba. The rooms that Selene furnished would look bare to us. In them were only the essential couches, chairs and tables. But these few exquisite pieces, made from Mauretania's ornamental citron-wood, were more in keeping with the richly-colored backgrounds the Romans liked than our modern upholstered furniture would have been. No mirrors hung on their walls. Instead, Selene had artists tint the woodwork red or yellow, and paint landscapes in each center panel, while the floors were covered with black-and-white tiles or glass mosaics of African scenes, as colorful as the frescoes on the walls.

The royal pair could not continue to build and design gardens indefinitely. The time came when their new home was finished. Even Juba could find nothing more to add. "Now you must start on your history of Rome," Selene said to him. "I'll see to ruling Mauretania."

Juba, who hated administrative work, was glad to leave the affairs of Mauretania in his wife's capable hands. It was an easier country to govern than Numidia. In Mauretania, there was no hatred of the Romans. Bocchus I, who ruled from B.C. 118-91, had hesitated between an alliance with Jugurtha of Numidia or Rome. Picking the winner, he was rewarded with a slice of Numidia after Jugurtha's defeat. His son supported Caesar against Pompey. After Thapsus, a docile vassal of Rome, Bocchus II ruled Mauretania until his death in 33 B.C.

Still, the country had its problems. Few of the *coloni* (colonists), had any idea of remaining long in Africa. Their one aim was to get rich quickly. They developed huge estates, raising wheat and olives and horses, then left them to a *vilicus* (manager) to supervise and returned to Italy. Farmed by slave labor, the conditions on these *villas rustica* were frightful. Smaller farms were worked by retired legionaries. After he had completed his twenty years of military service, a legionary was given a small tract of land, and he became a farmer. Corrupted by years of brutal fighting, these veterans of Rome's wars were a tough lot, arrogant like the native Mauri, people originally from Asia Minor, who roamed along the base of the Atlas with their sheep.

The Romans had managed to get along fairly well with the nomad Mauri, their Italian speculators and military colonies, by leaving them strictly alone. Now it was up to Mauretania's young queen and her scholarly husband to handle this mixed population to the advantage of Rome.

* * * *

When he conquered Greece in 83 B.C., and brought back to Italy Aristotle's library, the Roman dictator, Sulla, started the fashion of collecting books. Now every rich Roman had his private library. It was a status symbol, like owning an automobile is today. At Caesarea, the windows of Juba's library looked out on the sea. Busts of his friends, Virgil and Horace and Ovid, stood on cupboards in which were stored Juba's books. They were all of them rolled-up sheets of papyrus, looking, when small, like a college diploma and, when large, like a roll of wallpaper. Long works, divided into several rolls and tied together in bundles, were kept in pigeon-hole sections, with the *titulus* (label) giving the title hanging down in front. In this pleasant room Juba sat at his desk every day now, working on his *History of Rome*—but writing a book in the century before Christ was an arduous task.

The sheets of paper that Juba used came from Egypt. As a child, Selene had seen the papyrus reeds from which this paper was made growing along the Nile. Two strips of papyrus pith pasted together, back to back, with the grain crossing at right angles, made a cream-colored sheet about six inches wide, on which Juba wrote with a reed pen and ink made from soot. If he made a mistake, he wiped off the surface with a damp sponge.

Day after day, Juba worked away on his history. He also wrote poetry on the order of Ovid's light verse, that Selene, secretly, did not think very good, but her husband loved doing.

Slowly, the *schedae* (sheets of papyrus) piled up on the desk beside him. Now it was the task of Juba's *librarii* (copyists) to assemble them in the proper order and mount them. The sheets were not numbered, folded, and fastened together on one side into a binding, as are the pages in our modern books. Instead, they were pasted side by side into a continuous strip, about twenty feet long. A spindle *(umbilicus)* having been attached to each end, the manuscript was rolled up with the text on the inside.

When his *amanuenses* (secretaries) brought him his work, in order to correct in it the errors sure to be there, Juba unrolled a portion of the papyri until he had a round, slender stick in each hand. Stretched before him was a column of text, written in the Greek alphabet. When he had read and corrected this, instead of turning a page as we do, Juba rolled away the part read onto the spindle he held in his left hand.

It was not possible to have the text on both sides of papyrus paper, as we do on the pages of our books, so many rolls were needed for one work. Then Juba had only a single copy of his history. His secretaries must transcribe the others from the original manuscript, until they had made the necessary number of copies required by the Sosii Brothers, Horace's publishers, who, Juba hoped, would add him to their stable of authors. Then he must correct each book separately, since no two copies would have the same errors. It was tedious work. His arms aching from holding out the rolls, Juba often wondered why he wanted to be a writer!

How could the reading of books be made easier and pleasanter, Selene wondered. And she made a suggestion. "Why not write on single sheets and stitch them together on one side, so they can be turned backward or forward, and you can write on both sides of the paper?" Juba liked the idea. He wrote the Sosii about it, but, apparently, it was too much of an innovation, for nothing came of it.

Meanwhile, Ovid was becoming famous as a poet in Rome, and Julius Antonius was writing verses. "Oh, Selene, if I could only have an evening with them!" Juba often exclaimed, remembering the jolly times in the taverns of the Vicus Sandalarius with his literary friends. "I feel so out of touch. I don't know what Horace is writing, or Ovid, or what they are playing at the theater. I want to go home." Home for Juba and Selene, after ten years in Africa, was still Rome.

So much had happened there during the eight years that they had been building Caesarea. For instance, in B.C. 21, the Emperor's only child Julia had married again. For a Roman matron to remain a widow after one marriage was unheard of, the law required her to remarry, but for two years after Marcellus' death, Julia's father searched and hesitated, since her husband would be his successor. Selene and Juba were shocked when Ptolemy wrote them whom Augustus decided upon—M. Vipsanius Agrippa, the man who for years had run his empire. Julia was eighteen, Agrippa, forty-two, old enough to be her father.

"Besides, he's married to Marcella!" Selene put down Ptolemy's letter to exclaim. She read on. It seemed that it was Octavia who had suggested to her brother that Agrippa divorce her daughter Marcella, although they had several children, and marry her daughter-in-law. Anything to prevent Julia from marrying Tiberius!

Ptolemy's next letter brought more startling news. The divorced Marcella had surprised everyone by marrying Selene's half-brother, Julius. "I don't imagine Marcella minded trading Agrippa for a husband twenty years younger," was Juba's wry comment.

In Roman circles, one wed often, because divorce was easy. Still, the way the Emperor married off his family, and then had them divorced in order to remarry them elsewhere, for political reasons, shocked Selene. That Augustus had given his niece, Marcella, to Julius showed how highly he regarded the young man. Antony's son by Fulvia had a brilliant future before him, people were saying—in the law, in politics, and as an author. Julius was writing a long poem on Diomedes, one of the Greek kings in the Trojan war. And Horace had dedicated his fourth ode to him.

"It's an unprecedented honor," Antonia wrote Selene. "We're so proud of Julius." Then she went on to tell her sister about a wedding soon to take place, her own, for Livia, forced to reconcile herself to the fact that Agrippa, as Julia's husband, would be the next emperor, was willing now for her sons to marry. In 19 B.C., Vipsania Agrippa had been old enough to be wed to Tiberius; and this summer of 16, Drusus was to marry Antonia, his boyhood sweetheart.

Selene longed to go back to Rome for her sister's wedding, but Juba was too proud to return to Italy until they were invited to come by the Emperor. They were bored, they were childless, they felt themselves exiled in North Africa and forgotten. So much was happening in Rome without them. Then, in the year 14, a wonderful surprise occurred. Ptolemy came out to Mauretania for a visit.

When he arrived in Caesarea, her red-haired, freckled little brother had grown so tall and handsome in his elegantly draped toga that Selene hardly knew him. Mauretania was no longer quiet and dull. She was busy and happy all day, planning banquets, issuing orders, receiving guests, doing everything possible to give Ptolemy a good time. He was twenty-two and had become a lawyer, but he was still keenly interested in sports. In Rome, Ptolemy spent more time at the Circus Maximus than he did at the Basilica Julia, the law court built by Caesar, where the attorneys pleaded their cases. He liked to hang around the sheds, among the blanketed horses in their stalls, talking with the drivers and stableboys.

Herod's sons, Alexander and Aristobulus, who had lived in Rome while being educated, had gone back to Judea. Two years ago, they had both married. Alexander made a fine match. The bride Herod chose for him was Glaphrya, the daughter of Archelaus, King of Cappadocia, a country in what is now eastern Turkey. His younger brother, Aristobulus, married his cousin Berenice, the daughter of his father's sister Salome.

Selene was glad the Jewish princes had left Rome. "That will be the last we'll hear of them, I hope," she told Juba. Unfortunately, the harm was done. Alexander and Aristobu-

HEROD'S

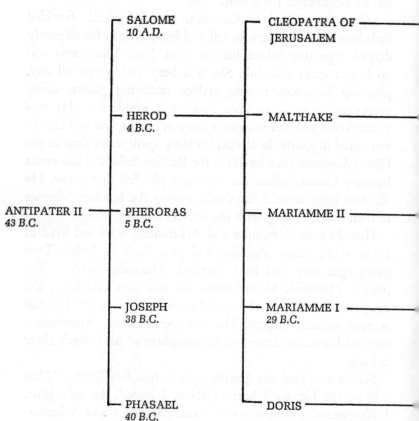

ANTIPATER II
43 B.C.

SALOME
10 A.D. — CLEOPATRA OF JERUSALEM

HEROD
4 B.C. — MALTHAKE

PHERORAS
5 B.C. — MARIAMME II

JOSEPH
38 B.C. — MARIAMME I
29 B.C.

PHASAEL
40 B.C. — DORIS

FAMILY

PHILIP
34 A.D.
m. SALOME

ARCHELAUS
18 A.D.
m. GLAPHYRA

ANTIPAS
39 A.D.
m. HERODIAS
*(The Herod who executed
John the Baptist. Tetrarch of Galilee
in the days of Christ.)*

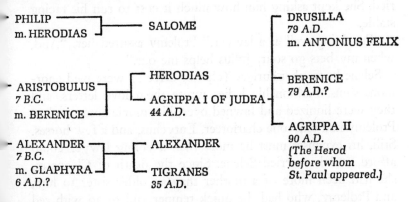

PHILIP
m. HERODIAS ⎦ **SALOME**

DRUSILLA
79 A.D.
m. ANTONIUS FELIX

ARISTOBULUS
7 B.C.
m. BERENICE ⎦ **HERODIAS**

AGRIPPA I OF JUDEA
44 A.D.

BERENICE
79 A.D.?

ALEXANDER
7 B.C.
m. GLAPHYRA
6 A.D.? ⎦ **ALEXANDER**

TIGRANES
35 A.D.

AGRIPPA II
90 A.D.
*(The Herod
before whom
St. Paul appeared.)*

ANTIPATER
4 B.C.

NOTE: This table is not complete. Herod married **ten**
wives and had fifteen children. The names
are those mentioned frequently in my book. The **dates**
are when they died.

lus had given Ptolemy a love of horse racing he would never get over.

There were four professional racing clubs in Rome—the Greens, White, Blues, and Reds, named from the colors worn by their drivers. Great rivalry existed between them. Ptolemy always bet on a team of the Greens. No Roman of any social position ever drove at these races—any more than he would fight as a gladiator. That was done by professionals. But many fashionable young men, like Ptolemy of Egypt, had their own racing chariots, their *aurigae* (drivers), and a stable of horses they entered in the races. The finest horses were imported from Mauretania. And Ptolemy, who found it dull living along with Octavia, now that Antonia was married to Drusus and Marcella to Julius, had come to North Africa to buy a pair of stallions.

Juba took his brother-in-law to visit the stud ranches that furnished cavalry mounts for the Roman army. Ptolemy had a good time in Mauretania. He enjoyed being with his sister again. At twenty-six, he found her beautiful, well educated, and charming. "A thoroughbred," Ptolemy thought. If only Selene wouldn't nag so! She worried because he wasn't married. She kept asking him how much it cost to run his racing stable.

"I'm doing well as a lawyer," Ptolemy assured her. "And, when my bets go sour, Julius helps me out."

Selene knew that aurigae (chariot drivers) were paid enormous sums. Fashionable ladies wrote them love letters, and they were lionized and fawned over, like movie actors today. Ptolemy had only one charioteer, Entychus, and a few horses. Still, his expenses must be more than a young lawyer could afford, and it worried Selene. Since the death of Cleopatra, she had been more of a mother than an older sister to him, and Ptolemy, who had the quick temper said to go with red hair, jealous of his independence, began to resent her interference. The time came when he could not endure his sister's questions any longer. Cutting short his visit, he returned to Rome.

After Ptolemy left, Selene and Juba settled down to boredom again. Feeling themselves exiled from Rome, too young and energetic to vegetate, they were ready to grasp at any excuse to escape from the paradise they had created for themselves.

In 13 B.C. the excuse came.

23

SELENE OUTSHINES JULIA

In spite of writing diligently, Juba had only reached the beginning of the civil wars in his *History of Rome*. As he worked on the original manuscript, each of his amanuenses (secretaries) copied the portion assigned him, for every duplicate must be made individually, the hundredth copy taking as much time and effort as the first.

Tedious as this was, an author's troubles in classical times were only beginning. Now Juba must get his work sold. In 13 B.C., he sent some of the finished rolls to Rome. The Sosii Brothers agreed to publish his book. But Cornelius Gallus, one of their editors, wrote him that there were countless errors in the copy they had received. Future work must be proofread more carefully.

Yet, speed was essential, Gallus added. Since Livy had made such a success of his history of Rome, other authors were trying to imitate him, and the Sosii Brothers must get Juba's book out before these. So why not let them do the copying of the rest of the edition? The Sosii Brothers had a large number of Greek slaves, trained to write nine lines a minute, who could duplicate a roll in an hour. All these matters were hard to discuss by letter. Couldn't Juba come to Rome so they could have a talk? Gallus didn't know how many copyists to put to work, for he didn't know how many books Juba wanted published, or how much to charge for them.

Here, at last, was the excuse Juba needed to return to Rome. "I must see the Sosii Brothers," Selene's husband told her, and he sent to Maecenas his letter from Gallus. Juba's former patron knew what he wanted. Maecenas went straight to the Emperor, and, shortly, a letter arrived from Augustus, inviting the rulers of Mauretania to pay him a state visit.

Juba rushed to show it to Selene. "We can go home!" he cried. "Just think, I'll see Ovid, Horace, and Livy again!"

With his wife bending excitedly over his shoulder, Juba composed his reply, being careful not to misspell a word, for the Emperor was insistent on correct spelling and grammar. Selene was trembling with joy. She felt as she had at fourteen —twelve long years ago—in Octavia's house in Rome, when she had danced around a rosebush on learning that she was to be a queen.

"This time, Juba, do you realize we aren't going to Rome as captives to walk in a conqueror's triumph?" his wife exclaimed. "We'll be received there as reigning monarchs."

These two, who as children had been led in chains through the Forum, would be returning as royalty to Italy, a country that did not compare with theirs in size. "Augustus will probably give a banquet for us. What shall I wear? Oh, I've never been so excited!" Selene danced about like a girl. Juba laughed as he caught his wife up and kissed her. He loved to see Selene happy. She had been so silent of late, worried, he knew, about her brother.

* * * *

Time flew on wings, now that they were going back to Rome. Two weeks later, the long, sleek galley of the King and Queen of Mauretania, with its purple sails and silver oars that flashed in rhythmic unison as fifty Nubian slaves dipped them into the water, was nearing the Italian coast. Before them lay the harbor of Ostia, crowded with ships that had crossed from Caesarea to bring to Italy the wheat, olive oil, and wine it could not do without.

When their boat docked, the officials of Ostia were lined up on the wharf among the amphorae (wine jars) to do the royal couple honor, and waiting was the imperial barge that Augustus had sent to bring them in style up the Tiber River. This was what Selene had dreamed of, the Queen of Mauretania held her lovely head high as she listened to the welcoming speeches.

By way of the Tiber, the royal pair made their formal entry into Rome. At the landing, to greet them, were the Emperor and Empress, and behind them, not only Octavia, Julius, the two Antonias and Ptolemy, but a large crowd of people, cheering madly. It looked as though all of the city had come to see them, or so Juba and Selene thought, as they stepped ashore.

Litters were waiting and they were carried through the streets of Rome to the Domus Palatina, where, as ruling monarchs on a state visit, it was proper that the King and Queen of Mauretania should stay with Augustus and not with Octavia. As soon as they crossed the threshold, gifts were exchanged. Juba and Selene had brought from Caesarea an antelope robe for Augustus and ostrich plumes for Livia; in return, Selene was given pearl earrings and Juba a jewel-studded sword.

From then on, their visit was pure joy. After her boring years in Africa, Selene reveled in the *convivia* (banquets) the Emperor gave for them. At these affairs, nine persons reclined, three to a couch, around a low table. Servants brought food to the open side. Augustus took the upper right seat;

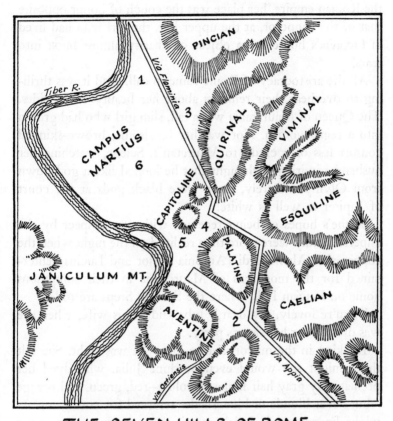

THE SEVEN HILLS OF ROME
The Capitoline, Palatine, Quirinal, Viminal, Esquiline,
Caelian, and Aventine. 1~Mausoleum of Augustus.
2~Circus Maximus. 3~Ara Pacis. 4~Forum
5~Theatre of Marcellus. 6~Pantheon.

and when Selene realized that, as the only reigning queen in the Roman empire, her place was the couch of honor opposite that of the Emperor, at the upper left, the girl who had lived in Octavia's house as an object of charity almost burst into tears.

All the aristocracy of Rome came to call. And it was thrilling to overhear their remarks about her beauty on all sides. The Queen of Mauretania was a tall, slim girl who had grown into a regal woman. Nor was her handsome, brown-skinned consort less of a credit to Mauretania. Selene, watching her husband admiringly, thought that he looked like a god down from Olympus. Surely, there were black gods at the court of Jupiter as well as white!

Selene's hopes of being received with new respect by the imperial family were more than realized on the night when the copper-rich Ahenobardi (Antonia Major and Lucius) entertained for the monarchs of Mauretania in their sumptuous home on Pincian Hill, where the Spanish Steps are today.

"You're lovely, my dear," Juba said to his wife, when she was dressed for her sister's party.

Looking in the mirror, Selene knew he was right. She felt that tonight she would even outshine Julia, who dyed her prematurely gray hair fantastic colors—red, green, and orange—but never blonde or blue, shades reserved for courtesans. As might be expected, Julia's marriage to Agrippa was not a happy one, although two little boys had been born to them. Married to an older man who bored her, she was amusing herself with Julius, Ovid, and a flock of other admirers, to the annoyance of her father, who did not approve of Julia's gay (and, possibly, immoral) life.

Selene felt a bit sorry for Julia that night. She remembered how once she had envied the Emperor's daughter. Now she was the lucky one. "I wouldn't change places with Julia for anything in the world," Selene thought, gazing fondly at Juba.

One of the most successful men at the party that evening was Julius Antonius. Due to the Emperor's liking for him, Julius had been made a praetor, and Marcella was proudly predicting that her husband would be a consul before long. Outwardly, at least, their marriage appeared to be a success. Tiberius and Vipsania also seemed to be getting on well. But the most happily married couple there were Antonia and Drusus.

After twelve years, Selene found her old sweetheart little changed. Tiberius was getting bald, she saw, but he was the same quiet, melancholy man, overshadowed by his more attractive younger brother. One would never think that the modest Tiberius was serving, with great distinction, with the Roman army in Gaul and Germany. "Oh, Selene, it's good to see you!" he exclaimed, as they strolled in the Palatine gardens. "You're the only person I could ever talk with!" They would never be lovers again, yet to the end of their lives, always good friends.

But it was with the Emperor that the Queen of Mauretania most enjoyed being, now that he treated her as an equal. "Do you realize that you're ruling the only independent Mediterranean kingdom, as you mother, Cleopatra, ruled the only country free from Roman domination in her time?" Augustus reminded her. And Selene glowed with pride. They spent hours together, two sovereigns discussing affairs of state.

"Selene, why haven't you and Juba had a child?" the Emperor asked, one day. "You've been married for twelve years. Why not see Antonius Musa? My doctor may be able to help you."

Octavian was complacent these days, for Julia's marriage to Agrippa had produced what he wanted—grandchildren. Gaius was born in B.C. 20, Lucius in 17, and their doting grandfather never rode about Rome without having Julia's boys in the chariot with him. After his death, they would inherit the throne.

Selene and Juba had about given up hope. They never mentioned having children any more. But now she had to tell her husband what Augustus had said, that he should be examined by the Emperor's doctor.

"Oh, no, Musa will want me to take cold baths, even in winter, that's his remedy for everything!" Juba protested. Still, hadn't Musa's spartan treatment worked with the Emperor? His Greek physician kept the delicate Augustus alive, he would live to be an old man.

The Romans survived mysteriously, practically without doctors, Pliny wrote sarcastically. Medicine was scorned as a career. Most physicians were Greek household slaves, who treated the sick with simple remedies and charms. There were doctors attached to the army, and surgery has developed further than medicine, due to their treatment of soldier's wounds. Many of the Romans' surgical instruments are similar to modern ones. There were also oculists, dentists, and even women physicians. But the only hospital in Rome was the temple of Aesculapius (the Greek god of healing), on an island in the Tiber.

Musa had Juba and Selene go there and be examined. To his surprise, Juba learned that his wife wasn't barren, the fault was his. He looked so ashamed when he told her that Selene threw her arms about his neck. "What does it matter? We don't need children, we have each other," she assured him. Then, for fear that her husband would see how brokenhearted she was, Selene fled from the room to have a good cry.

They tried to forget their disappointment and think of other things. Augustus and Livia gave several literary evenings for Juba, who read his poems before a roomful of distinguished guests. The scholarly King of Mauretania was back in the intellectual circles he loved, discussing books in the taverns of the Vicus Sandalarius with Ovid and other writers, and conferring with his publishers. The Sosii Brothers had agreed to issue his *History of Rome* in two parts. The first would take the reader up to the civil wars, as far as Juba had gone. In the second, he wanted to digress a bit and trace the Roman institutions back to their Greek origins.

Now, surely, Juba's writing career would go better. The Sosii Brothers kept a large staff of transcribers, called a *scriptorium*, and thirty copies of a work could be made simultaneously as a reader dictated to them. They took great care to have their books free from errors. Competent correctors read each one, copy by copy.

Having decided upon the number they could sell, the Sosii copyists were put to work on Juba's history in great secrecy. No roll must leave their establishment until the whole edition was ready, for there was no copyright law in Roman times, and anyone could bring out a pirated edition.

How much should they charge for the book? Juba's editor, Gallus, thought not more than twenty cents in American money. The Sosii Brothers could afford to sell it so cheaply because authors in classical times received no royalties. Only rarely were they paid. Any profits went to the publisher. And, copied by slave labor, it cost the Sosii Brothers nothing to bring out Juba's work. Nor did they have to pay an illustrator. There were no pictures in Greek and Roman books.

Juba protested. He reminded his editor that the writings of Cicero, Virgil, and Horace brought high prices. An autographed copy of Virgil's *Georgics* had recently sold for the equivalent of a hundred American dollars.

"You're not Virgil, young man," Gallus replied. "This is your first effort. We can't expect much of a sale until you build up a reputation."

24

ANTIPATER OF JUDEA

WHILE JUBA CONFERRED with his publishers, Selene was visiting with Octavia, Antonia, and Ptolemy. It distressed her to find Antipater, the eldest son of Herod of Judea, in Rome. He had come to Italy to ingratiate himself with the Emperor. And Augustus, being fond of the rascally Herod, was paying his first-born marked attention.

Selene, who met Antipater everywhere, had disliked him on sight. He was a surly, uncouth fellow, for his mother Doris, Herod's first wife, was an ignorant peasant girl who had caught his youthful fancy, while Alexander and Aristobulus were the sons of Doris' successor, Mariamme, a Hasmonean princess. The two younger boys had been educated in Rome, but not Antipater, which made him feel inferior to his half-brothers and insanely jealous of them.

Glaphyra, Alexander's wife, had caused further friction in Herod's palace at Jerusalem, for she felt herself superior to her in-laws, being the daughter of King Archelaus of Cappadocia. Herod's family were not even Jews, but "common up-start Arabs," Glaphyra said, and Antipater was not capable of being king of Judea, but only a chariot driver, which was all his limited education had fitted him for—an insult that infuriated her brother-in-law.

As the eldest son, Antipater was entitled to the throne, but Herod kept him in suspense, and he had come to Rome, hoping to get the Emperor's support. Antipater planned that he would then return to Judea and crush Alexander and Aristobulus. He was determined to ruin them both.

Meanwhile, the Jewish prince was cutting quite a dash in Rome. One thing Antipater did well was drive a chariot. Having brought horses with him from Jerusalem, he entered in all the races at the Circus Maximus. Selene, who had disliked Ptolemy's friendship with Alexander and Aristobulus, was relieved to find that her brother had no love for Antipater. A fierce rivalry had developed between the two young men at the race track.

Selene enjoyed the excitement of a chariot race as much as anyone, and it was with happy anticipation that she went one day with Ptolemy to the Circus Maximus. As they took their seats, the huge open-air ampitheater in the valley between the Palatine and the Aventine Hills was already filled with people and the first bets were being placed. Chariot races were the only events in Rome that outdrew the *munera gladiatoria* (gladiatorial combats).

"I especially wanted to come today," Ptolemy told his sister, "because Antipater is driving, and I hope to see him get beaten."

As the sound of trumpets was heard, everyone turned to watch the *pompa* (procession) enter. A parade of two-wheeled chariots, drawn by four horses abreast and driven by *aurigae* (racing charioteers) in short tunics, the colors of their stables, slowly circled the U-shaped arena. "That's my team," Ptolemy pointed out to Selene four black stallions, their harness hung with bells. "And there's Entychus, my charioteer, driving." He also showed her Antipater's team.

They belonged to rival *factiones* (racing clubs). Ptolemy was a Green; Antipater, a Blue.

The parade over, the spectators went wild with excitement as four of the *quadrigarum* (four-horse chariots) lined up and the first race began. The arena was divided for two-thirds of its length by a low wall, called a *spina* (backbone), on which stood an obelisk that Augustus had brought from Egypt. Everyone in the audience had his eyes glued on his favorite, cheering madly for the Greens or the Blues, as the four charioteers whipped their teams around the *metae* (goal posts) at either end of the central spina. The skill of a driver was shown in turning them as closely as possible and keeping the inside track. The thrill-hungry crowd sat hoping for a "shipwreck," as the Romans called a spill. No rule prevented an auriga from blocking another as he thundered by, or hooking wheels and swerving to upset a rival.

The chariots must circle the track seven times. Ptolemy's gradually took the lead, leaving the three others behind in the dust. The race seemed won. Then, on the last *curriculum* (lap), a strange thing happened. Ptolemy's driver, Entychus, had turned sharply around the meta, the post at the end of the oval, and started back on the final stretch, when his horses began to slow down. Behind him came galloping Antipater's team. They crossed the *calx* (finishing line) two horse-lengths ahead of Entychus' chariot.

"We've won! Antipater won for us!" the Blues in the stands shouted. Ptolemy was in a rage. He was sure his hated rival had won dishonestly. "Selene, did you notice how my horses suddenly grew tired? By Jupiter, I'd swear that Antipater had them drugged!"

For days after the race, the Egyptian prince brooded over his defeat. Antipater was jubilant. "Why don't you drive your own chariot, Ptolemy? Or are you such a coward you must have Entychus do it?" he sneered. "Let's have a race, with both of us driving, and see who is the better horseman. Or are you afraid?"

Selene was greatly alarmed when her brother repeated this conversation to her. Knowing how dangerous chariot racing was, she said to him, "Of course, you won't do anything so foolish. Pay no attention to what that wretched Antipater says, he only wants to see you break your neck."

Ptolemy promised to be careful. Still, Selene worried about him. Nor was Antonia, now, the gay companion she had always been. Drusus had been made *procurator* (governor) of Gaul. Antonia was busy getting herself and their two-year-old son, Germanicus, ready to go there with her husband. Selene watched Antonia's little boy with pain in her heart. If we only had a child, she thought wistfully. Now they would never have one.

"Juba, I can't stand Rome another minute," his wife said forlornly. "Let's go home."

So they went back to Caesarea—and boredom. Juba worked on the second part of his *History of Rome* with little enthusiasm, for the first installment was selling badly. He read Ovid's *Amores* (Love Poems), a best seller in Rome, and tried to imitate his witty couplets. But Juba knew little about debauchery, wine, and the girls. The Sosii Brothers refused to publish his verse. "Perhaps, I'd better give up writing," Selene's husband said to her bitterly.

Again, they looked forward to the days when the mail from Rome arrived. Antonia's chatty letters, penned for safety in a private code known only to themselves, came regularly every month and told Selene all the gossip. They meant everything to her. But in B.C. 12, a *nuntius* (messenger) arrived with a letter from Antonia that Juba hated to show his wife. As his eyes ran over the papyrus roll, his lips trembled.

"What's wrong?" Selene asked, reaching for the letter. Juba held it behind his back. "It's about Ptolemy," she said.

"Is he dead?" The tears in her husband's eyes told her he was.

Antonia wrote them what had happened. It seemed that, just as Selene feared, Ptolemy was finally forced by Antipater to compete with him in a chariot race. There were four other chariots in the race, but when the crowd saw Ptolemy of Egypt driving, as well as Antipater of Judea, they knew the contest could really be between these two bitter rivals. So it was. As around and around the track the six teams went, Ptolemy's four black stallions were finally in the lead. Then, the ghastly accident occurred—! Antipater had overtaken Ptolemy on the last turn. Passing him on the right, Antipater crowded Ptolemy's horses against the meta. To the horror of the crowd, his chariot turned over. The four oncoming chariots, unable to stop, piled up on top of him.

Dropping Antonia's letter, Selene took a few unsteady steps and sank down on a chair. "I knew it would happen, those dreadful sons of Herod!" she sobbed. Selene had loved her brother dearly. She would even miss the worry he had caused her. Selene felt as she had when, as a child, she had a nightmare and woke up screaming. Cleopatra would come and hold her daughter's hand and say, "S—sh, it's nothing, just a dream." But now her mother wasn't here to hold Selene's hand, and this wasn't a nightmare. Ptolemy was dead.

The following year, when Octavia passed away, the last close link that Juba and Selene had with Italy was broken. After that, they no longer talked of going back to Rome. Africa became their home.

* * * *

12-9 B.C. were years of mourning in the imperial family. In 9, Antonia lost her dearly-loved husband. The Roman legions had invaded Germany, as far as the Elbe River, with Drusus in command. The popular young general died there, as the result of a fall from his horse, leaving Antonia with two sons, Germanicus and Claudius, and a daughter Livilla. Three years earlier, Agrippa, racked with gout, had died at Baia. Julia was left with four children (Gaius, Lucius, Agrippina, and Julia), and pregnant with a fifth (Posthumus Agrippa).

It did not surprise anyone that Julia's father wanted her to marry again, but whom did he pick for his daughter's third husband, due to Livia's pleadings? *Tiberius!* Selene and Juba were shocked. Tiberius was forced to divorce Vipsania (the mother of his son Drusus) and marry Julia, whom he had always disliked. As a result of this disastrous marriage, Tiberius, never a genial man, became even more morose and bitter. But Livia had achieved her ambition. As the Emperor's son-in-law, her eldest child was next in line to the throne after Julia's boys.

Many were the changes that Selene and Juba found in Rome, when they returned there in 5 B.C. Virgil, Horace, and Maecenas had died. And this visit was quiet in contrast to the gaiety they had enjoyed there eight years ago. The second volume of Juba's *History of Rome* was published that year, without making any great stir in literary circles. But it wasn't to see his publishers that he had come to Rome. "At the temple of Aesculapius, we've perfected an operation that may help you," Musa, the Emperor's doctor, had written him. "At least, it's worth trying."

This time, the royal couple stayed at Capua, in Campania, with Antonia. The inconsolable widow of Drusus had retired to the country with her children. "Who could replace my Drusus? I shall never marry again," Antonia told Selene. Nor did she, in spite of the law which compelled a Roman widow to find herself another husband.

It was very different with Julia. Tiberius, to escape from an unhappy marriage, had isolated himself on the island of Rhodes. And Julia was not a girl to sit alone and mourn.

Enjoying herself recklessly, she had become the leader of the wild younger set. If Julia had not been the Emperor's daughter, nobody would have cared how she chose to amuse herself. But since she was, Julia's immodest tunics, her drinking, and her lovers (the favorite, to Selene's dismay, being her brother Julius) were the talk of Rome.

Augustus, who posed as a model of virtue, had always insisted that the imperial family be an example to the Roman people. Especially must Caesar's daughter, like Caesar's wife, be above reproach. So, for a long time, he refused to believe what was public gossip. Finally, in B.C. 2, unable any longer to ignore Julia's conduct, which was becoming scandalous, in shame and anger, the Emperor was forced to face the truth and, some thought, punish his daughter too severely. Tiberius was still living away from his wife in Rhodes, so Augustus divorced Julia in her husband's name and banished her to Pandataria, a barren island thirty miles off the coast of Campania. Julia's lovers were severely punished. Some were exiled. But it was Julius Antonius toward whom Augustus felt the most bitter. The man to whom he had given his niece in marriage, whom he had made consul, then governor of Greece, was condemned to death. On learning the verdict, Julius, always an epicure, gave a lavish banquet for his friends and then drank poison.

"There's more to it, I'm sure," exclaimed Selene, when the news of her brother's death reached Mauretania. Had Julia been found to be more than just a disgrace to the family? Was it possible that she and the ambitious Julius Antonius had been plotting to seize the throne from her father? Otherwise, why was their punishment so severe?

What lay behind the latest scandal in the imperial family was something about which Selene and Juba could only speculate. Antonia wrote them how shocked they all were. "Marcella is taking her husband's death very hard. Scribonia

(Julia's mother) has gone to join her in Pandataria. It's a horrible place. Poor Julia! She is forbidden to drink wine or have any new clothes. I wonder how long her father will keep her there. . . ." Then Antonia dropped such an unpleasant subject to inquire about Selene's health. "Has anything happened, darling? Or is it true what you suspected? Oh, I hope so!"

Her stilus raced over the wax tablet, as Selene replied to Antonia. After twenty-three years of marriage, a mother-to-be wrote proudly, "I'm pregnant!"

25

CLEOPATRA'S SON-IN-LAW

BETWEEN 8 B.C. AND 1 B.C., two baby boys were born—one in
a stable in Judea, the other in a palace in Mauretania. The
birth of the infant born in the humbler circumstances, a man-
ger at Bethlehem, alarmed King Herod, for he feared that this
child might some day cause Judea to revolt. His dissolute life
made the Jews hate him, and they longed for the time when
a descendant of David, one of Judea's great kings, would become their ruler and free them from Herod and the domination of Rome. The birth of a baby called Jesus (Joshua in
Greek) at David's birthplace, Bethlehem, the village where it
was said that this leader (the "Messiah") would be born, ful-
filled the prophecy concerning His coming.

So, informed that a child had been born at Bethlehem who
was to become King of the Jews, Herod gave orders to kill
all male babies (Matthew 11:16). But the infant Jesus escaped
with His parents to Egypt. It is said the first place at which
the Holy Family stopped was Heliopolis, where, at the temple,
Cleopatra had planted the cuttings of the balm-of-Gilead
Herod had given her when she passed through Judea.

Now what about that other baby, Cleopatra's grandson,

born in 1 B.C. at Caesarea, in Mauretania, and about the same age as Jesus? (No one knows the actual year of His birth). With totally different backgrounds, the lives of the two boys would be similar in many respects.

Even before she knew the sex of her child, Selene named the fetus Ptolemy after the brother she had lost, for her doctor Euphorbus (a brother of Antonius Musa, the Emperor's physician), summoned by Juba to Mauretania, predicted that the Queen would have a son. And she did. After twenty-four years without children, a fact that had greatly saddened her, Selene gave birth to a chubby, brown-eyed boy. His middle-aged parents were wild with joy.

With his wife occupied with the baby, Juba had time to devote to his writing, but hour after hour he sat at his desk wondering, "What shall I write about?" His *History of Rome* was not selling well. "Titus Livius (Livy) is writing a history of Rome to end all histories of Rome," was the excuse the Sosii Brothers gave him. They refused to publish any more of it.

When Juba stormed into the nursery where Selene was playing with Ptolemy, his publisher's letter in his hand, his wife had never seen him so upset. Selene soothed her husband as best she could. "The Sosii may be right," she said gently. "Since Livy has made himself the historian of Rome, why don't you do a book on Africa? Remember that history of Numidia, in Punic, your grandfather Hiempsal wrote? Why don't you translate it into Greek and Latin?"

"And compete with Sallust? Oh, Selene . . ." Juba's tone of utter discouragement, more than his words, alarmed her. "I don't think I'll ever write another book or even an occasional ode . . ." For wasn't there all that poetry of his the Sosii Brothers had sent back—Juba suspected—unread?

Their editor Gallus, however, liked the King of Mauretania personally. And, in the year A.D. 1, he wrote him a suggestion.

"The Emperor is sending his grandsons, Gaius and Lucius, on an expedition to Arabia, and we've been asked by the army for information on the country. You're just the person to write such an itinerary. Does the idea appeal to you?" Juba was indignant. He looked up from Gallus' letter, his dark eyes blazing. Here he was longing to write a history that would bring him lasting renown, or witty verse to make him famous like Ovid, and what did they want from him? A guide book!

"Selene, what am I supposed to do? Tell the distances between towns? Where there are temples and baths and the army can stop for supplies?" Juba sputtered. Unlike the Greeks, the Romans were interested in geography only as a help to their military campaigns. For the use of the army, countless copies of Agrippa's huge map, which was engraved in marble and displayed on a wall in the Forum, had been made on papyri. They distorted the shape of the known world, but showed the empire's 80,000 miles of paved roads, the facilities available to travelers in the towns along the way and other practical information.

"If I go to Arabia, Selene, I will have to be gone a long time," Juba said hesitantly, but he was already looking forward to the days at sea. An ocean voyage had soothed him more than once when life displeased him.

Little Ptolemy was too young to be taken on such a trip, Euphorbus thought, and Selene refused to leave her precious child. Besides, she had never liked the sea as Juba did. So he went to Arabia without her. The country was more interesting than he had thought it would be and the trip invigorated him.

Back in Caesarea, Juba sat down to write his army manual on Arabia, but he made it more than a dry account. Along with the information the army asked for, he gave the reader a vivid description of the country and told of the birds, animals, and plants he had seen. Incense burned in great quantities in their temples and homes came from resinous trees in southern Arabia. And the Romans were curious to know more about that mysterious land. Juba's book, dedicated to Gaius Caesar (Augustus' elder grandson), had a good sale in Rome.

Selene was delighted. "Juba, why try to be a second-rate Ovid?" she said. "Write about the things that really interest you."

"Such as what?"

"Oh, that way to Asia you were telling me about. If you found a navigable river across Africa, you'd be famous."

Urged to by his wife, Juba decided to make the trip, although it mean exploring the unknown. The Phoenicians had sailed up the coast of Gaul to Britain to obtain tin. But those great mariners were not interested in voyages of discovery, only in trade, and they established a blockade at the Pillars of Hercules, as the Straits of Gibraltar were then called, so that only their own ships could sail out into the Atlantic. To further discourage competitors, the Phoenicians spread fantastic stories about the perils beyond the Straits, where, if a ship sailed too far west, fierce winds drove it right off the edge of the world. In those days, the earth was believed to be a flat disk with a precipitous void beyond.

But by A.D. 2, the Phoenicians' blockade of the exit to the Mediterranean having been broken, Roman ships were venturing out into what were almost unexplored waters. Hanno of Carthage had gone down the West African coast as far as the present Guinea. How much further on did land extend? It was thought then that Africa curved around in an arch at the equator. Could one go by ship from the Atlantic to the Indian Ocean? That was what Juba sailed from Mauretania to find out. Strabo and other 1st century geographers believed that, halfway down the "bulge" of the continent, a river, filled with hideous, howling monsters that could swallow a ship at one gulp, flowed through the center of Africa from east to west.

Looking for that passage to Asia, Juba skirted the coast of modern Morocco. The crude maps of his day were based on information received from sea captains blown off their course, rumors, and wild guesswork. Juba never found that legendary cross-Africa river (possibly the Niger), but he made another discovery. It was a feat of great daring. Ancient geographers thought that the Pillars of Hercules were close to the western limit of the world. And Juba's sailors believed that, in taking his ship out into the Atlantic Ocean, so far from land, their captain was heading them all straight for a drop into a bottomless abyss. He paid no attention to their threats of mutiny, and sailing west for several days, came upon a group of islands (the Canaries or Fortunate Islands), eighty miles off the West African coast, opposite southern Morocco.

Walking along these shores from which Columbus was to sail to America, Juba found quantities of shellfish (*murex trunculus*), the mollusk from which the Phoenicians made their purple dye. These shells were so hard to find by now, and therefore so expensive, that a pound of wool, so-dyed, cost a thousand *denarii* ($200). Consequently, all-purple robes were worn only by royalty. Having cornered the dye market, the Phoenicians had kept the location of their murex beds a secret, but Juba believed that he had come upon a new source of supply. He returned home to establish, at the present Moroccan port of Mogador, an industry that was to be immensely profitable to Mauretania.

While her husband wrote of his discoveries to Rome, Selene taught the workmen she later sent out to the Fortunate Isles just how to extract the dye. The big, spiny shells must be opened soon after the mollusk was found, for the precious fluid was secreted in small glands that dried up after death. These color sacs were extracted and steeped in salt water for five days. The liquid was then boiled in vats. At first color-less, it changed to a rich purple. The wool or silk was left in the vats for five hours, taken out and dried, then given a second dipping. This made the twice-dyed Tyrian purple, which the Romans valued so highly that it became a sign of rank, and produced a phrase to describe royal blood—"born to the purple."

The Fortunate Isles were probably known to the Carthagin-ians, but Rome first learned of them from Juba of Mauretania, whose account of one of his expeditions there was preserved by the elder Pliny. "They are situated six hundred miles from the *Purpurariae Insulae* (Purple Islands or Madeira) . . . the first is named Junonia (now Lanzarote). Another Capraria (Grand Canary) is infested by quantities of giant lizards . . . In view of these islands is Ninguaria (Tenerife), named from its snow-clad volcano; and Canaria, so called from the multi-tude of *canae* (dogs) of great size to be found there . . ." writes Pliny in his *Natural History*, quoting from the report Juba sent to the Emperor. He also tells us that the King of Mauretania brought home two of these big wild dogs. They became Selene's favorite pets, although they fought with the crocodile she liked to lead about on a leash.

After Rome fell, during the Dark Ages, many of the places visited by Juba and other explorers of his day were forgotten. In the 14th century, the discovery of Madeira and the Can-ary Islands would be attributed to Portuguese and Spanish navigators. But Juba of Mauretania, Pliny says, was the first person actually to see them. His expeditions made him famous as an explorer. On another trip to the Fortunate Isles he found the *roccella tinctoria*, a dye-producing lichen peculiar to the Canaries; and the cactuslike *euphorbia canariensis*, which he named after his doctor.

Juba had interested Euphorbus in botany. The two men

climbed the Atlas Mountains, where, Juba wrote to Rome, he had found the euphorbia growing. He told of the plant's value as a purgative. Our *euphorbia regis jubae* is named after him. No longer did the King of Mauretania wonder what to write about, he became a prolific author, turning out books in Greek on botany, history, geography, grammar, the theater and painting. Selene found herself married to "one of the great scholars and writers of his age," so Pliny calls him.

In 3 A.D., Juba was doing a book on the theater. For years he and Selene had been importing actors from Greece to perform Aeschylus' tragedies and the comedies of Aristophanes in their open-air theater overlooking the Mediterranean. To adorn the grounds, marble statues of gods and goddesses were needed. Juba set out for Greece to get them. It was the first of many such trips to the Aegean he was to make. The dream of most Romans was some day to see Greece. And Juba fell in love with it. Month after month, he lingered on in the studios of the Athenian sculptors, superintending the carving of the marble statues, the molding of the bronze figures that he ordered to take back to Mauretania.

His ship loaded with treasures, Juba still did not come home. King Archelaus of Cappadocia, also a lover of Greek art, had invited him to stop by for a visit at his island-palace, off the coast of Cilicia. Selene learned, to her dismay, as the months passed and Juba did not return, that this was where he was— and the attraction holding him in Asia Minor was Archelaus' daughter Glaphyra. Once the wife of Herod's son Alexander, Glaphyra was now his widow, thanks to her brother-in-law Antipater.

Having caused the death of Selene's brother Ptolemy, Antipater had returned to Judea, where he undertook to ruin his own brothers. Herod, growing old, was ill and suspicious. In 7 B.C., he believed Antipater when he said that Alexander and Aristobulus (who had returned to Jerusalem with a deep hatred of their father for having slain their mother, Mariamme) planned to kill him while out hunting, pretend that it was an accident, and seize the throne. In a frenzy of rage, Herod had both his sons strangled. Berenice, Aristobulus' widow, was married off to an uncle; and Glaphyra and her two small boys, Tigranes and Alexander, were sent back to her father.

Antipater was now king of Judea in everything but name, for Herod, riddle with disease, was dying. Not fast enough, though, to please his eldest son. In 4 B.C., Antipater tried to hurry matters by poisoning his father. But servants warned Herod of the plot. Antipater was arrested and cast into a dungeon under the palace. As the Jewish historian, Josephus, tells it, the end of these two wicked men (five days apart) reads like fiction—but it actually happened.

Which of them will die first? Half crazy with pain from his disease (dropsy), Herod tries to commit suicide. He lifts a knife to plunge it into his breast, but his attendants prevent him. The commotion in the palace is heard by Antipater, who, thinking his father is dead, tries to bribe the jailer to set him free. The man runs to the dying Herod and tells him. "Kill him at once!" shouts the King. So Herod's last murder is committed. Five days later the man who killed his wife, his three sons, as well as countless other people, is dead.

"Herod the Great," as history calls him, died on March 13, B.C. 4, and since only a few months before his death Jesus Christ is now thought to have been born, that is the year from which the Christian era should properly be dated.

Selene was glad to hear of the death of Herod. How she hated him and his sons! Especially Antipater, who had caused the death of her brother Ptolemy. She had hoped never to have anything more to do with that detestable family. Now, seven years after Herod passed away, thanks to Juba, her life was to be linked with them again.

* * * *

In 40 B.C., Mark Antony deserted Cleopatra, pregnant with twins, and married Octavia. Now, forty-three years later, Cleopatra's daughter faced a similar abandonment. For in Cappadocia, if we are to believe Josephus, Juba of Mauretania took as his second wife the widow Glaphyra, King Archelaus' daughter.

The two marriages, though, were very different. Antony's Egyptian marriage to Cleopatra, a foreigner, was not recognized in Rome. Fulvia having died, Mark Antony was technically a widower when he married Octavia, while Selene and Juba had been united in Roman nuptial rites. So we are left wondering, as Selene must have wondered, why Juba should thus humiliate her. In Rome, divorce was easy. A Roman might marry and remarry, but he was allowed only one wife at a time. In Numidia, a man was permitted as many wives as he could afford. Juba I had maintained a large harem. So perhaps his son, in spite of his Roman education, was not as Romanized as he had thought he was.

These were bitter days for Selene. As her mother had done when abandoned by Antony, she ruled her kingdom and brought up her little son as best she could. Often she must have said to herself, as Cleopatra did—"I never want to see that man again!" Some day, Selene imagined, Juba would come home. And then what? Would he bring Glaphyra and her two boys by Alexander of Judea with him? Would he expect her to live in the same house with his second wife?

Juba had been gone a year when Selene, looking out of the window at the Mediterranean one day, saw a tall, dark-skinned man striding up from a boat that had tied up to the dock. The walk was unmistakable, yet, for a moment, Selene thought she was seeing things. It was no hallucination, though, for Ptolemy had seen his father, too, and was running to meet him. She saw Juba catch his son up in a bear hug and place the boy on his shoulder. Then the two continued up the path.

Selene's first glance had told her what she wanted to know. *Juba was alone.* At least, it would appear so, unless Glaphyra had remained on the ship until Juba could persuade Selene to invite the woman on shore. What was she going to do now? Surely, her unfaithful husband couldn't expect her to welcome him home with open arms!

In a panic of indecision, Selene took a swift glance in her mirror. Horrors! After a year's absence, why did Juba have to come home on this day of all days, when she had never looked so hot and bedraggled? But nothing could be done now about her appearance. He stood in the doorway.

"Is Glaphyra with you?" Selene asked.

"No, and she isn't coming to Mauretania, ever. That's all over, Selene. I came back to Caesarea to tell you. Now I shall go away, some place where you'll never have to see me again, if you want me to. You must hate me."

"No, I don't hate you, so stay in Mauretania. We need you badly, Ptolemy and I."

Selene could not have said anything more disarming. Sick with remorse, Juba had been afraid to come home, expecting a flood of reproaches. And well he deserved them. Now he saw his wife, her face white, staring at him with those big blue eyes that he had never been able to forget, even during his infatuation with Glaphyra. She was so frightened that he was no longer frightened at all.

"I'll never see Glaphyra again," Juba promised. And he held out his arms.

Selene hesitated. Surely, she must at least act cold and distant and teach Juba a lesson. But, no, the next thing she knew, there she was, her arms around his neck, holding him tightly, convulsively, as if he might escape from her again. "Oh, I love you so! It has been lonely without you," whispered Selene, who hadn't expected to say any such thing. For an answer, her husband only pressed his lips hungrily against hers.

A daughter, Drusilla, was born to them nine months later.

26

❧❧❧❧❧

BY THE SEA AT TIPAZA

SELENE AND JUBA had made Mauretania into a model Roman colony. Not only did the Italian *coloni* (immigrants) who crossed the Mediterranean to work on the wheat farms and in the olive groves find in Caesarea temples, baths, and race courses like those in Rome, but, to make them feel at home, the ancient festivals were faithfully observed.

The chief event on the Roman calendar was the Saturnalia, held on the seven shortest days of the year in honor of Saturn, god of the harvest. During this week, beginning on December 17th, the Romans observed the winter solstice, marking the emergence of the earth from darkness and the start of lengthening days. It was a time of brotherly goodwill, of joy and merrymaking, like the present Christmas season. Schools and shops were closed; gifts were exchanged; and the houses were decked with evergreens (an emblem of immortality), as a sign of faith in the return of light and life to a darkened world.

In the 4th century A.D., Pope Liberius, hoping to attract pagan converts to the Christian faith, chose the holiday time of the Saturnalia, when the Romans were used to celebrating, and declared December 25th to be the birthday of Our Lord. Feasts, the carrying of small lighted trees in processions, the decking of houses with greenery to give courage to the sun in its struggle for life, and other features of the pagan Saturnalia became today's Christmas customs.

In the palace at Caesarea, Twelfth Night in January was another happy occasion. The sun having regained its power and routed the forces of darkness and evil, Selene saw to the taking down and burning of the evergreens, their magic accomplished. In April, she helped Drusilla and Ptolemy paint eggs; and the children tried to see which of them could roll an egg the greatest distance down a grassy slope without cracking it. (A Roman game that is still played annually on the lawn of the White House, the home of the President of the United States.) For Easter is a holiday that is older than Christianity. On the day of Eostra, goddess of planting and growth, the Romans gave their friends eggs dyed in various colors, symbolizing the new life that returns to the earth in April.

Another Roman custom observed in Mauretania was the law forbidding the burning of the dead within the walls of a city. The Appian Way, for miles outside of Rome, is lined on both sides with burial places. So in North Africa, Selene and Juba began to erect their tomb, seventeen miles east of Caesarea, on the road to Tipaza. Standing on the highest hill along the coast, the beehive-shaped mausoleum was designed by Juba in the Punic style, like the tomb of his royal ancestor Masinissa at Lacus Regius, back in the High Atlas.

By 6 A.D., it was finished. "Just in time," Selene thought. Euphorbus had warned her, at forty-five, not to have another child. After Drusilla's birth, Selene never regained her strength. A wasting illness developed (probably cancer) and, like a great actress, Cleopatra's daughter played her last and best scene.

Juba wished to go in search of the source of the Nile, a mystery that would intrigue explorers until 1858, when an Englishman, John Speke, discovered the Victoria Falls in Tanganyika. Growing weaker daily, and not wanting her husband to see her die, Selene assured him, "Darling, I feel so much better!" One last kiss, then, with sunken cheeks rouged and her brightest smile, she sent him away on a long journey, and bravely faced death alone.

Cleopatra had not feared to die. She had brought up her daughter to believe in the pharoahs' faith in immortality. So Selene was not sad at leaving this world for another, where Juba would soon join her. It was in a happy mood that she set out for Tipaza, a month after her husband's departure, against Euphorbus' advice, to inspect the tomb that would hold the urn containing her ashes. The Romans cremated their dead. Burial in the earth did not become the custom until Christian times.

Driving seventeen seemingly endless miles, lying in a spring-less carriage jouncing over rutted roads, exhausted her, as Euphorbus had warned it would. But Tipaza was finally reached. From the bed in her carruca (traveling coach), Selene looked at the round building, decorated by sixty Ionic half-columns, and crowned with a pyramid, outlined against the blue African sky. And her thoughts went back to another mausoleum in Alexandria in which she had hidden with her mother and Ptolemy from Octavian. She thought how she had deceived him about the snake. She thought how she had walked in Octavian's triumph and met Juba. She thought of their wedding and how Juba had taught her to admire what was good in the Romans and ignore what was bad, and how they had loved each other for over thirty years. She thought of Glaphyra, too, and how Juba's unfaithfulness could have wrecked their marriage had she not wisely chosen to ignore it. And she spoke aloud. "Come, death," Selene said. "I'm willing to go. I've had a happy life."

She died two days later, on March 3, 6 A.D. Jesus Christ was a boy at the time, growing up in Nazareth.

Surrounded by flowers and burning incense, the body of the Queen of Mauretania rested on a funeral couch of ivory and gold, covered with a pall of purple silk, in the palace at Caesarea until the day of her funeral. Then, led by a band of musicians and followed by wax images of Selene's famous ancestors—Cleopatra of Egypt, Mark Antony, and Alexander the Great—a line of carriages escorted the Queen to her last resting place by the sea at Tipaza.

It was Euphorbus who delivered the eulogy at the grave. Since his father was absent, seven-year-old Ptolemy, weeping bitterly, threw a handful of earth on his mother's remains. Then men picked up the couch and placed it on a pyre, and, with torches, lighted the perfumed wood, so the pyre and the body were consumed together. After the fire had died down, the ashes were collected in a bronze urn to be placed in the tomb—and the funeral was over.

But the Roman dead were not forgotten. After his return to Mauretania, the grief-stricken Juba always took Ptolemy and Drusilla to Tipaza at the end of May, to place violets, her favorite flowers, before their mother's funeral urn. The decoration of graves on Memorial Day in the United States occurs on a date nearly corresponding to the Romans' *Rosaria* (rose festival), when they remembered and honored their dead.

27

NEVER AGAINST ROME

When halfway up the Nile, Juba had heard that Selene was ill. His staff, to spare him, did not tell the King she was dead. "My poor wife, she needs me," Juba said to an aide. "Pack at once, we must get back to Caesarea." No one dared confess to him the truth. So when the King of Mauretania learned of his loss, upon reaching home, the shock was overwhelming. He no longer wanted to live.

Trying to forget his grief, Juba immersed himself in his studies. He went frequently to the Aegean and became a famous collector of Greek art. Bringing back shiploads of treasures, he made Caesarea into the handsomest city on the southern shore of the Mediterranean, its buildings adorned with fluted columns, mosaic floors, and statues of marble and bronze. He also founded the town of Volubilis, near modern Rabat, today the most notable Roman ruins in Morocco. But all his activities seemed pointless to him. Without Selene, the joy had gone out of living. During the Roman *Matronalia* (Mother's Day), March first, and on her birthday, September second, he shut himself in his room and would see no one.

Lonely and unhappy, Juba traveled continually, but on his

trips to the Aegean, there was no stopping off in Cappodocia now to see Glaphyra. His infatuation was over, and she had become the wife of another man, Archelaus of Judea. In A.D. 5, Herod's fourth son, Archelaus, fell so violently in love with Glaphyra that he divorced his wife in order to marry her.

Herod the Great murdered his three eldest sons. But he had fifteen children by ten wives. At his death, Herod left to Archelaus, the eldest of his surviving sons, Samaria and Judea; and Antipas and Philip, Archelaus' half-brothers, inherited Galilee and Perea. The Jews hated the Herod family as much as they did the Romans. When the Judeans rose in revolt, Archelaus butchered three thousand of them in one day alone. That is why Joseph, on his way back from Egypt with Mary and Jesus, on being told that the courts of the temple at Jerusalem were strewn with corpses, was afraid to return to Judea. "He came and dwelt in a city called Nazareth" (Matt. 2:23), and Christ spent His childhood and youth in Galilee.

As brutal as his father, Archelaus had made the error of marrying Glaphyra, the widow of his murdered brother, Alexander. Such a close union horrified the Jews. They thought it immoral. In 6 A.D., at their request, the Romans banished Archelaus to Gaul, where he died. Did Glaphyra go into exile with him? We hope so, but, at this point, the woman who must have caused Selene many a sleepless night disappears from the pages of Josephus' history. With Archelaus exiled, Judea became a province, ruled by a succession of Roman governors. The fifth of these would be Pontius Pilate.

Josephus, his contemporary, tells us that, from Galilee, Antipas watched the downfall of Archelaus with trepidation, for he had made the same forbidden marriage as his older brother. In defiance of Jewish law, Antipas had married his niece Herodias (daughter of Aristobulus), the divorced wife of his brother Philip. It was this Antipas who put to death John the Baptist, for telling the tetrarch to his face that it was sinful for him to be living with his sister-in-law (Mark 6:17). It was before this same man that Christ was sent by Pontius Pilate. He was the "Herod" in Jerusalem at the time of Jesus' crucifixion.

* * * *

Finding Caesarea too lonely a place without Selene, Juba continued his travels. In 9 A.D., he went to the Black Sea to console an exiled friend. "How strange life is!" Juba thought. "After envying Ovid all these years, now I'm sorry for him." For the year before, on the grounds that his *Ars Amatoria* (The Art of Love) had shocked the Empress Livia, the poet's pleasant life in Rome was interrupted by an imperial edict, banishing him to Tomis (Constanta, in Romania), then a dismal hamlet at the mouth of the Danube River.

Juba couldn't believe that Ovid's *Ars Amatoria*, which had run by this time through several editions, was the real cause for his exile. "Of course, it wasn't," the poet said. It seemed that he had come by accident upon Augustus kissing Terentia, Maecenas' wife, in the Palatine gardens. Ovid was known as a gossip, and, before he could tell all Rome that the Emperor was far from being the paragon of virtue he liked people to believe, the poet's *Ars Amatoria* was banned, his work on the *Metamorphoses* was interrupted, and he was sent away. Juba found his friend, bored to death in Tomis, composing melancholy verse, dedicated to Augustus, in the hope of persuading the Emperor to let him return to civilization. Augustus remained implacable. He never forgave Ovid or his daughter Julia. Both of them died in exile.

There was no danger that Juba's writings would be censored. He had taken Selene's advice, to revise his grandfather

Hiempsal's notes, and, having studied ancient Punic manuscripts, was working on a book about Africa that would bring
him great renown. About to leave one day for a trip into the
Atlas Mountains, the scholar-king of Mauretania called for his
horse, stepped toward the front door, and was suddenly con-
fronted by a curly-haired, brown-eyed boy. "I want to go
with you," Ptolemy said.

"No, it's a dangerous journey and you're too young, only
ten," his father replied. But his heart swelled with pride.
Ptolemy showed a determination and courage reminiscent of
his mother.

"I'm not afraid, I want to go."

Juba said no more. He walked beside the tall, handsome boy
out to the courtyard, where the king's huntsmen waited on
horseback and a groom held his mount. "Get Prince Ptolemy
a horse," Juba ordered. Father and son rode away together,
and from then on, Ptolemy became his father's constant companion.

* * * *

The camel did not reach the west coast of North Africa
until about the time of Julius Caesar. Mauretania, in those
days, was not a camel but an elephant country. And Juba
was concerned over the way the herds were being wiped out.
First the Carthaginians had captured wild elephants for military purposes, using up thousands of them in three wars with
the Romans. Since then, hunters were after them constantly.
There was a great demand for ivory and, in the ampitheaters
of Rome, elephants, lions, and tigers were needed to fight each
other or against armed gladiators for the amusement of the
bloodthirsty crowds. The slaughter of five thousand animals
during a single day of games was not uncommon. In Mauretania, where once lions, leopards, elephants, panthers, ostriches,

and monkeys roamed, only the North African monkey, still to be found in Gibraltar, has survived to our day. Even as early as the 1st century A.D., Juba and his son had to go back into the High Atlas to find much wildlife.

Evenings by the campfire, Ptolemy's father told the boy stories about the elephants that he was putting in his book. For instance, how Hannibal of Carthage left Spain with thirty-seven of them to crush Rome, and all the big-eared African animals died crossing the Alps, and how Hannibal rode down into Italy astride the only survivor, an Indian elephant. And how at Thapsus, Ptolemy's grandfather, Juba I of Numidia, had placed his elephant cavalry in front of his infantry, so they would frighten the Romans' horses.

"Horses are afraid of the scent of elephants," Juba told his son. "Your grandfather's elephants might have won the battle for him, if Caesar's archers hadn't caused a stampede by shootings arrows dipped in burning wax at them. Stung by the fire, they ran amok, trampling to death more friends than foes."

Apt to be indiscriminate in the damage they did, causing havoc in the enemy's lines until they were turned back and then doing the same in their own, elephants had become almost obsolete in warfare. But, along with lions, panthers, and leopards, they were being sent to Rome to be used as circus animals. Some would be taught to do tricks and dance in a ring. Others would die in combat with lions and tigers. Juba took his son to Hippo (now Bone, in Algeria), from where most of the beasts destined for the greedy ampitheaters of the Roman world were shipped.

Like his mother, Selene, Ptolemy loved animals. Seeing the poor creatures penned in cages below deck in the galleys, often without sufficient food and water, he cried out indignantly, "It's barbaric! Father, why do you allow it?"

"Because I must," replied Juba gently. "I love animals, too.

But, my son, there is one thing you cannot interfere with—
Rome's insatiable demand for *panem et circenses* (food and
games)."

His father explained to Ptolemy how caravans from Central
Africa brought up to the port of Hippo, for export to Italy,
gold, ivory, ostrich feathers, and wild beasts. Juba deplored
the fact that the elephants, lions, and leopards were going to
Rome to be slaughtered. "But nothing can be done about it,"
he said regretfully.

Even in Caesarea, the games had become increasingly brutal.
When they came into town from their outlying farms, the
Italian colonists wanted to be entertained by bloody wild-
animal shows and gladiatorial fights. In the theater Selene
and Juba had built, the audience, bored by Greek dramas, demanded music hall skits and burlesque comedies. Juba never
went to the games now, and seldom to the theater, although
he had written a book on the subject.

Ptolemy hated this side of Roman life. He often said to his
father, "When I become king, I'll stop all this cruelty. I'll
put an end to the combats in the arenas and to the slavery
on the farms. I'll—"

"Softly, softly, my son, don't get so excited!" Juba warned.
"You cannot fight Rome. Never forget that, or they'll destroy
you, as they destroyed your grandmother, Cleopatra."

To be kind to man and beast was radical talk in this cruel
age, the 1st century A.D. In a few years, Jesus of Nazareth,
a grown man now, in His late twenties, would gather twelve
devoted Apostles about Him and go through Galilee, preaching this same doctrine, "Love thy neighbor—" In Mauretania,
Juba knew better than to attempt any reforms. He was proud
of the fact that, for nearly half a century, he had governed
Mauretania so thoroughly in accord with the wishes of Rome
that it was practically a free nation. Wanting to keep it that
way, Juba opposed any changes, for he feared that an uprising

against Rome would destroy Mauretania's independence completely.

"Work with Rome and they'll work with you," Juba often said to Ptolemy. "Fight Rome and you fight them alone."

Then, in 23 A.D., another funeral procession wound its slow way along the coast road from Caesarea to Tipaza. Selene and Juba were together again. But now there was nobody to warn Ptolemy any more.

* * * *

The horse ranches, wheat farms and olive groves of Mauretania, owned by rich men who lived in Rome, were operated by slaves under a *villicus* (manager). He was usually a hard taskmaster, who kept his laborers busy. Slaves from Central Africa were not yet needed. The Romans had plenty of white prisoners of war. The slave quarters were underground dungeons—dark, filthy, and heavily barred. From dawn to dusk the wretched creatures worked in chains, watched by an Italian overseer, armed with a whip.

After his father died and Ptolemy became King of Mauretania, at twenty-four, he made an inspection tour of these farms. He went down into the tunnels under the arenas, where, prior to their appearance on the sanded floor above, the wild animals were kept. Their pens were twenty feet below ground, with slots high up in the walls to allow food to be dropped to the half-starved beasts. But not much. They must be kept hungry to be sufficiently ferocious, when they were released from the tunnel, to attack their pinioned victims.

Ptolemy was shocked. He ordered better treatment of the slaves on the farms; he stopped the bloody combats in the arenas; and he shut down the port of Hippo. If Juba had been alive, he would have warned, "Watch out, Son, you can't do this to Rome!" as he had often said to him in days gone by.

But Juba was dead. The export of wild animals dwindled, almost to a trickle. So did the flow of grain, wine, and olive oil, the basic fat of Mediterranean cooking. The farms could not be worked without forced labor.

There was an immediate outcry. The estate owners complained to Rome. "Our young king is mad!" they told Tiberius. For in 14 A.D., Augustus, after a reign of over forty years, had passed away, and, since Julia's boys had also died— Lucius at Masilla (Marseilles) in 2 A.D.; and Gaius, in Armenia, two years later—Livia had achieved her ambition. Her son Tiberius, by now a tired, embittered man in his sixties, was emperor.

Fortunately for Ptolemy, Tiberius never forgot his first love. As long as he lived, the old Emperor protected Ptolemy, Selene's son, from his own subjects, even when there broke out in North Africa the riots his father had feared. From 24-29 A.D., Mauretania, at peace under Juba II for forty-seven years, boiled over. Encouraged by King Ptolemy, the slaves on the farms revolted and murdered their overseers. It took all the Third Augusta could do to crush the uprisings. Even then, Tiberius refused to listen to the outraged estate owners and punish their young monarch with his crazy liberal ideas.

Toward Jesus of Nazareth, also stirring up trouble for them in Judea, the Romans acted swiftly. Who was He? Not a king, like Ptolemy of Mauretania, only an obscure individual from Galilee. But Jesus claimed to be a king—the King of the Jews. That was enough for Rome. It made Him a rebel against the Emperor Tiberius, who alone had the right to appoint the rulers of Judea. When Jesus came to Jerusalem to celebrate the Passover, the Romans arrested Him for treason.

The punishment for such a crime against Rome was crucifixion. But Pontius Pilate, the governor of Judea at the time, believed Jesus to be innocent. Herod Antipas was in Jerusalem for the Passover. Learning that Jesus was a Galilean,

Pilate had Him taken under guard to Antipas, tetrarch of Galilee, as belonging to his jurisdiction—hoping to shift the blame for Jesus' death on Herod. But Antipas, too clever to be compromised, promptly sent Jesus back. The mob shouted at Pontius Pilate, "Crucify Him! If you let this man go, you are not Caesar's friend." And the Roman governor gave in.

Jesus was seized by Pilate's soldiers and taken to the hill of Golgotha, outside the walls of Jerusalem, where He was nailed to a cross and hung between two thieves. Considering Him merely another rebel getting the usual punishment, Pontius Pilate did not think Jesus' death of sufficient importance to mention it in his report to Rome.

Who would have thought then that it would become the greatest event that has happened in the history of the world and that, two thousand years later, people would ask, "Ptolemy? Did Cleopatra have a grandson?" For, at the time, all the talk in Roman circles was about the uprisings in Mauretania. But, as long as Tiberius lived, no one dared raise a hand against Ptolemy.

Then, in 37 A.D., Tiberius, almost eighty, caught pneumonia; and Caligula hastened his uncle's death with a pillow. Now there was no one to protect Cleopatra's grandson.

28

HIS AFRICAN COUSIN

THE DESCENDANTS of Selene's two sisters successively ruled the Roman empire. Antonia Major was the grandmother of Nero. Antonia Minor became the mother of Claudius and the grandmother of Caligula. These three emperors followed Tiberius. But in what order? Since the throne was not hereditary, the succession was always a matter of dispute. It led to feuds and intrigue, even to murder. And in the spring of A.D. 37, when Tiberius was taken ill with pneumonia at Cape Misenum, while on a visit to the West Coast naval base, all Rome wondered who would succeed him. Tiberius' only child, Drusus II, was dead. So was his nephew Germanicus, the son of Antonia and Drusus, who had died in Syria at the age of thirty-four.

Named in honor of his father's German victories, Germanicus married Agrippina, the daughter of Agrippa and Julia. Of their nine children, only one son was still living. Gaius had been born while his parents, Germanicus and Agrippina, were with the Roman legions on the Rhine. Caligula (Little Boots) was a nickname given him by the soldiers for his wearing as a child small *caligae* (army shoes) instead of sandals.

The name stuck to the boy after the death of his father in Syria, when he came to live in Rome with his great-grandmother Livia, and, after she passed away, with his grandmother, Antonia. But March of 37 found Caligula at Cape Misenum. Tiberius' son, Drusus, had died, leaving a boy of eighteen named Gemellus. Unable to return to his island retreat at Capri, the Emperor, realizing how ill he was, had invited his grandnephew (Caligula) and his grandson (Gemellus) to his bedside, to try to decide which of them he wished to name as his heir.

Gemellus was the nearer of kin, but he was a stupid youth, while the handsome, twenty-five-year-old Caligula was the grandson of Drusus Senior and the son of Germanicus, two national heroes. His sister-in-law, Antonia, for whom Tiberius had great affection and respect, because she was not only Selene's sister but also the widow of Drusus, the brother he had dearly loved, was trying to persuade him that her grandson, Caligula, would make the better emperor. So Tiberius had not yet made up his mind. Lying in bed on the night of March 15th, he asked both young men to come and see him in the morning. "I'll choose the one who enters the room first," he told his doctor, Charicles.

The next day, Gemellus overslept, and Caligula came to the sickroom ahead of him. Tiberius was glad, for he knew his choice would please Antonia. "My boy, I hope—you'll make a good emperor," he said to her grandson. "Rule wisely . . . and well . . ." Then, the strain of speaking being too much for the sick man, he sank back exhausted on the pillows.

Caligula acted quickly. Tiberius called weakly for help and a struggle followed, when he felt his nephew's fingers on his throat. But his cries were soon muffled. Picking up a pillow, Caligula pressed it down hard on the old man's face and held it there, until the weakly tossings arms and the legs beneath the bedclothes were still.

The Emperor's nephew thought he was alone in the room. But, no, eyes had been watching him smother the sick man with his own pillow. Horrified at the sight, Tiberius' doctor had hidden himself behind a screen. Caligula spied Charicles in his hiding place and dragged him out. Weeping, the old man fell upon his knees, pleading for his life. But he had seen too much. Would the doctor expose him? To prevent Charicles from talking, Caligula ordered his tongue cut out, before he was killed, and his body flung into the Tiber. All this was done very secretly, of course. And, at the funeral, when Antonia's grandson, in an all-black toga, followed the corpse as the chief mourner, the crowds, delighted to have a young and handsome emperor in the place of old, sad-faced Tiberius, gave him an ovation.

Nurtured on stories of his mother's real or imagined wrongs, Caligula felt no remorse at having murdered his uncle. It was an act of revenge. Everyone knew that Tiberius had been jealous of his nephew's popularity with the army. And Agrippina firmly believed that her husband, Germanicus, was poisoned in Syria, on orders from the Emperor. Obsessed with the idea, she became involved in a conspiracy to overthrow Tiberius and place Caligula's elder brother on the throne. The plot failed. Agrippina and her son were arrested and banished to Pandataria, the same island-prison off Campania to which Agrippina's mother, Julia, had been sent. They soon perished. Her son was executed and Agrippina, granddaughter of the revered Augustus, had one eye knocked out by a guard. She ended her miseries by starving herself to death.

Agrippina passed away on October 18, A.D. 33. Four years later, Caligula's first act as emperor was to sail out to Pandataria, bring the ashes of his mother and brother back to Rome, and place them in the mausoleum that Augustus had built for the imperial family. The next ashes to be placed there were those of Caligula's grandmother, Antonia. The most beloved

woman in Rome, Selene's favorite sister died on May 1, A.D.
37, at the age of seventy-three, six weeks after Caligula became emperor. It was a great pity. Had she lived, Antonia
might have restrained her grandson in some of his excesses,
for he had great respect for her. But Caligula was soon no
longer responsible for his actions. Epileptic from childhood,
shortly after mounting the throne, he had a mental breakdown. From then on, Caligula acted like a madman. His favorite pastime was going to the jails to watch criminals tortured and put to death; and to the arenas, to see them burned
alive.

But Caligula, in spite of his scandalous behavior, was more
popular with the Romans than Tiberius had been, for he was
a lavish spender on games and gladiatorial combats. The people had disliked Tiberius, a miser who spent little on himself,
because he did nothing to beautify Rome (a city he detested).
He cut down on the bloody games (which he hated), and
refused to let the governors overtax and plunder the provinces
—qualities that would make any ruler unpopular. Now life,
under Caligula, became a continual carnival. The Romans delighted in the antics of their crazy emperor.

Encouraging Caligula in his vices was another member of
the Herod family—Marcus Julius Agrippa, the son of Aristobulus, who had been named after M. Vipsanius Agrippa, a
friend of his grandfather, Herod the Great. When, in 7 B.C.,
his father Aristobulus was killed, little Agrippa was sent to
Rome to be educated, and he grew up with the imperial family. Antonia liked the smart, handsome Jew, and he was a
boyhood friend of her son Claudius and her grandson Caligula.
When the latter became emperor, he made Agrippa the ruler
of Galilee and Perea.

Agrippa, who found living in Palestine dull, was usually
in Rome. One day in the fall of A.D. 40, he was seated in
Caligula's magnificent new palace on the Palatine, listening to

the Emperor's troubles. After three years on the throne, the extravagant Caligula had squandered all the surplus in the treasury saved up by the careful Tiberius.

"What shall I do?" the Emperor asked. But he was only thinking aloud, for Caligula would do what he had often done before, order a millionaire to kill himself and appropriate his fortune. It was better yet to confiscate the treasury of a conquered country. And Agrippa offered a suggestion. "Why don't you depose Ptolemy and make Mauretania a Roman province? Why should it continue to be an independent kingdom, the only one in the empire?"

The idea was tempting. Unlike the other client nations dependent upon Rome, Mauretania had been free ever since Augustus gave the present Morocco and western Algeria to Cleopatra Selene as a wedding present. It would be an easy matter to find an excuse to oust her son. Then Caligula could put the riches of Mauretania in his pocket and adorn his new palace with the art treasures with which he heard that Ptolemy was surrounded. Those marble and bronze statues brought by Juba from Greece were coveted by Caligula even more than the wealth of Mauretania, for, like most rich Romans, he fancied himself as an art collector. Mauretania was noted for its exports—horses for the Roman armies, purple dyes for the togas of the emperors, and citron-wood for the making of exquisite furniture. And Caligula longed to own a certain dining table of citron-wood, inlaid with ivory, which he had been told Ptolemy possessed.

"I could send an army—" the Emperor began. But Agrippa had a better idea. "Why go to all that trouble? Why don't you invite Ptolemy to come to Rome? If—perhaps on his way home—something happened to him, wouldn't you inherit Mauretania? Ptolemy is your cousin. His mother and your grandmother were sisters. He has never married and has no children. So, at Ptolemy's death, my dear Caligula, you, as his heir, become the ruler of Mauretania. All, very legally—"

"And I'll get his citron-wood table!" the Emperor exclaimed. "Agrippa, let's write and invite Ptolemy at once. Cousins should get better acquainted."

* * * *

There is no way of knowing if Ptolemy of Mauretania had heard of Our Lord, but he practiced without realizing it the Christian doctrines. A passionate defender of the poor and oppressed, Ptolemy had tried, without much success, to introduce reforms in Mauretania, abolishing all slave labor. He issued orders that, in the gladiatorial contests, nobody was to be killed, not even condemned criminals. And, recently, he had further antagonized his people by passing the first conservation law in history, to safeguard the wildlife of Africa.

"The elephants eat our crops. Why are we forbidden to kill them?" Ptolemy's indignant subjects wrote the Emperor. "The ivory hunters kill the elephants, take the tusks, and leave the meat to rot. But if we kill an elephant to protect our food supply, our king puts us in jail."

While Tiberius ruled, such protests went unheeded. But now, with Caligula on the throne, there was no one to protect Selene's son. So when he received the Emperor's letter summoning him to Rome, Ptolemy was not surprised. He only wondered why he had not been sent for sooner, to account for his humane actions.

He packed for the journey with care, selecting his finest jewels and his most costly purple togas, embroidered with gold, for he wanted to be a credit to Mauretania. But when the day came to sail, Ptolemy asked himself, a bit nervously, "I wonder what Caligula is like?" He had heard of the Emperor's eccentricities—how Caligula had the heads removed from statues and replaced them with likenesses of himself; how he gave banquets at which his horse Icitatus was the guest of honor; and at the circus, when there was a shortage of condemned criminals to be fed to the lions, he had some of the audience seized and thrown into the arena. Ptolemy hoped such tales were exaggerated. How could the grandson of his Aunt Antonia, whom his mother had loved, be utterly bad?

Ptolemy arrived in Rome a week later. Caligula had sent his imperial barge down to Ostia to bring the King of Mauretania up the Tiber, and he stood on the wharf to greet his guest as he stepped ashore, just as Augustus had welcomed Ptolemy's parents when they visited Rome in 13 B.C. Caligula was good-looking, tall and blond, but there was a wild look in his eyes that frightened Ptolemy. Nor did he like M. Julius Agrippa, always at the Emperor's side, for Ptolemy knew that the Herods of Judea had never been friends of his family.

Still, what was there to fear? "Dear Cousin Ptolemy, welcome to Rome!" cried Caligula, kissing him on both cheeks. After which, eager to impress his guest, he took the African King to reside at his fine palace on the Palatine.

To his relief, Ptolemy found that he hadn't been invited to Rome to be scolded, but, on the contrary, to be royally entertained. There were banquets, theatrical performances, and a cruise on Lake Nemi, aboard Caligula's pleasure-galley, that contained every conceivable luxury, including baths of warm, scented water.

Where once the Palatine had on it only a few houses, the hill was now covered with palaces and government buildings, and the Forum below was fairly choked with temples. Ptolemy wanted to see the Via Sacra, along which his father had walked in Caesar's triumph and his mother on Augustus' day for Egypt. He went to look at the mausoleum of the Julio-Claudian family on the Campus Martius, which contained the funeral urns of many people of whom Selene had told her son—Augustus, Livia, Octavia, Agrippa, Drusus, and Antonia. Eventually, though, came the occasion which Ptolemy dreaded, when he must go to the amphitheather with Caligula and witness the games in his honor.

"It will soon be over," Selene's son consoled himself by thinking. "In a few days, I'll be going to Ostia to sail for home. And won't I be glad!"

The Emperor, cordial at first, had by now grown cold and distant. Ptolemy wondered why. Did Caligula, who fancied himself to be the best dressed man in Rome, resent his African cousin wearing handsomer purple togas than his? Or was it because every time the King of Mauretania appeared the crowds cheered him more than they did their own ruler?

That afternoon in the arena, seated beside Caligula in the imperial box, Ptolemy tried to smile and appear interested in the performance so that his visit to Rome would end pleasantly. But it made him cringe to see the ravenous panthers, lions and tigers, driven out of the ramp leading up from their underground cages, being whipped to make them turn on the helpless people chained to posts around the ring. The trumpets blared loudly to drown out the screams of the victims; the audience shouted with delight; but Caligula looked bored, and before the revolting spectacle was over, dozed off to sleep.

A crash of cymbals wakened him, as the next act began, and in marched the *dimachaeri* (professional gladiators). They stopped before the imperial box, calling out to the Emperor, "*Te morituri salutamus!*" (We about to die salute you!) Then the fights began.

Before long, Caligula took it into his crazy head to go down into the ring and challenge one of the fighters. Knowing better than to strike back at his royal attacker, the gladiator, after waiting a decent time, dropped to his knees and raised his arm in sign of surrender. "*Mitte!* (Let him go!)," the mob shouted, for the man had conducted himself well. But Caligula lifted his fist with the thumb down. That meant death and he ran the kneeling gladiator through with his sword. Then, as the *libritenarri* (arena attendants) dragged away the body and raked over the bloodstained sand, the Emperor strutted back to his box, to be greeted effusively by the fawning Agrippa. Ptolemy turned his head away, in disgust.

"I can't be polite any longer," he thought. "I'd better go home, before I tell Caligula what I think of him."

That evening, the African King announced to his host that he was returning to Caesarea the following day. As soon as they were alone, Agrippa said to Caligula, "Well. how about it? Shall I give Chaerea the order?" Gaius Cassius Chaerea was the prefect in command of the praetorian cohort, the Emperor's bodyguard. "Yes," replied Caligula, still angry over the contemptuous looks he had received from Ptolemy after his "victory" over the gladiator.

By morning, the Emperor, whose deranged mind was always somewhat confused, had forgotten his conversation with Agrippa. When Ptolemy left for Ostia, Caligula stretched out both arms to embrace him. "Good-by, dear cousin, you must come to Rome often," he said, kissing him.

Agrippa, however, did not forget what Caligula had said. Ptolemy of Mauretania never reached Ostia. By order of the Emperor (relayed by Agrippa), a mile and a half from Rome —close to the place where, about twenty years later, St. Paul, beheaded nearby, was buried—Ptolemy was dragged from his carriage by Chaerea's soldiers. Trying to escape, he ran to the shores of the Tiber. But the men caught up with him, and, forcing the African King over a steep bank, they cut off his fingers while he tried to hold on. Ptolemy fell into the river below. As he struggled from the water, the soldiers ran down to the edge of the stream and beat his brains out.

There is a tradition that, periodically, the despairing shrieks of Cleopatra's grandson can still be heard at the lonely spot by the Tiber where he perished—murdered by the men sent by Caligula to escort his "dear Cousin Ptolemy" safely to the coast.

29

THE LAST OF THE CAESARS

It took three generations to do it but Herod the Great had full revenge on Cleopatra for taking the Jordan Valley from him. Rhodon, Herod's agent in Egypt, betrayed Caesarion to Octavian; Herod's son, Antipater, caused the death of Cleopatra's youngest child, Ptolemy; and it was Herod's grandson, Agrippa, who gave the order to Caligula's soldiers to murder her grandson.

Eventually, Agrippa told the Emperor that his African cousin had, unfortunately, had an accident on the way home. Ptolemy was dead. Caligula was "surprised"—and pleased. Mauretania was now his, and he sent agents to Caesarea to strip the city of its fabulous art treasures. Especially, that citron-wood dining table must be brought to Rome. But Caligula was never to see it, for his evil deeds caught up with him.

Hating the Emperor for his cruelty, Cassius Chaerea, Cornelius Sabinus, and others of the praetorian guard had been discussing among themselves how to assassinate him. Caligula's murder of the harmless King of Mauretania revolted even these callous soldiers. "It's time we rid ourselves of that madman," Chaerea told his companions, and he volunteered to strike the first blow.

On the night of the 24th of January, A.D. 41, the Emperor sat chatting with his wife, Caesonia, and his Uncle Claudius, the second son of Antonia and Drusus, a man of about fifty. Seeing his chance, Chaerea walked up behind Caligula and stabbed him in the back.

Staggering to his feet, the wounded ruler tried to escape, but the rest of his household troops fell upon him, and Caligula dropped to the floor. Then everybody pounced on him. Sabinus finished off the hysterical Empress Caesonia; but it was Chaerea, whom Caligula had enjoyed humiliating by mimicking the prefect's high-pitched voice, who revealed the depth of his hate by picking up Drusilla, the Emperor's baby girl, by the heels and dashing her brains out against the wall.

Their orgy of killing over, the assassins realized they had acted too impulsively. Caligula lay dead. Who was there to succeed him? Just then, Chaerea happened to notice the tips of two sandals protruding from beneath a curtain. He drew back the silken folds. There stood Uncle Claudius, white and trembling. He had hidden himself, thinking that he too was about to be murdered.

Chaerea pulled him out and said jokingly, "Our next emperor!" To his surprise, nobody laughed. The other soldiers liked the idea. Claudius was considered a fool, but he was popular with the army, being the only living brother of their late hero, Germanicus. Herod Agrippa was in Rome at the time. He persuaded the senate that, for want of anyone better, the middle-aged Claudius should become emperor.

Rewarded for his support by Claudius with the gift of Judea and Samaria and the title of king, M. Julius Agrippa, already in possession of Galilee and Perea, became the ruler of all of Palestine, formerly held by his grandfather, Herod the Great. He endeared himself to the Jews by doing his utmost to stamp out the new Nazarene religion, based on the idea that the Messiah had come and been crucified under Pontius Pilate. And there began during Agrippa's reign the persecution of Christ's devoted followers. After beheading James, the brother of John, the first Apostle to die for Jesus, Agrippa arrested Peter and would have killed him too, but for his miraculous escape from prison (Acts: 12).

With Palestine quiet under the stern rule of Agrippa, the first great enemy of the Christian church, trouble flared up elsewhere in the Roman Empire. In North Africa, the Third Augusta was busy putting down an attempted revolt. After Ptolemy's death, his subjects had hoped they would be allowed to continue to be a semi-independent kingdom, with Drusilla, sister of their late king, as queen. Rome squelched any such idea and Mauretania became a province in A.D. 42.

"What shall I do with Drusilla?" her Cousin Claudius must have wondered. Tacitus says that the Emperor married off Selene's daughter to the widowed Antonius Felix, a Greek freedman, formerly the property of his mother, Antonia. Not much is known about Drusilla. If Cleopatra Selene died in A.D. 6, a year after the birth of her daughter, as is generally thought, Drusilla would be thirty-seven at the time of this marriage. What had she been doing all these years? She only reappears in history as Felix's second wife.

For Cleopatra's granddaughter to marry a Greek ex-slave, set free by her Aunt Antonia, was not such a bad marriage as might be supposed, however, for Felix was the brother of the notorious Pallas. As Claudius' financial secretary, Pallas had amassed a huge fortune. Through his influence, Antonius Felix was appointed procurator of Judea. He was the Roman governor there in A.D. 56, at the time of St. Paul's arrest.

This Jew from Tarsus named Saul (or Paul, as the Gentiles called him) was imprisoned by Felix as a dangerous agitator. But when he saw him, a bald-headed, little man, with

a scrubby beard, "but the face of an angel," the Roman procurator was impressed. So much so, the Bible says, that, "later
he sent for Paul and heard him concerning the faith in Christ."
(Acts 24:24). Felix married for the third time another Drusilla, a daughter of Herod Agrippa. It was this Jewish Drusilla,
not Selene's daughter, who listened with him to what Paul
had to say.

One wonders what happened to the first Drusilla?

Two centuries later, a Queen Zenobia of Alexandria
claimed to be descended from Cleopatra's granddaughter and
the Roman governor of Judea. During the reign of Aurelian,
when the Romans conquered Egypt, Zenobia, like Cleopatra,
tried to kill herself rather than be taken as a prisoner to Rome.
She was unsuccessful and, "loaded with jewels," graced the
Emperor's triumphal procession. Then, instead of dying of
grief or being strangled, the fate of most captives, the beautiful
Zenobia won Aurelian's heart, and, with her two boys, ended
her days on an estate at Tivoli which he gave her.

Down to the time of Aurelian, Roman Emperor A.D. 270-5,
is as far as Cleopatra's line can be traced, even dubiously, so
let us return to Agrippa.

* * * *

St. Luke tells us that M. Julius Agrippa died suddenly at
the circus in Judea, during some games in honor of Claudius,
and it was before his son, Agrippa II, that Paul was taken as
a prisoner by Porcius Festus, the Roman governor who succeeded Felix (Acts 12). Although a Jew, Paul was a Roman
citizen. He knew his rights, and had made his famous request:
"*Caesarem appello!*" (I appeal unto Caesar!) When he stood
before Agrippa, Paul told him how, as an orthodox Jew, he
had persecuted the Christians, until, on the road to Damascus,

the vision of Jesus rebuked him and, ever since, he had been preaching the Gospel.

Agrippa granted Paul what he asked for, the right of any freeborn Roman to be heard by the Emperor Nero. So in August, A.D. 58, Paul was taken to Rome in chains, accompanied by Luke, and joined Peter, who was already there, organizing the infant church. Although forced to live as a shackled prisoner under house-arrest for two years, Paul continued to preach to all who would listen to him (Acts 27:28).

Augustus and Tiberius had allowed only the Roman gods to be worshipped, but Caligula, through indifference, let many foreign cults build temples in Rome. Christianity had not yet begun to attract the aristocracy. It was still a religion for the lower classes, and, since there were not many of them, the followers of Jesus were not considered to be dangerous by Nero, the present emperor.

Nero, who had succeeded Claudius four years ago, was the great-grandson of Antonia and Drusus; the grandson of Germanicus and Agrippina; and the son of Agrippina II (sister of Caligula) and Cnaeus Domitius Ahenobarbus, a son of Antonia Major. So, through both his father and mother, Nero was descended from Selene's two sisters (if the reader is still following me). Antonia Minor had married the admirable Drusus, while for her older sister, Antonia, an equally distinguished husband was selected. A consul in B.C. 16, then in command of the Roman army in Germany, Lucius Domitius Ahenobarbus belonged to the immensely rich Ahenobarbus family—the Bronze Beards, they were called, because their wealth came from copper mines in Asia Minor and they all had red hair. The son of Antonia and Lucius, Cnaeus, married Agrippina, daughter of Germanicus. And they became the parents of a red-haired baby, L. Domitius Ahenobarbus, known to history as Nero.

Agrippina longed to see her son become emperor. So,

Cnaeus having died, she set out to seduce her Uncle Claudius. The Emperor was married to his third wife, Valeria Messalina —a beautiful redhead of twenty-five, more than thirty years his junior. A granddaughter of Antonia Major, she was lovely to look at, but so depraved a person that the word "Messalina" is used today to describe a wicked woman. Scheming to replace her, Agrippina told her uncle that Messalina was plotting to murder him and place one of her lovers on the throne. The gullible old Emperor, easily convinced by Agrippina of Messalina's guilt, had her killed. In 49 A.D., he married his thirty-four-year-old niece. The town, Colonia Agrippina, now Cologne, Germany, was named in her honor. Agrippina II was born there, while her parents, Germanicus and Agrippina I, were on the Rhine with the army.

Married to Claudius, Agrippina urged him to set aside Britannicus, his son by Messalina, and adopt her Nero as his heir. When Claudius was foolish enough to do this, Agrippina needed him no longer. She disposed of her tiresome old husband by feeding him a dish of poisoned mushrooms, or, as Tacitus puts it, "Claudius ate the mushrooms, after which he ate no more."

A big stout fellow with red hair, Nero was only seventeen in A.D. 54, when he became emperor. Agrippina thought she could dominate him as she had Claudius. But Nero was to be no obedient son. He soon asserted himself by falling in love with a Greek freedwoman named Claudia Acte. Married at sixteen to the daughter of Claudius and Messalina, Nero was bored with the sweet Octavia. He informed his mother that he wished to divorce her and make Acte his wife. "A former slave for my daughter-in-law? Never!" cried Agrippina. And she broke up Nero's first serious romance by introducing him to Poppaea Sabina, an auburn-haired society beauty. Acte, realizing that Nero no longer loved her, quietly disappeared.

Poppaea's husband, N. Salvius Otho, was sent off to govern

Lusitania, the most distant of the Roman provinces. But there remained two more obstacles to her becoming empress—Nero's wife and, especially, his mother. Knowing that, as long as Agrippina lived, Nero would never be allowed to marry her, Poppaea nagged and wept until the Emperor gave in to her wishes. Tacitus writes: "Nero agreed that she (his mother) must die. But how? Poison seemed best, but Agrippina had made herself almost immune to it by dosing herself regularly with antidotes." So Anicetus, Admiral of the Fleet at Misenum, suggested to the Emperor a safer way to get rid of her. "I could have a boat built that would sink while at sea. If your mother drowns, who will suspect you?"

Nero was delighted with the idea. In March, he always went to his villa at Cape Misenum, near Baiae. That spring of 59, he invited Agrippina, who was staying at Antium (Anzio), thirty miles below Rome, to visit him. After entertaining his mother royally, he sent her home in a specially constructed boat that fell to pieces a half mile from land. Everything went as planned—except that Agrippina managed to swim ashore. On reaching Antium, she sent a message back to Cape Misenum. "I miraculously escaped shipwreck, dear Nero. But I am home safe and well. You are not to worry."

The Emperor was in a panic. "She knows!" he thought. He had better send men to kill his mother, before she came after him. "Go quickly," he ordered Anicetus. "And, this time, don't fail to do it."

When Anicetus and his sailors broke into her house, Agrippina faced them defiantly. "If you've come to ask about my health, tell the Emperor that I'm feeling better. If you've come to kill me, I refuse to believe that Nero gave the order—" She never finished the sentence, for Anicetus ran her through with his sword.

Hated by everyone, Agrippina's death was not greatly mourned, but the Romans were shocked by the brutality with which Nero rid himself of his wife. Octavia was banished to Pandataria, and her head was chopped off. He married Poppaea two days later.

Even then, his people might have forgiven the Emperor his hideous crimes if, on the windy night of July 18, A.D. 64, a fire had not broken out that lasted nine days and nearly destroyed Rome. Nero rushed back from the seaside resort of Antium to help fight the flames—but it was rumored that he had stood on the Palatine above the inferno, playing his lyre, while, with delight, he watched Rome burn. When the fire died down, half the city was gone—also Nero's palace on the Palatine. He built himself a more ostentatious one, his famous *Domus Aurea* (Golden House). Named from its gold-tiled roof, the vast building overlooked a lake where the Colosseum now stands. Shocked by Nero's selfish extravagance, when so many were homeless, people said the Emperor had set the fire himself to clear a square mile of land on which to build a new palace.

Nero blamed the arson on the Christians. It was treason to worship Christ and not the Roman emperor. So he made the fire his excuse for persecuting the new sect. Peter was arrested and imprisoned with Paul in the Mamertine. Tradition says that the two men were led out of prison together, to die on the same day (*circa* 67 A.D.). Peter was crucified in Nero's circus, the site now of St. Peter's Cathedral. Paul, because he was a Roman citizen, escaped crucifixion. He was beheaded a mile and a half from Rome, on the road to Ostia, where Cleopatra's grandson met his tragic end.

Christians, sewn into skins of animals, were thrown to the wild beasts in the arenas. Covered with tar, they were burned alive as human torches to light up Nero's gardens, while he and his friends feasted and drank. But, eventually, his insane cruelty disgusted even the tough-skinned Roman people and

—at last, the army. In 68 A.D., the legions in Spain revolted and proclaimed their commander, Galba, as emperor.

Deserted by everyone, even the praetorian guard sworn to protect him, Nero fled to the suburban home of a former household slave of his, named Pharon. No longer the swaggering playboy-emperor but a haggard, broken man, Antonia Major's grandson waited there, hoping, after dark, to get to Ostia and escape to Egypt on a ship. Instead, a slave, sent by Pharon into the city, returned with the news that soldiers were searching for Nero. The senate had sentenced him to die.

"How?" the Emperor asked Pharon, in terror.

"By being stripped naked, your neck fastened in a forked stake and whipped to death."

"I'll kill myself first!" Nero picked up his sword, then put it down. How did one commit suicide? This man who had caused the death of his mother, his two wives, Octavia and Poppaea, and so many others, did not know the answer. "Show me how to do it," he begged.

"It's easy," Pharon replied. "Hold the point of your sword to your heart, under the ribs, then fall forward on it."

The trembling fugitive still had not found courage enough to end his life when galloping horses were heard approaching. The soldiers, sent by the senate, had discovered Nero's hiding place.

As they pounded on the door, the Emperor managed to pierce himself with his sword, and the soldiers, finding that the fugitive had "honorably" killed himself, were willing that his remains should have a decent burial. They went away. Pharon was washing Nero's body when he heard a knock on the door. On opening it, he saw a lovely, dark-haired woman.

"I'm Claudia Acte," she said. "May I speak with the Emperor? I heard he had fled from Rome and was here, so I've come, thinking that he might need me. I'm an old friend of his."

When Pharon told her that Nero was dead, Acte burst into tears, for she still loved him. She went with Pharon to stand beside the bed on which lay the corpse of the man who had wronged her. Nero was only thirty-one, but he had become obese from dissipation, his face coarse and brutal. To Acte, though, he was still her handsome, red-haired lover. She knelt and prayed for his soul.

It was not to the Roman god Jupiter that Acte prayed, but to Jesus Christ, for, after Agrippina had broken off her romance with Nero, the former Greek slave girl had turned to religion for comfort, and St. Paul converted her to Christianity. All these years, Acte had been part of his congregation, worshipping in secret with the Christians, and several times barely escaping being thrown to wild beasts.

Later, when Acte could control her emotions, she helped Pharon prepare Nero's body to be cremated in his garden. All the Emperor's fine friends had turned against him. It was Acte and Pharon—two humble ex-slaves—who, when the fire died down, took his ashes to the tomb of the Domitii family, at the foot of Pincian Hill.

Standing on the terrace of the Borghese Gardens, overlooking the Piazza del Popolo—where visitors now come to watch the sun set behind St. Peter's—few of them notice a church, below on the square, to their right. S. Maria del Popolo was built in the 12th century over the site of the mausoleum of the Domitian family, in order to try to exorcize the ghost of Nero, which, on stormy nights, is said to wander the slopes of the Pincio to this day, wringing his hands and bewailing his sins.

So perished the last ruler of Julius Caesar's line. The Roman emperors who came after him were army men, without a drop of the blood of Caesar or Augustus in their veins. With

Nero ended the Julio-Claudian family that had dominated Rome for over a century and given it one dictator and five emperors. So in A.D. 68 finishes a story that began in B.C. 48, when, in Alexandria, Cleopatra stepped out of a rug and smiled at Caesar.

Notes of a Researcher

PART 1

THE DUST THAT WAS CLEOPATRA

Gibbons spent twenty-three years working on his *Decline and Fall of the Roman Empire*. When he finished it, the historian wrote that he was sorry to be taking leave of "an old and agreeable companion, but glad of the recovery of my freedom." He wasn't glad for long, I imagine. This was in 1787, and after twenty-three years of pushing countless quill pens over countless sheets of paper, Edward Gibbons' days of "freedom" must have stretched empty and endlessly before him.

I do not claim I spent the same length of time on the research for and the writing of *Cleopatra's Children*, but it was several years. As I worked day after day, often in utter discouragement as the remarriages and repeated names of the Julio-Claudian dynasty grew confusing, I wondered why I had attempted such a long and involved subject. Still, I stuck with it and now, the book finished, like Gibbons, I part with regret from "an old and agreeable companion." And my thoughts go back to a morning in Kenya, East Africa, when the inspiration to write *Cleopatra's Children* came to me.

Having finished my nineteenth book, *Marie Antoinette's Daughter*, I went with my husband Tom to Africa. I was passing through one of those dry periods that every writer dreads and had nothing in mind for the next book. Was I written out? All the way up the East African coast from Cape Town, the possibility frightened me. Frustrated and unhappy, as I always am when not working, I reached Mombassa. From this port in southern Kenya, we were to go inland to the Tsavo National Park.

The morning of our departure found us at a grocery store. Our white hunter, as the safari guides like to be called, was packing his Land-Rover with supplies for our journey, since the game reserve furnished huts but no food. While he was dashing in and out of the store, Tom and I stood on the quay of the harbor, watching some little lateen-rigged boats, with long overhanging bows, high poops and an open waist, setting bravely out to sea beyond Fort Jesus Point.

His car loaded, our white hunter came to tell us that he was ready to leave. "They're nice, those Arab trading dhows," the guide said, his eyes following mine. "They've been riding the wind to India for two thousand years."

"Yes," I told him, excitedly, "since Caesarion tried to escape from Octavian."

"Caesarion? Who's he?"

"Cleopatra's son. He was at Berenice with Rhodon, his tutor, trying to get away to India, but he didn't make it. The monsoon died down."

"Cleopatra's son? I didn't think she had any children. But I know Berenice, that's a port north of here on the Red Sea. Say, folks, we'd better get going, if you want to reach Tsavo before dark."

A happier woman, I climbed into his Land-Rover, for I

wasn't written out. I had an idea for another book. We had come to Kenya to photograph its wildlife and, as I chased through the bush with my camera after elephants, giraffes, and rhinos (hoping they wouldn't turn and chase me!), I often thought of those Arab dhows laden with ivory, animal skins and spices, being carried by the seasonal winds across the Indian Ocean today, as they have been for two thousand years. By now, the plot for *Cleopatra's Children* was clear in my mind.

I first went to Egypt when I was ten years old. My parents rented a dahabeah and, for two winters, we cruised on it up the Nile. In those days, the leading hotel in Cairo was Shepheard's. Originally the pasha's harem, when De Lessep was building the Suez Canal and tourists began coming to Egypt, it became a hotel—by 1907, one of the most famous in the world—filled with European royalty, Russian grand-dukes, and titled English people, but few Americans. We were quite a curiosity. To charter a dahabeah on the Nile was the fashionable thing to do. I remember stopping at Thebes to visit the temple of Ammon, as Cleopatra and Caesar did, and going by donkeyback out to the temple of Hathor, at Dendera, to see the bas-relief of Cleopatra and her son.

"That boy was to have inherited the world," my father told me. "Instead, the Romans murdered the little fellow."

I felt very sorry for poor Caesarion. Ever since, I have read every word I could find about him. So when I began to write *Cleopatra's Children*, it seemed as though I had been doing research for this book all my life.

Cairo, founded in 969 A.D. by the Arabs, did not exist in Cleopatra's day, but the pyramids did. You can go out to Heliopolis, where, at the temple of the Sun, Cleopatra planted Herod's balm-of-Gilead trees, *Balsemodendron Gileadense*, said to be descended from some the Queen of Sheba gave King Solomon, and see a sycamore marking the spot where the Holy Family are believed to have lived during their exile in Egypt.

Otherwise, Heliopolis is a commercial suburb of Cairo. Nor is Alexandria any longer the city of marble that Cleopatra knew. Only the Heptastadium, the mile-long mole that Ptolemy I built out to the island of Pharos, which divided the harbor in two, still exists. The east basin is now little used. Ships dock in the ancient Eunostos (Harbor of the Happy Return), and the visitor to Egypt today steps ashore on the old Heptastadium. No longer a mole of quarried stone, but a wide dirt embankment, the Heptastadium has made the island into a peninsula and most of present day Alexandria is erected on it. On the western tip is a lighthouse. But the Pharos raised by Ptolemy Philadelphus, one of the wonders of the ancient world, stood on the eastern end of the former island (the site of the present Fort Kait Bey).

Under the fort, the foundations of the old lighthouse can still be seen. The tallest building ever erected in B.C. 300, the white marble Pharos soared in a series of three towers, each one smaller than the one below. Square at the base, the second story was octagonal, and the third was round. Donkeys laden with wood trotted up an incline roadway, inside the tower, to feed a huge fire kept burning at night. Reflected by a mirror, its flames could be seen thirty miles out at sea. The Pharos Light survived the earthquakes of 1303 and 1396, but finally collapsed into the sea, and Fort Kait Bey was built on its ruins in the 15th century.

Earthquakes have so altered the coastline here that the Alexandria of Cleopatra's day is now largely under water. Layers of soil overlie the old streets and houses. The island of Antirrhodus has disappeared. And Lochias Point has almost eroded away. The present Rue de la Porte de Rosette corresponds to old Alexandria's main street, along which Caesar used to canter with his hands behind his back, to show off his fine horsemanship. It ended at the Canopic gate. Beyond lay the suburb of Nicopolis, laid out by Octavian on the plain east of the town where he defeated Antony.

Most tourists in Alexandria ask the same question, "Where were Cleopatra and Antony buried?" In the Soma, Plutarch tells us, with Alexander the Great. Since Cleopatra's mausoleum on Lochias Point was unfinished at the time of her suicide, Octavian had the royal couple interred in the old cemetery of the Ptolemies. What became of Alexander's remains is a mystery. His body was brought from Babylon, where he died in B.C. 323. It was embalmed and laid in a gold sarcophagus in the Soma. Needing money to crush a revolt, Ptolemy IX melted down Alexander's gold coffin to pay his mercenaries, and placed the mummy in a glass one, that Strabo mentions seeing when he visited Alexandria. So, as late as A.D. 24, the Macedonian king must still have been lying there.

What happened to Alexander's mummy after that? No one knows—or what became of the remains of Cleopatra and Antony. The Soma was probably looted during the Arab invasion in A.D. 640, and by the 8th century, even the location of the cemetery had been forgotten. Archeologists think that it may have stood on the site of a Moslem church on the corner of the present Rue Nabi-Daniel and the Rue de l'Hôpital Grec. The Arabs refused to allow a dig there. So perhaps, under this old mosque, the dust of what was once one of history's most glamorous women lies undisturbed. Who knows?

The only ancient monument left in Alexandria is Pompey's Pillar. The name is due to the mistaken belief, in the Middle Ages, that it marked the tomb of Pompey the Great. Actually, the Egyptians erected the Corinthian column in A.D. 302, as a landmark for sailors.

Nor have the two obelisks that once flanked the temple of Serapis, patron god of Alexandria, any connection with Cleopatra, although they are known throughout the world as

Cleopatra's Needles. Originally from the temple of Karnak at Thebes, the sculptured granite pillars were first erected by Rameses II before the temple of the Sun at Heliopolis (in the days of Moses), and stood there until Roman times, when they were taken to Alexandria to decorate the Serapeum. After the temple burned down in A.D. 366, the two obelisks were set up in the Forum. They remained there until the 19th century, when, along with a third one brought from Thebes by Thutmosis III and erected by him at Heliopolis, they were given by Egypt to France, England and America, where the three of them are now. They have lost their gold tips, but you can see the Paris obelisk in the Place de la Concorde; the London one on the Thames Embankment; and New York's in Central Park.

Lake Mareotis, where Antony and Cleopatra liked to fish, looks the same as it did in their day. Its shores are still lined with papyrus reeds—*biblos* to the Greeks, and the source of our words "Bible" and "books," because the pages were made of papyri. Otherwise, to recreate the Alexandria that Cleopatra knew, and where St. Mark preached the Gospel, Tom and I had to stretch our imaginations, but not in Rome. As we stood on the Capitoline overlooking the ruined Forum, once the center of the Roman world, we saw many of the places mentioned in *Cleopatra's Children*, right there, before our eyes.

Six centuries before Christ, the Romans built the temple of Jupiter on Capitoline Hill, now replaced by Michelangelo's Palazzo Senatorio, the City Hall of Rome. Below it, captive kings were murdered in the Mamertine prison; and their bodies were thrown into the *Cloaca Maxima*, the sewer of ancient Rome that still flows through the Forum. In this notorious jail, at present an underground chapel for the Church of San Giuseppe dei Falegnami (St. Joseph of the Carpenters), Jugurtha and Juba II were imprisoned. Also, later, Peter and

Paul. A spring of water was shown us, supposed to have flowed at Peter's bidding, so that he could baptize his guards.

The Via Sacra winds through the Forum, past the ruins of the house where Caesar was living on that fatal Ides of March. Stumbling over these actual stones on which we were walking, Cleopatra's frightened children were led in chains in Octavian's triumph. And where the Sacred Way ends at the foot of the *Capitolium* (the seat of government, from which we get our word "capitol") was the spot where Selene first saw Juba.

One day, my husband and I climbed the Palatine Hill to have a picnic. South of us lay the long oval of the Circus Maximus, where Ptolemy of Egypt was killed in a chariot race. Beyond it ran the Via Appia, Rome's first paved road, by which Paul of Tarsus came from Capua (Acts 27). While across the loop of the Tiber, we could see the ridge of the Janiculum where Cleopatra once lived. In his will, Caesar left all his land there, on the west bank of the river, to the Roman people. It is still theirs to enjoy. The summit of the Janiculum has been laid out as a park.

On the Palatine, Rome began. A band of shepherds made this hill beside the Tiber their camp. They named it for Pales, goddess of flocks; and the site where the emperors lived became in time the Palatine, which gave us our name for "palace." Here, after Cleopatra's death, Selene and Ptolemy found refuge with Octavia; and Juba worked in the temple of Apollo. Augustus' library adjoined the small, unpretentious house on the southwest slope of the hill from where he governed the empire. Perhaps because of an unhappy boyhood spent at his stepfather's, Tiberius built himself another home on the northwest side of the hill, overlooking the Forum, where Caligula, who greatly enlarged it, was murdered, and the trembling Claudius became emperor, much against his will.

Tom and I were no sooner seated on a bench that day, and

had taken our sandwiches from their paper bag, than the lean, battle-scarred cats that infest the Palatine (and all Roman ruins) crept out from their dens in the stones. Soon we had about us a circle of half-wild animals—gray, tabby, black, white and mixed—eyeing us hungrily. Who could resist their pleading eyes? When they had nearly consumed our lunch, an old lady came up the path, carrying a sack of food. She was evidently expected. At the sight of her, more toms and their mates appeared—about fifty, no less—from their holes in every corner of the ruins.

"That's the Cat Lady, she comes every day," said a guard, who was passing by. I could imagine her—poor, lonely, perhaps hungry herself, but sharing the little she had with these unfortunate felines.

There was talk of sending some of Rome's homeless, unwanted cats to a suburban refuge, maintained by the Society for the Protection of Animals, the guard told us. "But not the cats from the Forum, the Colosseum, or the Palatine ruins. Those we must never touch. The Palatine without cats would be like St. Mark's Square in Venice without pigeons!"

After lunch, Tom and I strolled through the ruins of the temple of Apollo and the *Domus Liviae*. The house belonged to Livia's first husband, T. Claudius Nero, and Augustus added it to the one he bought overlooking the Circus Maximus. Destroyed in the great fire of A.D. 64, the site of these buildings was first discovered in 1869, but the dig there did not begin until 1956, and the work is still going on. Huge areas of the Palatine are only partially excavated. I thought of Cleopatra's daughter as we walked through the ruins. Selene often came to the Domus Palatina, to be among the guests at Augustus' literary evenings and hear Virgil and Horace read from their works. In this house she was married to Juba.

Livia, who had inherited silver mines in Spain, was very rich. Yet she wove her husband's togas, and shared his abstemious life, without a complaint. When Augustus died in A.D. 14, Livia was seventy-two years old. She outlived him by fifteen years. Leaving the Palatine, she went to spend her last days in her villa at Prima Porta, nine miles north of Rome, on the Via Flaminia. Livia continued to be the First Lady of Rome (her son, Tiberius, being a widower), and she was held in great respect. She was a cold, efficient woman, never very affectionate, but her marriage to Augustus had been a happy one. She nursed her husband through a succession of illnesses and tolerated a rivalry with Maecenas's wife, Terentia. Augustus loved her dearly. He died in Livia's arms, on the 19th of August, the month to which he had given his name.

The Empress Livia passed away in A.D. 29 (about the same time as Jesus), and her ashes were placed in the mausoleum that Augustus had built on the Campus Martius—a circular drum of concrete, once faced with white marble. On the top of the tomb originally stood a bronze statue of the Emperor. Two obelisks (now in the Quirinal and Esquiline Squares) guarded the entrance to a corridor leading into a central chamber, where the ashes of Augustus and his family were preserved in bronze urns, placed around the walls in a series of niches. The first to be buried there in 23 B.C. was Marcellus, whose premature death is lamented by Virgil in the Sixth Canto of the *Aeneid*, the reading of which so affected his mother that she fainted.

The ashes of other people mentioned in *Cleopatra's Children* also once reposed here—four emperors (Augustus, Tiberius, Claudius, and Caligula), as well as Livia, Octavia, Agrippa, Drusus, Antonia, and Germanicus, but not Julia. Her unrelenting father forbade Julia's remains to be placed with those of her family. In 410 A.D., when the Visigoths captured Rome, they plundered this tomb of the Julio-Claudian dynasty. All of the imperial ashes disappeared. Since then, the circular building has been used as a fortress, a bull ring, and a concert hall.

Near by, on the piazza, we were to see some of these characters in my book, almost in the flesh, for the members of the imperial family were carved on a monument erected to celebrate Augustus' return to Rome in B.C. 13, with Spain crushed at last. The doors of the temple of Janus, open during a war, were closed for the first time in two hundred years. And the Romans rejoiced that peace would now settle upon the empire. Hence, its name—*Ara Pacis*, Altar of Peace.

A Roman friend, who took us to see the monument, told us that, in 1937, the altar had been discovered under the Palazzo Fiano on the Corso, which overlies the ancient Great North Road, the Via Flaminia; and how it was moved by Mussolini's engineers to its present location, across the street from the mausoleum of Augustus. The altar stands within an enclosure of white marble. On it, a frieze of life-sized sculptured figures shows the imperial family on January 30, B.C. 9, walking in a procession to its dedication.

"Can you identify these people you've been writing about?" the Roman asked me. "I'll help you. That is Agrippa, the tall man with a fold of his toga over his head. The child clinging to him is one of Agrippa's boys, probably Gaius."

"Then the woman with her hand on Gaius' head must be his mother, Julia. Is the young man in the short military tunic, Drusus? If he is, that's Antonia, turning to face him, holding their son Germanicus by the hand."

Our friend pointed out to us Octavia, believed to be the woman behind Antonia and Drusus, with a finger on her lips; and, to the right of Drusus, the Empress Livia. In the foreground were the Ahenobarbus family. The handsome, shapely woman was thought to be Antonia Major, he said, with her son (Gnaeus) and her daughter (Domitia). Their father, Lucius, had his hand raised over his daughter's head. Gnaeus

—the small boy grasping the folds of Drusus' cloak—grew up to be the father of Nero.

"As these portraits were carved during the lifetime of the imperial family, they're probably good likenesses," the Roman said. I thought so, too. Standing before that relief on the Ara Pacis, the people I had been writing about in *Cleopatra's Children* became for me, not just names in history, but living men and women. I will never forget that happily-married couple, Antonia and Drusus, smiling at each other. Their love was here, immortalized in stone.

"But where are Selene and Juba?" I asked. "Surely, those two belong with the imperial family."

"They were in Africa," Tom reminded me. "Let's go there and look for them." So, on another trip, that is what we did.

PART II

RENDEZVOUS WITH SELENE

Tiberius was the Caesar of the Crucifixion. That is why Christian writers made him out to be such a monster. Actually, he should not be held responsible for what happened in distant Judea, on a day, *circa* A.D. 29 (the actual date of Jesus' death is uncertain). Tiberius was then at Capri, living as a recluse. He loved islands. He had gone to Rhodes to escape from his unhappy marriage with Julia, and only left it when he was forced to return to Rome and become emperor. Tired of ruling, he fled to Capri and, for the last ten years of his life, isolated himself on that rock off Sorrento, where he had been happy with Selene.

Gossip, of course, said the usual things. Was Tiberius' real motive in retiring to Capri so that he could enjoy in seclusion his secret vices? This is most unlikely. Except for excessive wine-drinking (a solace for his loneliness), he had always led an abstemious life. It is hard to believe that, in his late sixties, the Emperor changed his habits and indulged in the orgies that Suetonius and Tacitus, who lived two generations after him, describe with such relish. Due to them, unfortunately, the image of Tiberius as a senile, old reprobate is the one that has come down to us. Few people know that, for thirteen years, he tried to be a good ruler; of his distinguished military career in Germany and Illyria; and that, but for his modesty, our month of November would have a different name.

Tiberius was born on the 16th of November, 42 B.C. In 18 A.D., a delegation from the senate came to inform the Emperor that his birthday month was to be called Tiberius, as Augustus had given his name to the month of August. Much amused, he asked them, "What will you do if there are thirteen Caesars?" and declined the honor.

Capri is haunted by the ghost of "the saddest of men," as Pliny calls Tiberius. When Tom and I are in Naples, we like to take a little steamer out to the island, to visit his Villa Jovis. One day, seated among its ruins, my husband asked me, "What are you thinking about?"

"I was wondering what Tiberius was doing on the day when Jesus was crucified. News traveled slowly then. He probably didn't have a suspicion of what was going on in Judea."

For Tiberius, that day must have been like any other. Possibly, he had read over a report from Pontius Pilate, saying that everything in Palestine was under control, and regretting there was no news from Jerusalem to tell him. Now, dozing in the sunshine, as old men do, the Emperor was dreaming of the past. Did he remember Selene, dead for about twenty years? Or was he thinking of Vipsania? She, too, had died. How could he recall his first wife, except with bitterness? After their divorce, Vipsania had married C. Asinius Gallus, his most relentless enemy.

So I believe it was of his first love, Cleopatra's daughter, that Tiberius thought fondly during his last days on Capri. Augustus had acquired the island from Naples, in exchange for Ischia. There are some ruins of a so-called "Villa of Augustus" at Anacapri. But it is doubtful that Augustus ever went there. The "Island of the Goats" (so named, because only goats dared to walk on its precipitous cliffs) remained practically deserted until Selene and Tiberius discovered the place.

One day, seated in a café on the Salto di Tiberio (the precipice where—so Suetonius would have us believe—Tiberius had people who displeased him pushed off the cliffs), Tom and I found ourselves surrounded by lovers—French, German, and English—holding hands as Selene and Tiberius did there, twenty centuries ago. They were the first lovers to go to Capri. Ever since, it has been a honeymoon island.

Over a dish of *aragosta* (lobster), Tom asked, "When are you going to take me to Algeria?" We had often visited North Africa in the past—even the Canary Islands that Juba discovered—but now that I was writing *Cleopatra's Children*, I was afraid to go back there. Would I be disappointed?

"Well, I suppose we can't put it off much longer," I replied. "So, all right, let's go."

A week later, we sailed from Palermo on a boat that, for size and discomfort, hardly differed from the Roman galley on which Selene and Juba crossed to North Africa on their honeymoon. After a seasick voyage, the white houses of Tunis were a welcome sight. But our unpleasant crossing was forgotten when, after a good dinner and a night's rest, we visited the Bardo Museum and were shown their collection of Greek art objects, found at the bottom of the sea.

Sponge fishing is carried on extensively along the Tunisian coast, chiefly by Greek divers. Coming into the harbor of Tunis, we had passed the anchored sponge fleet, most of the little wooden boats being from Rhodes. On their decks sprawled big, bearded, half-naked men—similar to the sponge fishermen who had discovered the treasures the director of Le Bardo had been showing us that morning.

"One day, back in 1907, some of our divers came upon what seemed to them to be big guns lying on the ocean bottom, three miles off Mahdia," the director told us. "But after a few plunges down among the sharks, the men found the barrel-like objects to be Greek marble pillars, protruding from the half-buried wreckage of a sunken boat."

Salvage operations began in the spring of 1907 and continued until 1910. It had been a three-year job to bring to the surface these objects we saw before us. Many divers were killed by sharks or died of paralysis, caused by working too long at the great depth where the Roman cargo ship lay on the ocean floor. The sixty marble columns (probably intended to be used to decorate a temple) proved to be too heavy to raise. But the divers found such a quantity of art treasures in marble and bronze, lying among the rotted timbers of the old freighter, that Le Bardo acquired a priceless collection which today fills two rooms in the museum.

Among the marbles, all a bit sea-eaten from being submerged for so long, the director called our attention to an exquisite Hermes. "Since this statue is signed by its creator, Beothus of Chalcedon, a sculptor known to have lived in Athens in the 2nd century before Christ, we believe the ship sailed from Piraeus," he said. "Running into a storm off Mahdia, the 400-ton merchantman, too heavily laden with marble and bronze, plunged straight to the bottom."

Obviously. "But where was it going?" I asked.

"We don't know," the director replied. But I did. To Caesarea, of course! To whom could this Roman cargo boat have belonged, if not to Juba of Mauretania? He was the only wealthy art collector along this coast.

Can't you see Selene, Juba, and little Ptolemy waiting on the dock at Caesarea for this freighter that never arrived?

Juba had told his wife about his purchases in Greece, and Selene had already planned where she would put them—the Hermes in their atrium, the winged cupid in the garden. Then, to their consternation, the days passed, then the weeks, while they wondered, where was the ship? Eventually, they realized, it must be at the bottom of the sea.

In Caesarea, my husband and I would be shown art objects Juba bought in Greece that did arrive. But on the way we stopped at Cirta, the ancient capital of the Numidian kings, where Selene and Juba lived on first coming to Africa. The city looks today much as they must have seen it. As then, the houses perch on cliffs that fall in a 800-foot plunge into the gorge of the River Ampsaga, now called the Rummel. The name of the town has also been changed. After Selene and Juba left for Caesarea, Cirta was made the capital of a Roman province, *Coloniae Cirtenses*. Later, the Christians came and Cirta was renamed Constantine, in honor of Constantine the Great.

"Don't expect Cherchel to be like Cirta," Tom said, when, after a stop at Timgad, built by the Third Augusta Legion in A.D. 100 (after the time of Selene and Juba), we drove west to Mauretania, now western Algeria and Morocco.

"No, I'm prepared for the worst," I replied. The little seaside resort of Cherchel was only sixty miles from Algiers, in these days of the automobile, practically a suburb. Also, much had happened there since Ptolemy's death in 40 A.D. Divided by Claudius into two parts—the west called Mauretania Tingitana from its chief city, Tingis (Tangier); and the east named Mauretania Caesariensis from its capital, Caesarea—after the fall of Rome, the country was overrun by Vandals and later by Moslem Arabs. In the 10th century, even the name of the city founded by Selene and Juba was changed to Cherchel.

Entering the outskirts, we saw our first ruins, those of the ampitheater where many followers of Jesus died for their faith. A Phoenician settlement in the 5th century B.C., then a Roman colony in the 1st and 2nd centuries A.D., Christianity spread rapidly here in the 4th and 5th centuries, until in A.D. 650, Mauretania was conquered by the Arabs. The descendents of its early inhabitants, the Mauri (in Spanish, Moors) still exist in Morocco and Algeria, under the name of Berbers.

"Well, here we are, at last!" I said to Tom. But we had hardly caught a glimpse of the arches of the old Roman aqueduct before we were fighting our way through a dense traffic of tramcars and buses. Ahead was the harbor. Once it had sheltered the fleet of triremes the Romans kept in Caesarea to guard from pirates the grain galleys crossing to Ostia. Then, turning into a side street, our chauffeur drew up before a shabby hotel.

Could this be the Caesarea that I had been dreaming about for years? I looked at the dusty little square, lined with cheap lunch bars and souvenir shops, and sighed with disappointment. Another illusion gone! Then we were told the name of the square, Place Romaine; and over the door of our pensione I saw its name, Hotel Juba. By the time we were ushered into our room overlooking a small tiled patio, we wouldn't have exchanged the Juba, rated "humble" by Baedeker, for the Ritz in Paris.

Its guests were not tourists but mostly anglers, in Cherchel to catch the tuna and sharks that prey on the sardines swept along the Algerian coast by the currents. Across the street, or within walking distance, was all that was left of the Caesarea that Selene and Juba created, for most of it lies beneath the modern Arab town. The fountain in the center of the Place Romaine was composed of marble fragments (notably four large heads) from their palace. And only a few blocks away were the ruins of the thermae they built, with bits left of the old mosaic pavement. Further out, on the Rue du Caire, we came upon the remains of their theater. The *scaena* (stage) is still there, but the twenty-seven tiers of marble seats were used by the French in 1845 to build a military barracks.

The amphitheater and the circus served as quarries for modern houses, but safe from harm in the museum are the statues that adorned the royal palace and Caesarea's other fine buildings. Most of them were purchased by Juba in the ateliers of Olympia or Athens, and they show him to have been not only a lover of Greek art, but a collector with a discriminating eye. Some are originals, such as the statue of Augustus in the courtyard of the museum, found on excavating the Roman theater. Others are copies of statues by Phidias, Polycletes, and Praxiteles.

"What if they are reproductions?" Cherchel's director said to us. "We're grateful to Juba for showing us the vanished Greek masterpieces from which our statues were copied."

Unlike the cargo of marble and bronze that sank into the sea off Tunis, these Greek art treasures reached Caesarea safely, and I could imagine with what excitement Juba and Selene saw to their unpacking. Where did they put the smiling Asclepius, "a copy of a statue by Scopas," according to the catalogue? And that muscular Hercules, "a reproduction of the 5th century Greek bronze by Myron?" Did these statues adorn the royal palace? Or stand in the Forum? And the one Tom and I liked best, an Apollo "copied from the bronze by Phidias?" Surely, Selene must have wanted that for her own garden.

"Look, Tom, it says *Juba as a youth*." I pointed out to him a replica of the bronze bust found in 1944 at Volubilis, Morocco, which is now in the museum at Rabat. Nearby were busts of Juba and his wife as older people. And we were shown a life-sized head of a beautiful woman with classical features, so the catalogue said, "identified in 1953 by M. Jean Charbonneaux as Cleopatra VII." Nonsense, this head is not of Cleopatra of Egypt (compare the features with those on her coins), but of her daughter Selene. I stood looking at the young queen of whom I had written in *Cleopatra's Children*. Yes, I thought, that's Selene, all right. It was exactly as I had imagined her.

Several days later, when Tom and I were about to leave for France, we drove out to the tomb that had once contained the funeral urns of the King and Queen of Mauretania. After two thousands years, what would we find there? Nothing, I knew, remembering the mausoleum of Augustus in Rome. But, at least, we wouldn't be plagued by tourists. Aside from a few people at the museum, nobody in Cherchel seemed to have heard of the last resting place of Selene and Juba. The spot was in ruins long before the Arabs came to Mauretania. They named their empty *sepulcrum* (grave) "The Tomb of the Christian Girl," because of a molding on one of the blind portals in the shape of a cross.

When we asked the way, the museum staff told us, "Seventeen miles toward Tipaza, you'll see a mosque. Turn right and follow the road up the hill."

It sounded simple enough. But the so-called road proved to be a cow path. Our decrepit, rented car bumped along up it for two uncomfortable miles, then gave a last groan and died. There was nothing for us to do but to get out, and, loaded down with a heavy picnic basket and a bottle of Chianti, trudge the remaining half-mile on foot. But when Tom and I reached the top, the view out over the Mediterranean was magnificent. Perched upon one of the highest peaks of the Sahel, a range of the Atlas, the mausoleum serves as a guide to sailors, the most conspicuous landmark on the whole coast of Algeria.

There, before us, was the burial vault of Selene and Juba, half concealed by dense underbrush. A round stone structure, crowned by a pyramid rising in steps, it resembled a huge beehive. Around the cylinder base, the sixty Ionic half-columns were intact. Otherwise, with shrubs and weeds growing out of its tiered cone, what Baedeker calls "the most important Punic monument left standing in North Africa" was the picture of desolation. Damaged by earthquakes in 1825 and 1867, and from bombardments by the Algerian navy, who used the royal sepulcher for target practice, it had been looted for years by native treasure hunters. Lured by reports of the vast hoards of gold and jewels buried with the rulers of Mauretania, the grave robbers bored two tunnels into it. Furious when they found that others had been there before them, they tossed out the funeral urns and took everything that could be carried away.

What riches this great stone beehive may have held no one knows. Only rats and scorpions inhabited it now, but I couldn't resist having a look. Seeing a hole on the east side, I groped my way down a flight of steps into the darkness. "Look out for snakes!" Tom cried. Most disapprovingly, he followed me with his flashlight. It was spooky. We had not gone far along the passageway that led down to an inner chamber when I felt something glide over my foot. Letting out a scream, I dashed back to the entrance.

Cured of any desire to do further exploring, we unpacked our sandwiches. As we ate them and drank Chianti, I thought how this spot must have looked when the royal funerals took place here, twenty centuries ago. I could imagine the grounds planted with shrubs and flowers, and there would be marble benches on which visitors could sit, for the Romans thought of their tombs as pleasant homes for the dead, in which they were not entirely cut off from their familes. Since the *manes* (spirits of the dead) continued to live there, they made the interiors of them as homelike as possible. The walls were decorated with frescoes, like the rooms in their houses, and any articles the living had enjoyed having around them were placed in their tombs.

The soul, the Romans thought, could only find rest as long as the dead were remembered. That is why the living regularly visited the graves of their loved ones to bring their manes offerings of food and wine. There was a tube or lead pipe that ran down from the surface to an underground receptacle, through which the wine and milk could be poured. Unless this was frequently done, the spirit languished, unhappy itself and bringing unhappiness to others. "To speak the names of the dead is to make them live again," was a Roman saying. "It restores life to those who have vanished." Even strangers were asked to perform this rite when passing a tomb.

It was growing dark, and Tom and I must be leaving, but first I wanted to say good-by to Selene. "What are you doing?" my husband asked, when, going over to the mausoleum, I poured what remained of the Chianti down a hole. "Wasting our good wine?"

"I'm not wasting it," I explained. "I'm giving Selene a drink. She's thirsty. It is a long time since anyone has visited her." And when we left to walk down the hill, I called out to their manes, "Rest in peace, Selene and Juba, you are not forgotten. I have written a book about you."

Annotated Bibliography

THE BOOKS OF JUBA OF MAURETANIA

It is for his literary works that Juba of Mauretania is chiefly remembered. Highly praised by his contemporaries, he became a prolific writer in Greek on a variety of subjects—history, geography, grammar, natural history, and the fine arts. Unfortunately, his books are all lost, except for a few fragments that have come down to us, due to their having been quoted by Plutarch, Pliny the Elder, and other classical writers. Because of this, Juba's work has survived in the books of others, although his own have disappeared.

From the meager bits that exist, it is evident that, not only did Juba do original research on the animals and plants of North Africa, but he incorporated in his books material from earlier authors, which he collected in his private library at Caesarea. This, in itself, was a valuable contribution. Just as his copies of the statues of Praxiteles and other ancient Greek sculptors are our only way of knowing what their original masterpieces were like, so many old Punic manuscripts that would otherwise have been lost were preserved through Juba's writings. The most important of his books were:

A Roman History. The first part told of the early days of Rome. Part two traced the Roman institutions to their Greek origins, comparing the customs of the Romans and the Greeks. There must have been more to this work, now lost, for Plutarch admits getting most of his material on Cleopatra from her son-in-law's history of Rome.

History of Arabia. From passages cited from this work by other authors, Juba's first travel book seems to have contained a history and description of Arabia, and all that was then known about its zoology, exports, etc. Pliny says it was the best account of the country he knew.

A History of Libyca (Africa). In this work, Juba used as source material ancient Punic authorities, including the book on Numidia by his grandfather Hiempsal. This must have made his history very valuable. It is from this book that most of the information collected by Juba, and quoted by Pliny in his *Natural History*, is taken. Pliny lists the scholarly king of Mauretania first among his authorities for his account of Africa—its geography, natural history, and mythology; his description of the Atlas Mountains; and his chapter on the African elephant. Juba was also an authority on the lion and the panther, that in his day were still to be found in Mauretania. The third book of this work is quoted by Plutarch. Others known to have used material gathered by Juba on the geography, fauna, flora, and precious stones of Africa and Asia, are Josephus and Strabo.

On the Stage. This seems to have been a collection of essays on everything connected with the theater. The fourth book was devoted entirely to musical instruments.

On the Assyrians. Nothing is known about this book, except that Juba wrote one.

On Grammar. The second book was cited by Photius in his Lexicon. In it, Juba gave the synonymous terms in Greek and Latin, and wrote on other grammatical subjects. Being a king did not exempt him from the jealousy of rival authors, for Juba's contemporary Didymus of Alexandria, the celebrated grammarian, attacked him in many of his writings. He found fault, especially, with this work.

We know the titles of the above books, but there must have been others. For instance, Juba is known to have written a *History of Painting* and a great deal of poetry. All his poems have been lost, which is just as well, for they were said to have been but a feeble imitation of his friend Ovid.

Besides the books mentioned above, many other references to Juba's writings are to be found scattered through the works of the Greek and Latin authors of the 1st century A.D., and the lexicographers, in which the king of Mauretania is often quoted, but without any indication of the particular book referred to. In Roman times, writers took what they wanted from the works of other authors, usually without giving them credit. It is remarkable that Juba was referred to by name as often as he was. It may have been because he was royalty, and kings seldom write books.

CLASSICAL SOURCES

DION CASSIUS (150–235 A.D.). *Roman History.* 6 vols. Translated by
Herbert Baldwin Foster. Troy, N.Y.; Patraets. 1905
The author, also known as Dio Cassius, was a Roman politician and
historian of Nicaea in Bithynia. He was consul at Rome (220–229
A.D.), then governor of Africa and Dalmatia. Dion spent twenty-two
years on this history of Rome, written in Greek, which covers the
years from 68 B.C.–54 A.D.

HERODOTUS (484–424 B.C.). *History of the Persian Wars.* Edited by
Manuel Komroff from the translation by George Rawlinson
made in 1858. New York; Tudor Publishing Co. 1928.

This is a book that Juba may have used as a guide when he wrote
his *History of Arabia,* for Herodotus was our first globetrotter and
travel writer. Born in Asia Minor, he went to Athens in 455 B.C., and
having visited Egypt, Phoenicia, Libya, Mesopotamia, and the Crimea,
began telling of his trips in public. Herodotus was such a success that
he traveled about Greece as a professional story-teller. In 44 B.C.,
he went to live in southern Italy, where he wrote the above book.
He died there. Herodotus' history is more than a dry account of the
Persian Wars from 500–478 B.C. In the course of writing about the
reigns of Cyrus, Darius, and Xerxes, he manages, by means of frequent
digressions, or what modern writers call flashbacks, to describe the
people and customs of the lands he had visited.

JOSEPHUS, FLAVIUS (37–100 A.D.). *A History of the Jewish War.*
Written in Aramic, translated into Greek. English edition by
William Whiston. London: Thomas Tegg. 1825.
Antiquities of the Jews. (Same as above).
Josephus' Autobiography. (Same as above).

Born in Jerusalem, Joseph Matthias (his real name) was the governor of Galilee. In 66 A.D., during the Jewish revolt against Rome, he
led the defense of Jotapata and held out for forty-seven days before
surrendering to Vespasian. Josephus made himself popular with the
Roman conqueror by predicting that Vespasian would become emperor. Later freed, he adopted Vespasian's family name (Flavius)
and became a Roman citizen. Josephus remained all his life an intimate friend of Vespasian and his sons, Titus and Domitian. He was
with Titus at the fall of Jerusalem in 70, and returned with him to
Rome.

While writing my book, both Josephus' *History of the Jews* and
his *Antiquities* were a help to me. He is the authority from which
many other writers about the Jews have taken their material. Josephus, in turn, drew heavily on the biography of Nicholaus of

Damascus, tutor in the king's household, who furnished him with contemporary, first-hand material, in writing about the family of Herod the Great. My main quarrel with him is that he gives no dates. And what about this paragraph? (*Antiquities* XVIII: 54). "Glaphyra was married to Alexander, the son of Herod, and brother of Archelaus, but since it fell out so that Alexander was slain by his father, she was married to Juba, the king of Libyca (ancient name for North Africa), and *when he was dead,* and she was living as a widow in Cappadocia with her father, Archelaus divorced his wife and married her, so great was his affection for this Glaphyra."

Writing only fifty years or so after Juba's death in 23 A.D., Josephus was so close to the above events that it is strange he should make such an error. Archelaus was banished to Gaul in 6 A.D., so how could Glaphyra have married him, *after Juba's death?* It shocks me to think that Juba married Glaphyra about 4 A.D., while Selene was still living, but apparently he did.

PLINIUS, GAIUS SECUNDUS, KNOWN AS "PLINY THE ELDER" (23–79 A.D.). 6 vols. *Historia Naturalis* (Natural History). London: Bohn. 1755.

Pliny was born in Como, Italy, and served in the Roman cavalry in Africa and Germany. He returned to Rome, studied law, and was procurator in Spain under Nero (70–72 A.D.). In the intervals between his official duties (scarcely a waking moment of Pliny's day or night was he idle), this amazing man wrote books on military tactics, history, grammar, rhetoric, and natural science. He died while trying to observe too closely the eruption of Vesuvius, in August 79 A.D.

Of his writing, only one work is extant—his *Natural History,* an encyclopedia covering anthropology, zoology, geography, and mineralogy. Pliny did little original research, but took his material from more than five hundred authors of antiquity—Juba of Mauretania heading the list. In his *Natural History* (Book V), Pliny lists the king first among his sources. His data on the history and habits of the elephant (VIII, Chap. 1–12) is said to have been taken entirely from Juba's study of the animal. Pliny also admits his indebtedness to the latter for: V, Chap. 10 (the Nile); VI, Chap. 37 (the Canary Islands); VIII, Chap. 37 (the crocodile); VIII, Chap. 17–21 (the lion); I, Chap. 12 (Arabia); XII, Chap. 30–35 (its myrrh and incense). In all, Juba is mentioned by Pliny thirty-eight times.

PLUTARCH (46 A.D.–120 A.D.). *Parallel Lives.* 5 vols. Translation called Dryden's. New York: Bigelow, Brown. 1903.

A Greek, Plutarch was educated in Athens; taught and lectured at Rome; then, returning to Greece, became a priest at Delphi. Plutarch is best known for his *Parallel Lives*, in which he gives the life of a Greek statesman or soldier, then the life of a distinguished Roman, and compares the two. These famous biographies are believed to be the expanded notes of lectures he gave while in Rome.

Plutarch lists Juba of Mauretania among the leading Greek writers of his day. He also calls him "the best writer among our kings," which Boissier says is "faint praise." Plutarch admits getting from Juba's lost *History of Rome* most of the material he used in writing his life of Julius Caesar. Since Shakespeare is said to have based his *Antony and Cleopatra* on Plutarch, isn't it fascinating to think that he actually drew his inspiration, not from Plutarch, but from an earlier author, Juba of Mauretania? Who could write about Cleopatra better than her son-in-law?

LIVIUS, TITUS (LIVY) (59 B.C.–17 A.D.). *The Annals of the Roman People.* Translation by W. N. Roberts. London: Everyman's Library. 1935.

The leading Latin historian of his day, Livy was born and died in Padua, Italy, but spent most of his life in Rome. Under the patronage of Augustus, he devoted forty years to writing this history. He began his *Annals* between 27–25 B.C. Published in installments, the book at once brought him fame. Thanks to Livy, the story of Romulus and Remus, the capture of the Sabine women, the summoning of Cincinnatus from the fields to be dictator, and other familiar stories of the early republic have come down to us. Poor Juba! It was with Livy's best seller that his similar work had to compete.

SUETONIUS, GAIUS TRANQUILLUS (A.D. 70–160). *The Lives of the Twelve Caesars.* Translated by Philemon Holland. Printed for the members of the Limited Editions Club. Verona, Italy; Stamperia Valdonega. 1963.

A teacher of rhetoric in Rome, Suetonius was a friend of the younger Pliny, whom he accompanied to Asia Minor in 112 A.D., when the latter became governor of Bithynia. Returning to Rome, Suetonius was first a lawyer, then private secretary to Emperor Hadrian (119–121). Most of his work is lost, but his *De Vita Caesarum*, which contains biographies of Caesar and the eleven emperors from Augustus to Domitian, has survived almost intact.

Suetonius' writing is unique because of the intimate details he tells concerning the private lives of the Caesars. Historical facts alternate with scandalous stories. This new way of writing biography has greatly influenced modern writers, for the debunking period did not start in the 19th Century with Lytton Strachey, but back in Roman times, with Suetonius. The Greek writers pictured their statesmen as heroes. But Suetonius shows us the Caesars (so he says) as they actually were. He is the source of most of the stories, probably exaggerated, and even untrue, told of Tiberius' scandalous life on Capri. As Hadrian's secretary, Suetonius had access to the government archives, and he enjoyed exposing the vices attributed to earlier emperors safely dead.

TACITUS, PUBLIUS CORNELIUS (A.D. 55–125). *The Complete Works of Tacitus.* (Translated from the Latin by Alfred John Church). The Modern Library. New York: Random House. 1942.

Tacitus was born at Interamna, in Umbria. In 78 A.D., he married the daughter of Cn. Julius Agricola, governor of Britain. He was quaestor under Titus (79); praetor under Domitian (88); consul (97); governor of Asia (112–6); and an intimate friend of the younger Pliny. Tacitus' extant works are: *Agricola*, a biography of his father-in-law, the conqueror of Britain; *Germania*, an account of the German tribes; *Historiae*, a history of the Roman empire from Galba to Domitian (a period covering part of Tacitus' own lifetime); and the *Annals*, which deals with an earlier period, from the death of Augustus to that of Nero.

Writing two generations after the Julian emperors, Tacitus obtained most of his information about them that he used in his *Annals* from the memoirs written by Nero's mother, the younger Agrippina. And he stressed their vices, rather than their good side. Why? We must remember for whom he was writing—their successors—the Flavians. Recent emperors, he dared not attack. Gossip was repeated, and exaggerated, without fear of being prosecuted for libel in Roman times, and finally became history. The general public, then as now, loved scandal. And Tacitus, like Suetonius, gave them what they wanted. For instance, what was that old rascal, Tiberius, doing out on Capri if he wasn't indulging in orgies? As for the revered First Lady, hadn't Livia probably murdered all those who stood in Tiberius' way—Julia's three boys and Germanicus—and hastened her husband's end by poisoning the figs Augustus liked to eat? Tacitus repeated these slanders, not bothering to say whether they were rumors or facts. He was writing a best seller.

IN FRENCH

ALBERTINI, M. EUGENE. (Directeur des Antiquites de l'Algérie). *L'Afrique Romaine*. Alger: P. Gaiauchain. 1922. *L'Empire Romaine*. Paris: Payot. 1929.

BOISSIER, GASTON. *L'Afrique Romaine*. Paris: Hachette. 1901.

BOISSIERE, GUSTAVE. *L'Algérie Romaine*. 2 vols. Paris: Hachette. 1883.

CAISE, ALBERT. *Explorations Archeologiques sur le Tombeau de Juba II*. Blida: 1893.

CARIPINO, J. *Le Maroc Antique*. Paris: Payot. 1943.

GAUCKLER, PAUL. *Musée de Cherchel*. Chartres: 1895.

GSELL, STEPHANE. (Inspecteur Général des Antiquités et des Musées de l'Algérie). *Histoire Ancienne de l'Afrique du Nord*. 8 vols. Paris: Hachette. 1930. *Cherchel (Antique Iol–Caesarea)*. Alger: 1952.

JULIEN, ANDRÉ. *Histoire de l'Afrique du Nord*. Paris: Payot. 1931.

SEVEN, ABBÉ. *Memoires de l'Academie des Inscriptions* (an account of Juba's life and his writings). 4 vols. Alger: 1889.

IN ENGLISH

ASSA, JANINE. *The Great Roman Ladies*. New York: Grove Press. 1960.

ASINOV, ISAAC. *The Roman Republic*. Boston: Houghton Mifflin. 1966. *The Roman Empire*. Boston: Houghton Mifflin. 1967.

BALSDON, J. P. V. D. *Roman Women*. New York: John Day. 1963.

BUTTERFIELD, ROGER. *Ancient Rome*. New York: Odyssey Press. 1964.

CARCOPINA, JEROME. *Daily Life in Ancient Rome*. New Haven: Yale University Press. 1940.

CHANLER, BEATRICE. *Cleopatra's Daughter*. New York: Liveright. 1934.

DUDLEY, DONALD. *The World of Tacitus*. Boston: Little, Brown. 1968.

EBERS, GEORGE. *Egypt* (translated from the German by Clara Bell). 2 vols. London: Cassell, Petter, and Galpin. 1881.

FERRERO, GUGLIELMO. *The Women of the Caesars*. New York: Century. 1911.

FRANZERO, CARLO MARIA. *The Memoirs of Pontius Pilate*. London: Alvin Redman. 1961.

GIANNELLI, GIULIO (edited by). *The World of Ancient Rome* (translated from the Italian by Joan White). London: Macdonald. 1967.

GIBBONS, EDWARD. *The History of the Decline and Fall of the Roman Empire*. 7 vols. London: Methuen. 1900.

GRAVES, ROBERT. *I, Claudius*. New York: Grosset & Dunlap. 1934. *Claudius the God*. New York: Harrison Smith. 1935.

GRANT, MICHAEL. *The World of Rome*. Cleveland: World Publishing Co. 1960.

HOFFMANN, ELEANOR. *Realm of the Evening Star* (A History of Morocco and the Lands of the Moors). Chapter II, People of the Purple Dye and the House of Masinissa. Phila: Chilton. 1965.

HOMES, WINIFRED. *She Was Queen of Egypt*. Chapter on Cleopatra. London: G. Bell. 1959.

ISNARD, H. *Algeria*. Paris: B. Arthaud, 1954; London: Nicholas Kay. 1955.

JOHNSTON, MARY. *Roman Life*. Glenview, Illinois: Scott, Foresman. 1957.

KEAY, DOUGLAS. *Cleopatra*. London: Mayfair Books. 1962.

LUDWIG, EMIL. *Cleopatra*. New York: Viking Press. 1931.

MARANON, GREGARIO. *Tiberius* (translated from the Spanish by Warre Bradley Wells). New York: Duell, Sloan and Pearce. 1956.

MCCABE, JOSEPH. *The Empresses of Rome*. 2 vols. New York: Henry Holt. 1911.

PAYNE, ROBERT. *The Roman Triumph*. London: Abelard-Schuman. 1962.

PEROWNE, STEWART. *The Life and Times of Herod the Great*. New York: Abingdon Press. 1956.

PLATNER, SAMUEL BALL. *The Topography and Monuments of Ancient Rome*. Boston: Allyn and Bacon. 1904.

PRATT, FLETCHER. *Hail Caesar*. New York: Harrison Smith and Robert Hass. 1936.

SANDMEL, SAMUEL. *Herod: Profile of a Tyrant*. Phila: Lippincott. 1967.

SERVIEZ, JACQUES ROERGES DE. *The Roman Empresses* (translated from the French by the Hon. Bysse Molesworth). 2 vols. London: Walpole Press. 1899.

THADDEUS, VICTOR. *Julius Caesar and The Grandeur That Was Rome*. New York: Brentano. 1927.

VAN SANTVOORD, SEYMOUR. *The House of Caesar*. Troy, N.Y.: Pafraets. 1901.

WEIGALL, ARTHUR. *The Life and Times of Cleopatra*. New York: Putnam. 1924. *The Life and Times of Marc Antony*. New York: Putnam. 1931. *Nero: The Singing Emperor of Rome*. New York: Garden City Publ. Co. 1930.

WHEELER, SIR MORTIMER AND WOOD, ROGER. *Roman Africa in Color*. London: Thames and Hudson. 1966. New York: McGraw-Hill. 1966.

WILLIAMSON, G. A. *The World of Josephus*. Boston: Little, Brown. 1964.

Index

ALICE CURTIS DESMOND

is the wife of former New York State Senator Thomas C. Desmond. They live at Newburgh, New York, when they are not traveling. Much of Mrs. Desmond's life has been passed in Europe, South America, and the Orient. She has visited Alaska, Scandinavia, and Russia twice; been to Australia, New Zealand, South Africa; and three times around the world. All of her writing is based on her liking for travel and history. She has written five books with Peruvian, Argentine, and Brazilian backgrounds, and two juveniles on Alaska. Several of her books have been translated into Portugese, Swedish, French, Flemish, Dutch, and German. She has also done the lives of six famous women, including Marie Thérèse, the daughter of Marie Antoinette, who was the only member of the French royal family to leave the Tower alive and became Queen of France—for ten minutes! Mrs. Desmond's seventh biography, *Cleopatra's Children*, is her twentieth book.

This versatile author's hobbies are painting, photography, collecting classical stamps, and the raising of orchids. One has only to read about her in *Who's Who in America* to realize how varied are her interests. She belongs to clubs of painters, photographers, and stamp collectors, and is a trustee of the Society of Colonial History and a Fellow of the Society of American Historians. Russell Sage College conferred upon Alice Curtis Desmond the honorary degree of Doctor of Letters. The Rochester Museum of Arts and Sciences made her an honorary Fellow for her historical writing.

Always, this enthusiastic and thorough author likes to combine travel with research. Her interest in Cleopatra began when, as a young girl, she spent several winters in Egypt. It has led her to trace the lives of Cleopatra's children, of which little hitherto was known. Many trips to visit every place connected with them has taken Mrs. Desmond to Rome, to Egypt, to Mozambique on the East African Coast (where the idea for this book came to her), and to the Roman provinces of Numidia and Mauretania, now Algeria and Morocco.

As a result of this lifetime of study and personal investigations, Cleopatra's four children, who resulted from the brilliant Egyptian's love affairs with the two greatest Romans of her day, come alive in this biography, as do the characters in Alice Curtis Desmond's other authentic biographies: *Martha Washington—Our First Lady; George Washington's Mother; Glamorous Dolly Madison; Alexander Hamilton's Wife; Bewitching Betsy Bonaparte; Sword and Pen for George Washington;* and *Marie Antoinette's Daughter.*